SUZETTE SAUCE

Vanilla sugar
Skin of 2 oranges
Skin of 1 lemon
Orange blossom wate
Kirsch
White Curaço
Juice of 2 oranges
Juice of 1 lemon
Butter
Rum

THE
HENRI CHARPENTIER
COOKBOOK

THE HENRI CHARPENTIER COOKBOOK

Recipes and Memoirs
of the world - famed French chef
who created Crêpes Suzette

PRICE/STERN/SLOAN
Publishers, Inc., Los Angeles

THE HENRI CHARPENTIER COOKBOOK

Originally published privately as
Food and Finesse, The Bride's Bible

Copyright © 1945 by Henri Charpentier
Copyright © 1970 by Price/Stern/Sloan Publishers, Inc.

Price/Stern/Sloan Editorial Supervisor — *Auriel Douglas*
Book Design — *Bernard Nagler*
Jacket Design — *J. Chris Smith*

Printed in the United States of America
By Stecher-Traung-Schmidt Corporation, San Francisco
Bound by The Cardoza Bookbinding Company, San Francisco

Photo credits: pages 18, 168, 202, 234, 262, Sanford Roth; pages 62, 171, 382, Globe Photos. Color: Crêpes Suzette and Roast Duck, James K. Polk, The Milk Marketing Board of England and Wales; How To Make Omelets and Scrambled Eggs, and Pudding, Anna Shaw, The Poultry and Egg National Board; Rack of Lamb, Grover Cleveland, American Lamb Council; Lobster, Charles Dillingham, South African Rock Lobster Service Corporation.

Standard Book Number — 8431-0083
Library of Congress Catalog Card Number: 67-26534

Published by
PRICE/STERN/SLOAN PUBLISHERS, INC.
410 North La Cienega Boulevard
Los Angeles, California 90048

For the completion of this book, I owe heartfelt appreciation to my collaborating secretary and good friend, Mary Katherine Kalk.

Henri Charpentier

LIST OF ILLUSTRATIONS

CONTENTS

HENRI CHARPENTIER
1880 — 1961

No chef in the world had a more colorful background than Henri Charpentier.

He began his long and distinguished career as a ten-year-old page boy on the Riviera, and served his apprenticeship as a Master Chef in the major dining capitals of Europe: *Hôtel de Paris* in Monte Carlo, *Maxims* and the *Tour d'Argent* in Paris, *The Café Royale* and *Savoy* in London, the *Metropole* in Moscow, *The Vier Jahreszeiten* in Munich, the *Quirinale* and the *Belle Meunière* in Rome. He was a student of Escoffier, Jean Camous and César Ritz, the famed hôtelier.

Among his European patrons and friends were Queen Victoria, who fed him bon-bons, Sarah Bernhardt, who offered her silk-edged handkerchief soaked in oil when he burned himself with hot soup, and King Edward VII, for whom he created Crêpes Suzette.

Adventurous and ambitious, Henri came to America in the early 1900s with his new bride. He worked in the dining rooms of New York City's most distinguished hotels until 1906 when he opened *The Original Henri Restaurant* in his home in the rural village of Lynbrook, Long Island. The small dining room had only two tables. Feloména, his wife, was in charge, while Henri continued to work in the city during the day to finance the new undertaking.

During its first year, The Original Henri's *took in only $500, but the Charpentiers were not discouraged. They were certain their restaurant would ultimately be successful.*

The turning point came when J. P. Morgan, one of the most notable financial figures of the time, discovered the delightful little dining place in the country, rumored to serve finer cuisine than in New York City. Other equally distinguished patrons soon followed.

Henri's grew and prospered until it occupied a rambling mansion on many

acres, with sunken gardens and promenades. Over the next twenty-five years it attracted the wealthiest and most noted of the world's celebrities.

Among others who made the forty-five-minute trip from New York City were Rudyard Kipling, William K. Vanderbilt, William Jennings Bryan, Theodore Roosevelt, Woodrow Wilson, Florenz Ziegfeld, Marshals Joffre and Foch and New York City's colorful Mayor, "Jimmy" Walker. The itinerary of every distinguished visitor to New York was considered incomplete unless it included a meal at Henri's.

"Diamond Jim" Brady, wearing $500,000 worth of precious gems and accompanied by two bodyguards, often paid dinner checks totaling $500 (the equivalent of $2000 today), adding an extra $100 tip for the waiter. Brady's checks were for food only, since he did not drink liquor.

The restaurant continued to prosper until the Eighteenth Amendment to the Constitution ushered in prohibition. In April, 1930, twelve government agents "swooped down on the mecca of ultra-society," as the press reported, "smashing hundreds of bottles on the premises and confiscating approximately $100,000 worth of rare wines and champagnes."

"Even the soup was made with wine," an incredulous agent testified in court.

Although the judge refused to close Henri's *because "it was too respectable," the further use of brandy or liquor in food was strictly forbidden. Since preparation of most dishes thus became a felony, prohibition put an end to the type of cuisine for which* The Original Henri's *was famous. It was also the beginning of the restaurant's decline.*

The wealthy and famous who had flocked to Lynbrook began drifting away. Many had already lost a great deal of money in the 1929 stock market crash. With the advent of prohibition, they were replaced by "a new crowd of fast eaters and fast dancers carrying bottles of gin and whiskey in their pockets."

The once gay restaurant became almost deserted, but remained open, adding an outdoor dance floor "abetted with fixtures of Japanese lantern effect." It also offered a depression-priced dinner for $1.50 and a printed menu for the first time.

In 1934, the French government and John D. Rockefeller, Jr., seeking an experienced restaurateur to open the *Maison Française* in brand-new Rockefeller Center, approached Henri, because "his name and food were of such quality that people from all over the world would patronize him." Seeing it as a marvelous opportunity to reestablish himself in the city, he accepted, selling some of the considerable property he had acquired over the years to raise the substantial capital required for so large an undertaking. His wife continued to oversee the dwindling Lynbrook operation.

Despite the avalanche of critical acclaim and publicity he received when the *Maison Française* opened, there were financial difficulties from the very beginning. An artist, rather than a businessman, he had failed to realize that the new café was too small for the rent he paid; the seating capacity should have been many times larger.

> *Charpentier also refused to compromise his standards. When his friends pointed out that, as a result of the depression, the once gay Hotel Knickerbocker and Manhattan had become office buildings, and legions of restaurants were closing, he would say, "Yes, I know all about economy, but I am not one who understands how to be economical with food. The food must be of the best."*

As the depression deepened, money became scarcer. In Lynbrook, it was difficult to make the payroll. Soon, it only had two waiters and they were idle half the time.

> *Finally, in April, 1935, the locks were changed on the doors of the* Maison Française *and Henri was evicted for non-payment of $12,000 in back rent.*

In 1935, 1936 and 1937 he struggled to rebuild *The Original Henri's*, earning money to keep it afloat by presenting "Champagne Suzette Dansants" at *The Casino* in Central Park, and later at Helen Morgan's famous *House of Morgan.* But few could afford to spend $1.00 for pleasure in those days, despite the allure of *Canapé Nicois, Crêpes Suzette* and *Coupe Champagne,* and these efforts were also doomed.

Henri tried, unsuccessfully, to sell some of his remaining real estate to pay back-taxes on the Lynbrook property. He had been offered $375,000 for twenty acres in 1926 but could not find a buyer in 1938 at $10,000. The property was confiscated and subsequently razed.

Weary of New York, Henri left for Chicago where he operated The Café de Paris *for a short time. After a few years he moved to Los Angeles where, following World War II, he opened a new* Henri's *on the fashionable Sunset Strip. Once again, it was a tremendous artistic triumph, but restaurant economics are severe and Henri was not geared to economizing. Only the finest ingredients could be used, and food costs were often greater than customers' checks.*

For the last fifteen years of his life, Henri presided over the type of restaurant he loved best. Located in Redondo Beach, the intimate room served a maximum of sixteen guests nightly, allowing him to personally supervise the preparation of each dish. There, he served a different type of royalty, Hollywood personalities such as Bing Crosby, John Wayne, Ingrid Bergman, Lauritz Melchior and Ethel Barrymore. Its popularity was so great that reservations had to be made four years in advance. Until 1970, it was run by his long-time assistant, Mary Kalk, who helped compile this book.

Privately printed in 1945 and distributed to a select circle of friends, the book's original title was Food and Finesse — The Bride's Bible. *It was dedicated to "the queen of the home — the charming American woman." Charpentier's purpose was to perpetuate "the disappearing art of gentle and gracious living."*

Since his enthusiasm for his adopted country was boundless, he deliberately departed from the age-old custom of naming recipes for members of the nobility, choosing, instead, to dedicate his dishes to famous Americans.

Flamboyant and courtly in speech and manner, Charpentier saw "the little bride, the queen of America, presiding without a crown, with her presence, alone, making a castle of the American home."

Thus, each recipe is designed to serve two — those two who, in his romantic heart, he envisioned as first sweethearts, later bride and groom.

Unlike most master chefs, Henri had the ability to write his recipes in a simple, concise fashion. Imagination and originality were their hallmark. He did not seek to impress the reader with the tiresome, complicated instructions typical of many gourmet cooks. Nor did he ever borrow or add to existing recipes to create the impression of originality. Each is his own creation. Each is truly an "Henri Original."

Price/Stern/Sloan takes great pride in publishing this volume of Henri Charpentier's recipes and boyhood memoirs and hopes it will help to preserve in some small measure an era when gracious living and culinary excellence were cherished standards.

PRICE/STERN/SLOAN Publishers, Inc.
Los Angeles

FUNDAMENTAL
PRINCIPLES
FOR ROASTING

IT IS IMPORTANT that you have your oven very hot, about 500° Fahrenheit, before introducing your meat, poultry, game, etc. Put a large tablespoonful of butter into the roasting pan, if the roast you are preparing is a small one. Let the meat remain in the hot oven for a few minutes, depending on its size, and when you see, at the first basting, that it sizzles, turn it over, and in a few more minutes baste it again. At this point turn your oven from 500° F. down to a moderate heat of 375° F.

Please do not read a newspaper or a novel when you are cooking. The oven should be on your mind constantly, and the roast inside must be basted very often to insure its success. The perfection of your gravy depends on it.

A roast of beef, if it is to be well done, takes approximately 20 to 25 minutes for each pound. Medium, about 16 minutes per pound, and rare, from 12 to 14 minutes per pound.

The roast which has been basted very often will give you the effect you desire. Juicy meat inside and brown outside. Generally beef, lamb and mutton should not be cooked too much. A real gourmet will always choose medium or rare cooked meat. He doesn't appreciate it well done. Pork and veal, however, *must* be well done, very well done. To satisfactorily roast pork it is necessary to add, in comparison to the fat surrendered, an equal quantity of butter. This should be added to the roast at different times *after* the fat has been rendered. It will give the pork fat a gelatinous effect and slow down its intense heat, which, if left by itself, would dry your meat and spoil your gravy. Stick a fork into the pork roast and baste over the holes where the incisions have been made. A whole onion that has been washed, but not peeled, should be added to the roast of beef, pork, lamb, poultry, etc., a half hour before it is taken from the oven to give it a grand and pleasant aroma. Do not salt any of the roasts too much while cooking them, they should be seasoned with salt and pepper just before leaving the kitchen. And the black pepper must be ground at the last moment, because it is not used to make the meat more sharp, but rather for the aroma it gives off with the steam.

After your roast has been taken out of the pan, pour the gravy into a bowl. Place your roasting pan on the fire on top of your stove and pour into it a sherry-glassful of sherry or white wine, claret or port. What you use, and how much, depends on the kind of roast you are making and the size of it. If it is very large add a little more, and if it is small make it a little less. Take a wooden spoon and stir the bubbling wine around, mixing it with the brownness of the pan. Add a generous piece of butter, a pinch of salt, a pinch of pepper, and a little chopped parsley. And, if you have one, a very finely chopped shallot. Then, pour the original gravy into the pan as a final gesture, stir it well, and serve it with the roast.

To roast poultry sprinkle salt only on the inside of the carcass in which one quarter of a raw onion, in one piece, has been placed. The onion will make an aroma inside the chicken. Put some butter in the pan and add more as it is being roasted. Be sure that the fowl is resting on a leg and a wing, in other words on its side, when you begin to roast it. It should be turned quite often, and basted on both sides every time it is turned. Five minutes before serving it place the chicken on its back, and with the bubbling butter baste the breast for several minutes to give it a nice brown color outside and juicy meat inside.

Fur-bearing game should be roasted under the same principles as beef, and at the same temperature, except when the game has been marinated, and then it demands a different kind of preparation. Pheasant, partridge, etc., should be roasted under the same principles as fowl, with the addition of a strip or two of lean bacon, which should be tied to the breast of the bird with a string. This is done to keep the moisture in the flesh, since a game bird is a berry eater; consequently its meat is drier than that of the domestic fowl, which doesn't have a steady diet of berries. Wild duck should be roasted very rare, and a piece of celery, a little parsley, salt and pepper should be placed inside the carcass. In this case rare means 8 minutes in an extremely hot oven of 550° to 600° Fahrenheit. A wild duck should never be cooked over 12 minutes. Do not cremate it. Do not confuse the wild duck with the domestic which demands from 1 hour to 1½ hours to be roasted properly.

A goose after roasting should have meat that is rose in color, in other words it must be done medium, contrary to a turkey which should be well done. In order to recognize when a roast or a fowl has obtained the desired point in roasting, take a fork, sink it into the roast or the leg of the fowl, and then touch the prongs to your cheek. If it is cold or warm it has not been roasted enough, but if it is hot, then it is ready.

INSTRUCTIONS FOR BROILING MEAT

FILLET AND SIRLOIN STEAKS, contrary to many hotels and restaurants, are often made too oily, too peppery and too salty. I suggest that the steak or fillet be placed in a very hot broiler which has been made extremely hot beforehand, without oil, without pepper, and without salt. After the meat has been under the heat for two minutes, turn it over and permit the other side to broil for two minutes. The two minutes used in broiling each side, without any ingredients at all, are important. They sear the steak and keep the juice a prisoner. With the completion of that first step, plunge a brush into melted butter (it must be good butter), and brush it on both sides. The meat should reach only a rare or medium state, because a fillet or steak that is very well done has lost much of its nutritional value. Do not test it with a fork to see if it has been broiled enough, but touch it with your finger, and if it is swelled, and resists the gentle pressure, your steak is ready to be eaten. If it has reached the rare or *à point* state, it has been perfected in true culinary style. Too many people spoil a good thing by ordering their food done this way or that when dining out. At the moment your steak has reached perfection in the broiler, it should be placed on a very hot platter or plate, and to this hot, swelling, juice-filled piece of meat add a generous piece of fresh butter, and finally a pinch of pepper and salt.

To broil a chicken, squab, guinea hen, etc., split it up the back first, and spread it out. The breast should be left intact. Wipe out the fowl with a cloth, do not wash it. Brush some butter on the bony side and sprinkle it with salt. Place it under the broiler with the bony side up until that side becomes a very dark brown. Then reverse it to the breast side, and again brush on some butter, and a sprinkle of salt.

Put it back under the broiler, and watch it as it takes a brown color so that it doesn't burn. Finish it by placing it in a hot oven with a generous piece of butter. Leave it there for 15 minutes, basting it continuously.

To broil a chicken that weighs from 2 to 3 pounds usually takes 15 minutes for the bony side and 5 minutes for the breast. And then another 15 minutes breast up in the oven. Two-thirds of all the broiling must be done on the bony side. The result should be a chicken that is juicy and tasty. When you can afford it, do not be stingy with your butter.

Lamb and mutton chops, like beef, should be rare. Pork and veal, whether broiled or roasted, *must* be well done. Game, with the exception of quail, is generally much better when roasted.

SAUTE INSTRUCTIONS

A SAUTÉ OR STEW should be made with finely chopped onion, a piece of butter, pepper, salt, spices and your meat or meats. For poultry or game the basic sauté principle is the same. Your pan, or receptacle, must be large enough so that the pieces of meat, fowl, etc., do not rest on top of each other. There must be room enough for each piece to contact the heat under the pan. Then each will become seared individually. At this moment butter should be added, the consommé, or water, or wine; or all of them together, depending on the kind of dish you are preparing. After liquids, vegetables, etc., have been added, it is always better to finish it in the oven to eliminate the flames underneath the pan, which might destroy it. This is a much safer way to successfully complete your sauté.

INSTRUCTIONS FOR BOILING MEAT

WHEN MAKING A BROTH, meat, onion, and spices should all be placed in a pot at the same time. The fire should be at its maximum. When the meat has been seared and obtains a light beige color, then add the water, the quantity of which should be gauged by the amount of consommé you wish. It all depends on the size of the meat, how large your pot is, the number of guests you are having, and the size of your family. And it will not be a table for two. This principle of searing the meat will give color to the broth, as well as more aroma and taste. The combination of spices, celery, onion, garlic, carrot and parsley is necessary to the boiling of any kind of meat or fowl. When it begins to boil, remove the froth and boil slowly until the meat is done.

The entire cuisine is like a symphony—each ingredient signifies a certain note of music. The simplest of kitchen melodies may achieve the heights by the concerted or individual efforts of the spices, aromatic herbs and flavor vegetables that include garlic, shallots, onions, etc. In the world of cooking they are indispensable. Let your preparation of food be in accordance with your taste, but don't forget, the basis should be common sense. Don't be confused by some persons who don't like this or that, whether they have tried it or not. Nature intended all foods to be necessary for the perfect health of the body.

HOW TO MAKE OMELETS AND SCRAMBLED EGGS

A VERY SHORT NAME, and one of the greatest in culinary art, the egg is widely used in making sauces, and is to the food domain what the potato is to the vegetable kingdom. The egg needs no introduction, and is used in the most refined sauces for thickening and for completing a dish that is made distinctive by its wonderful taste. The egg has become the friend of all its food associates from soups down to *pâtisseries,* not forgetting hors-d'oeuvres. And when the *plat de résistance* is presented in the scrambled or omelet form, it has become, because of the eggs, one of the masterpieces of the culinary art. No wonder the rooster crows with such dignity! In saluting the arrival of the early morning sun he is announcing to the world that his chicken coop is in order and that his hens are ready to lay eggs in such abundance that, scrambled or in omelet form, they could fill every plate in every family in the universe.

In order to make a good omelet, one that is appreciated, do not beat the eggs too much. Salt and pepper them, and stir gently three or four times, or, just enough to break the yolks. Place a piece of butter into an omelet pan and when it becomes very hot stir them gently into the pan with a fork. When they thicken from contact with the butter and heat, begin to roll them down with your fork to form the omelet. Tip the pan and place another piece of butter at the point where you left off rolling it. The omelet should be soft inside and brown outside. This result is only obtained by not being too stingy with your butter, and in using it the way I have instructed. A piece placed on top just

29

before you begin to roll it into shape will immensely improve the softness and taste. An omelet of any kind, no matter what the recipe, must basically be started under the principle used herein.

Too many people scramble eggs directly into the frying pan. I call such a dish a spoiled omelet and an awful scramble. To be at their best, scrambled eggs must be prepared in reverse of the omelet. They must be separated from contact with the fire by the use of a double boiler, contrary to the almost direct flame which is necessary to the latter. An aluminum double boiler should not be used, since it will spoil the color and taste. Aluminum utensils should not be used in the preparation of white sauces or egg sauces. Beat the eggs thoroughly to a liquid. Place a generous piece of butter into the upper part of the double boiler after the water has started to boil. When it becomes hot pour in the eggs. Let them come into contact with the butter for a moment, and then begin to stir them with a wooden spoon. When they have thickened to the consistency of heavy cream, add another generous piece of butter, and then stir very fast. The finished scrambled eggs must be swelled and thickened; soft, but not running. I hope you will enjoy them; in tasting them I hope you will be able to distinguish between grub and real food. Any recipe concerning scrambled eggs should be followed through in this same manner.

QUALITY RATHER THAN QUANTITY

FOOD MUST HAVE QUALITY. There are only two categories into which it can fall: excellent and poor. That which is for human consumption must be good; the poor, or secondary food, Nature intended for the animals and for fertilizer.

In your kitchen a good quality of food, rather than a great quantity, should prevail. And use no more than you need. The mere thought that you are cooking and assembling appetizing dishes from superior grades of food should give you pleasure, should attract you. Devote yourself to cooking with enthusiasm. To find you have succeeded in creating a dish which gives pleasure and is satisfying to those for whom you cook, whether family, friends, or employer, will give you great contentment. A cook, man or woman, that carries the title by profession, who doesn't put ambition and finesse into the preparing and serving of food would be much better off renouncing his or her position so close to the range. The best recipe in any culinary book must be accompanied by food of good quality and an intelligence that will make of it something tasty and refined; although economical, it will still have aroma, and should be presented with finesse.

Cream, butter, wines, spices and herbs are the most important ingredients to the completing of a fine cuisine. In my opinion fats, oils and flour should be employed only when the five necessities mentioned above cannot be afforded; they are not used in preparing a first-class dinner.

Uncooked oil is easily digested. It is only after it is cooked that it is difficult to assimilate.   If you have no butter , pour the uncooked oil onto the vegetables *after* they have been cooked, strained and seasoned with salt and pepper. It will add to the taste of the hot vegetables. *Do not* heat them after the oil has been added.

Flour is necessary to make good bread and cakes, but it should not be used for sauces or gravies, since it has no chance to become thoroughly cooked in the short time it is on the fire. Besides that, a sauce or a gravy prepared with flour is most difficult to digest. With the exception of the farmer, whose work facilitates digestion, there are many whose stomachs are not strong enough to support such a concoction, and so, indigestion results.

Water, which is the greatest of all liquids and necessary to life itself, is the only one from which a good sauce or gravy cannot be made. Water does its share in the cleaning, dissolving and tenderizing of various foods; its great duty, as far as cooking is concerned, stops there. At that point butter, cream and wines step in. To thicken sauces, white sauces especially, one or more egg yolks should be used. This will also improve the quality. For gravies use one tablespoon of wine, one tablespoon of cream and a similar quantity of butter. The addition of a pinch or two of salt and pepper will produce the finest accompaniment to meats and poultry. A smaller quantity of cream should be added to the gravy that is served with rare meats. Sauces and gravies are to cooking what blood is to man. Good blood generally makes a fine human being; likewise, good gravies and sauces, added to quality meats, make the perfect cuisine.

Finesse to me is everything. It is the beginning, the end, the soul of service; but I include in my definition of finesse a quality of thanks from the one who receives. For those who do not thank you—well, for such—ladle out the food with your eyes closed. That would be, using an American phrase, serving him right.

A FEW WORDS
CONCERNING STOCKS

THE RECIPES IN MY BOOK are not complicated. They may be quickly combined and will facilitate the fine art of cooking for the American woman.

The making of stocks requires lengthy preparations and large quantities of meat, poultry, fish, vegetables, etc. And plenty of bones. This is not a book for restaurant use but rather for the table for two; for a new America with the spirit of the old. It is entirely unnecessary for the little bride, for whom this is really written, to burden herself with the making of these foods. If she will keep a small bottle of magic meat extract handy on her pantry shelf, and use it when needed, it will eliminate many long hours of work for her and will assist in the creating of sauces which are necessary for the perfect cuisine. America, the wonderful, is practically the only country in which extracts of meat, etc., are available in small quantities.

But, in case you have any remaining beef or veal bones, or the carcass of any fowl, put them into a pot with a quart or a quart and a half of water and let them boil slowly and you will have a few cups of consommé.

Left-over cooked foods may be used as hashes, *arlequins,* hors-d'oeuvres, sandwiches, canapés, etc. But too much left-over food is a poor bargain. I repeat, food is at its best when you wait for *it* and not when *it* waits for you.

ADVICE FOR A LADY
WITH A
MARKET BASKET

APPLES

Split the stem. If it is soft and sappy it is a good apple, probably tree-ripened.

GRAPEFRUIT

Those with unblemished thin skins are most desirable. If there are black spots where the fruit was attached to the stem, beware.

ORANGES

Test for fragrance by scratching skin with finger-nail. As a general rule unblemished, brilliant skins are indications of ripeness and, consequently, of flavor.

PEACHES

Take those which are fragrant. Peaches with beautiful skins and no odor are usually tasteless.

MELONS

Open and taste. There is no other way to be sure of the quality of this variable fruit. Fragrance is a fairly sound test, however.

ASPARAGUS

Stem should be smooth near the cut and pink-white in color.

ARTICHOKES

Slice off the blackened end of the stem. If the cut shows white and moist they are fresh.

BROCCOLI

Take that which has short, crisp stems.

CABBAGE

Young and tender cabbage has closely packed leaves and only slight odor. Watch out for splits. They indicate worms at the center.

CARROTS

Should be firm and the tender green portion near the leaves cover only a narrow margin. If the green has spread the vegetable is overgrown and probably tough.

CAULIFLOWER

Flesh should be tightly packed and white. When it has spread, another and unsavory growth has begun.

EGGPLANT

The stem and attached green segments should adhere firmly to the skin; the pulp and seeds should be white. If the segments have begun to detach themselves the plant has started to spoil and the inside will be spotted with black.

OYSTER PLANT

Should snap crisply. If it bends before breaking the plant is fibrous.

LETTUCE

Should be firm and crisp. If it has been plunged in water to revive it the inside will be soft.

MUSHROOMS

Raise the skin. The flesh should be white. If it is dark the mushroom is spoiled.

PARSLEY

If fresh it will be fragrant.

PEAS

Press finger-nail into pod. If sap does not appear in the wound the peas are not fresh.

RADISHES

The center leaves should be small and the flesh crisp.

SPINACH

Select straight leaves of deep green hue. Curved leaves mean over-growth.

STRING BEANS

Fresh string beans have solid stems. Avoid those of anemic pallor.

SWEET POTATOES

Select those with smooth skins. If there are little rootlets attached the sweet potato will be fibrous and unpalatable.

TOMATOES

If vine ripened the tempting odor can be detected at arm's length.

TURNIPS

Test with finger-nail. If incision does not fill with liquid the turnip will be stringy.

WATERCRESS

Leaves should be brittle and so brilliantly green they appear varnished.

CHESTNUTS

Fresh, raw chestnuts suitable for cooking wear tight skins. If the skins can be rubbed off easily the chestnuts are probably stale.

BEEF

Beef should be streaked with fat.

CHICKEN

A young and tender chicken is soft to the touch at breast bone and second leg joint. Contrariwise, if those places feel tough the chicken is old.

LAMB

Look for meat of a delicate pinkness. Lamb that is red in color is of poor quality.

PORK

Meat should be very white, with plenty of fat.

FISH

Eyes should be brilliant and tongue moist. The fish should be very slippery, not sticky.

CRABS

A live crab is a good crab.

MUSSELS

Select the heavy ones.

OYSTERS AND CLAMS

Rap the shells together. If they sound like stones the inhabitants are alive and edible.

COFFEE

The crack in the bean should be almost invisible. If widely spread the flavor and aroma will be diminished.

HOW TO KEEP FOOD IN GOOD CONDITION

EGGS, BUTTER, CREAM, AND MILK should always be kept together, but separated from other foods.

Fish should be kept in solitude, because it will announce, by its smell, that it is no longer an inhabitant of the sea. It must be buried in ice, but not in the ice-box.

Cheese should be kept as a hermit or it will be a bad neighbor to the rest. Fowl should be kept separate from game, lamb, or mutton, since the meat of fur-bearing animals will more or less contaminate everything else. Eggs, butter, cream and milk if placed among other foods will become curious and will taste also of other things.

Vegetables, after they have been taken from the plants or vines, may be assembled and kept together without the fear that they will exchange tastes. One will not spoil the other. But on the vines it is different. Some of them are enemies, and, if they get too close to each other, will confuse their origins.

Fruits are friendly and may be associated in the same basket. A cool place instead of one that is icy will improve them. Nevertheless, the refrigerator is indispensable in certain climates and is a necessity which enables the community to keep nutriments in good condition. Thanks to the refrigerator we have the chance to keep many foods that are not in season. Thanks to it, also, the temptations and desires of many people are satisfied.

Flowers, also, like to be kept in a cool place—a place where they might play peek-a-boo with the sun, which will give them more luster.

HOW TO KEEP
COLD DISHES

It is a great mistake to put hot chicken, lamb, pork, fish, etc., into the refrigerator as soon as they have been removed from the fire. That roasted chicken, pork roast, etc., or boiled fish, etc., ought to be kept in a cool place that is protected from dust and flies, a place that the sun cannot reach to cause contamination by its heat. Then you will appreciate the fact that it will be juicier and tastier. The ice-box or refrigerator will absorb the flavor of your cooked meats; your cooked salmon will be about as savory as a piece of wood.

Vegetables, including potatoes, should be treated in the same way, and, when they are freshly cooked, should be eaten the same day and not placed in the refrigerator. A cool place is necessary where the temperature does not reach more than 75° and no less than 60°.

THE PANTRY SHELF

A WELL SUPPLIED PANTRY contains these necessities which will aid in producing a symphony in the kitchen:

Salt

Peppers—black, white, whole black, red and paprika

Sugars—granulated, brown, powdered and vanilla.

Vinegars—plain, tarragon and wine.

Mustards—English and American (prepared and powdered).

Sauces—Worcestershire, catsup and chili.

Flavor Vegetables—onions, garlic and shallots.

Spices and Herbs— allspice (whole and powdered), cinnamon (powdered and stick), thyme, mace, nutmeg, cloves (whole and ground), ginger, turmeric, saffron, curry, coriander, sage, bay leaves, basil, marjoram, savory, chervil, fennel, rosemary, dill, tarragon, capers, cardamon.

Extracts—meat, vegetable and fish.

Beverages—coffee, tea, chocolate and cocoa.

Oils—olive and any other good cooking or salad oil.

Legumes—dried beans (navy, red kidney, and black), dried peas and lentils.

Vanilla Beans or Extract

Other Staples—flour, baking powder, baking soda, cornstarch, molasses, maple syrup, rice, currants, raisins, gelatine, tapioca, grated cheese, cereals, crackers, broad and thin noodles, spaghetti, vermicelli, macaroni and assorted jellies.

In the refrigerator—eggs, milk, cream, butter, oranges, lemons, bacon, mayonnaise, French dressing and salad greens. Oranges and lemons have many uses; keep a few on hand to use in the preparation of sauces. Their skins are indispensable in the perfuming of sugar.

For cooking purposes hold on hand-1 bottle each of sherry, port, claret, white wine, rum, brandy, kirsch and curaçao. A few bottles of domestic claret should always be kept in reserve for enjoyment at the table.

THE PREPARATION OF GOOD COFFEE

THE FIRST REQUISITE for delicious coffee is necessarily the quality of the bean. Coffee of a cheap quality will not improve by boiling it in water. Generally speaking, America possesses, by importation, the finest coffees in the universe, with prices so reasonable that the inferior brands shouldn't ever find an available market. One good cup of that splendid beverage will leave a more pleasant memory to your taste than four cups that are no good. I advise you to have one good cup and forget the other three.

If you don't have the latest in coffee-makers, use the principle that was first employed in making it. That is: boil the water until it is rolling and then add the coffee. When it has boiled up to the top of the pot, turn the fire out. Then add 2 tablespoons of cold water; this will cause the bubbling coffee to go down and clarify it more quickly. The quantity of coffee used depends on whether you prefer it weak or strong. Generally 2 heaping tablespoons to 2 cups of water will be sufficient for two. If you can afford it one additional tablespoon would make it still better.

The pot, to begin with, must be very clean. The coffee must be like flowers, fresh. If it is at all possible it should be ground just before using. Do not reheat the already prepared coffee which has stood for more than twenty minutes; it will lose its aroma and completely destroy its taste.

The same principle is followed in the making of "farmer coffee," with the exception of the water. Instead of 2 cups of water use 3 cups of milk.

CAFE DIABLO FOR TWO

Boil 2 cups of water and 2 tablespoons of sugar. Separately measure and mix 2 tablespoons of finely powdered coffee (ground almost to the consistency of flour) with 1 teaspoon of sugar. Pour this slowly into the sugar water which has reached a rolling boil, stirring it slowly with a spoon. The water and coffee are mixed under the same principle as chocolate. Pour it immediately; straining is not necessary. Sprinkle a few drops of orange blossom water into each cup of coffee. Large candied gum drops, any flavor but mint, are generally served with it.

TURKISH COFFEE FOR TWO

Prepare 4 small cups of very strong black coffee. A silver bowl is necessary for this recipe. Heat it until it becomes very hot. Dip 2 lumps of sugar into Angostura Bitters and then place them into the preheated bowl. Add a small piece of stick cinnamon, 2 bay leaves and 3 cloves. Into this, thinly cut the skins of ½ lemon and ½ orange (no pulp). Then add 1 pony of brandy, 1 pony of curaçao and 1 pony of kirsch. Make the contents of the bowl flame by touching it with a burning match. Immediately extinguish it by pouring in the 4 small cups of already prepared strong black coffee. Strain and serve. This coffee is also called "Coffee Royal" since it was created for the first time by King Henri IV of Navarre.

WINE ON THE TABLE

WHAT IS WINE? Since the beginning of time it has been called the "liquid of health." In France people consider it as a part of their food, not as alcohol or an intoxicant; it is found on the table for any occasion. In America people are becoming better acquainted with this wonderful liquid, the price of which, at the present time, is too exorbitant. A gallon of wine should not cost $4 or more. In the early days of the Original Henri I purchased it from George Dubois for myself and my employees for forty-two cents a gallon. There was wine on the table in the kitchen at all times, a custom which I found eliminated drunkenness. Because it is too expensive this wonderful natural drink is passed up for hard liquor.

A campaign should be made by the government to facilitate the purchase of wine rather than hard liquor. If the grape growers and merchants of our country do not wish to coöperate with the government by selling it cheaper, then the government should employ all the help necessary to grow and maintain arbors which would produce wine for civilian consumption. There would be fewer drunkards.

Wine should not be considered an alcoholic beverage, but should be looked on as a food. For centuries it has been given to children. I myself was raised on it, and from the time I was four have had a daily glass of claret, prohibition or no prohibition. I felt I was simply exercising common sense in violating an uncivilized law which stupidly forbade the drinking of a beverage that is as old as Christ.

A good wine reaches an alcoholic content of 12% or more; an inferior from 9% to 7%. There is no such thing as a 4% wine. One could not descend so low as to drink 4% and call it wine. In a few words, it is like a human being; it must be permitted to grow to the fullest extent of its quality, just as a human should to the fullest extent of his intelligence.

The proper wine greatly enhances the individual flavors of the various foods it accompanies, and serves to eliminate other beverages which do not belong with certain dishes. For example: a cup of coffee is excellent at the end of a meal, but, from the point of view of the specialist in fine food, hardly makes a suitable accompaniment for the dishes which make up a splendid dinner. The spices and delicate flavors so carefully created are lost in such a combination while a glass of dry wine would be delightful to your palate and greatly increase your appreciation of the dish you are eating. When a cocktail is to be served before dinner, it should be taken ten to fifteen minutes before the meal. Two cocktails previous to dining is the limit for one who appreciates a good dinner; more will not help digestion.

Dry white wines should be served with oysters or shell fish, broiled fish and most plain food without sauces. When sauces accompany fish or sea foods, a sweeter white wine should be chosen.

With an entrée, serve a claret or vin-rouge. For example: with a sweet bread *cocotte grand-mère,* or lamb in different forms, sauté of chicken or any kind of food with sauce—sweet, piquant or aromatic—these wines will aid in appreciation of the individual tastes of these dishes.

With roasts, including poultry, beef, pork or game, red Burgundies are best.

Salad should always be neutral. No wines whatever, or any other liquid, should interfere with the mystery of those wonderful mixed greens.

With cheese, which is one of the most particular friends in every menu, a port wine is the best choice. Before proceeding to the innumerable desserts that you may add to your menu, a rest period of fifteen minutes is recommended after the cheese course.

With Crêpes Suzette serve Château Yquem, the wine that kings have chosen as an appropriate accompaniment to this royal dessert.

Pâtisseries, tarts, *mendiants* such as figs, dry raisins, almonds, walnuts, hazelnuts, petits fours, dry cakes and fruits, should be accompanied by Champagne. This bubbling wine, every glassful of which represents the sun, offers the toast and wish that every one of its bubbles, as it breaks, will bring happiness to the whole world. In every nation, on every continent, Champagne is chosen for this expression. It is the wine of Romance, of conversation; it facilitates the expression of a full heart and enables each to speak in his own language.

Coffee comes last, like fireworks, to express itself in the finale of a beautiful dinner. It is apropos to take it black, as a large cup with cream or milk would not be appropriate at the end of a superb dinner. Cognac or cordials should be served with it.

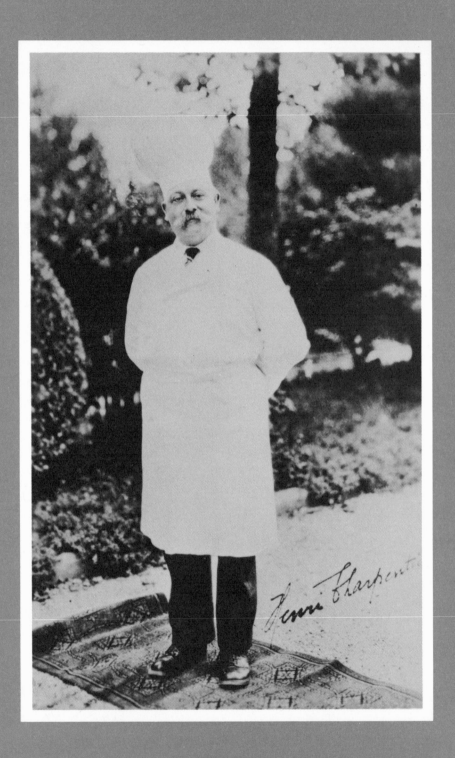

Chapter One

WHAT IS LIFE?

I, HENRI CHARPENTIER, have been, and still am, the pupil of the three great masters of hostelry and the culinary art: César Ritz, Auguste Escoffier, and Jean Camous. In memory of those three great gentlemen, who have passed on, I would like to pay homage before it is too late. Today may be ours, but tomorrow belongs to the unknown. I have therefore decided to add a few lines, in the great tradition of restaurateurs, concerning food, and to also add experiences and knowledge, which began for me at an early age in my little village of Contes on the French Riviera in the Alps, and which I am still collecting after more than half a century.

In the latter part of September in 1890 I was introduced to the fascinating aromas emanating from the kitchen of the Hotel Cap Martin. On that memorable day I stood on tiptoe to appear taller in front of the manager, the very much appreciated Mr. Charles Ulrick, the Czechoslovakian born *hôtelier* who engaged me on the recommendation of Jean Camous, my foster-brother. I didn't give my age and he thought I was already in long pants. I had great assurance. In my opinion if I had had a pipe in my mouth my face would have looked like that of a grown man. But I was only ten.

Born of the very finest of French parents, fate deprived me of them in the early days of my life. My mother was eighteen when I was born and my father was fifty eight. This same fate, in exchange, placed me with the kind family of Maman and Papa Camous, their three children, Jean, Celestin, and Césarina, and the old Giroumetta, gentle mother of Papa Camous, who, on my arrival as a small baby in that good home, was already past 100 years of age. It was a great privilege to grow among those lovely people and to have danced, as a little boy, with Giroumetta a few weeks before she died. She was 107 and I was 7. I felt a great loss at the death of this wonderful grandmother who had accepted me, the little orphan, without my having been of blood relationship. She took me, as the rest of them did, sincerely to her heart, and would have quarrelled with anyone who ever said that I was not one of her family. Maman and Papa Camous, Jean, Celestin, and Césarina raised their hands in approval of the old lady's expression. The death of my own parents was replaced to such an extent that I never felt I was an orphan.

In the little school in our village my wonderful professor, François Draghui, with his heavy beard and light pay of fifty francs monthly, taught all the boys, including myself, to be polite, to be generous, and to be, at all times, gentlemen. He could not teach them how to become wealthy, because by looking at his own monthly pay he reached the easy calculation that in the life God had given him, although joined to that of his lovely wife who taught the girls, it was unlikely that he would ever become wealthy, and certainly an impossibility that he would ever be listed among the millionaires. All because the first teachings of those two lovely people were constituted in the three words: honesty, sincerity, and kindness. Three words which are the enemies found on the road to becoming wealthy.

Those words were repeated also by the very humble priest of my village, Don Albini, who wore three pairs of eyeglasses. One pair was worn close to the eyes, and the other two pairs, pince-nez, were worn on top of the first. Both were tied by black ribbons. The gentle Père Don Albini practised the same three words: honesty, sincerity, and kindness. He represented one of the finest soldiers in the army of God's believers. A gentleman with the intelligence and the knowledge to become a pope, but in his own kind heart the only ambition it pleased him to remain was that of being a soldier of God. During those many, many years in which he served Him, he baptized the little fellows, married the young couples, and buried those who died, young and old. Using the same prayers and pomp for each one who died, he accompanied the procession from the church to the cemetery, and there in his eyes, we remarked very often, were a few tears which he said were perspiration from the sun on his glasses. And then he softly said, "There shall be a resurrection. We will meet again, for there is no death." With those simple words, Père Don Albini encouraged everyone.

That grand old priest brings to mind several stories, the first of which I shall bring to you now.

It was spring in Contes, one of those beautiful Sundays in April for which the French Riviera is so famous. The countryside was green and lovely; violets and daisies formed an enchanting panorama, and all the beauties of Nature were conspiring to intoxicate me. The violets, peeking through the grass, were intermingled with the daisies that wanted to show their superiority by having height, but could not reach them, either in quality or perfume. The *paquerettes* also wanted to be among the blossoms that embellished the spring day. The blue of the violet with its fragrant odor, the white of the daisy with its golden button in the center, the *paquerette* entirely yellow, and the grass in its green tenderness, all spoke the language of God, noiselessly. Each nodded to little Henri and said, "This is our life, what is yours?" With their voices singing in my heart, I left them most reluctantly. I had to hurry to my afternoon class of catechism before the vespers so I would not be tardy. Facing the priest, Don Albini, with great courage and audacity, I said, "Monsieur le curé, I would like to ask you something."

"Ah!" he said, "you again. Hm-m-m, hm-m-m. Well, what is it?"

As I looked at him, and saw his long nose supporting those three pairs of eyeglasses, he looked to me like a tree, frozen and full of ice in the wintertime. I was to find out later in life that his nose, at that moment, really did look like a frozen tree whose branches were composed of those black ribbons. I didn't know if I dared to laugh or not. Instead I asked, "Monsieur le curé, what is life?" From his slightly stooped position he straightened up, and bit his lips; then slowly he took off the first pair of pince-nez, cleaned both sides with his red handkerchief and placed them in the right side of his belt. Slowly, graciously he did the same with the second pair, and placed them in his upper pocket. At that moment he looked to me like a Cossack. If those ribbons had been white instead of black his uniform would have resembled one still more closely. With his finger he pushed the third pair to his forehead, and there for the first time I saw the clear, twinkling eyes of Père Don Albini. Into my little head came the thought, "Don Albini is not sincere, because he wears three pairs of eyeglasses and to look at me he needs none." Then he bent down to me, and with his strong hands vigorously took hold of my ears and raised me off the floor, like a rabbit. Then he put me back on my feet, saying ferociously, "Don't you know there is a great deal of mystery that we have no right to penetrate?"

I could not go and ask the flowers what it was that constituted life, because in their language they would have laughed "ho! ho!" and "ha! ha!" at me. I had had enough of penetrating the mystery of life on that first day when my inquisitiveness brought me nothing but sore ears. But stubborn and curious, at this time of my life, I thought of the three men in my whole village who represented knowledge, and who would have a solution for anything no matter how difficult. One of the three, I thought, would have the answer to any question that I might ask. The first was the curé, who, I thought by representing God, should be the first to be called upon. And so I had called on him.

Now the second was Monsieur Draghui, my professor, who educated and prepared me to be a free human being, instilling, by his teachings, ideals which are the foundation for a perfect civilization. The third was the mayor of the village, who was chosen and elected by the community. After these three little Henri had no more enlightened ones to call upon.

So the next day, Monday, I arrived at school with the feeling of

Maman and Papa Camous

pain still in my ears. Those aching ears gave me the courage to get for myself, maybe, a new spanking from the teacher, that is, if he had the same thoughts as the priest. I said to myself, "Bah! Pulled by the ears or spanked on the pants, it's worth it to learn, at least, what life is." And full of resolution and courage I raised my hand to ask the question of the teacher.

"Monsieur Draghui, I would like to ask you something."

He said, "Step to the front of the class, Henri."

On the wall behind his desk was a sign that read *"Silence, debout, assis."* The humming noises of the schoolroom ceased, and I got ready to ask the same question, which, twenty-four hours before, I had demanded of the priest. Monsieur Draghui caressed his beard and waited. The class in its anxiety wondered what it was going to be. I gave the kids a quick glance and turned again to Monsieur Draghui. Looking directly at him, I said, "Sir, I ask you to tell me, what is life?" One great laugh, like the crack of a whip, escaped from those 110 boys. At that moment, very slowly, and with great dignity, Monsieur Draghui turned to face them.

He said, "Boys, I demand silence, and no laughter." Then he raised me to his desk so the kids might look at me.

He said, "Here's a little fellow who demands things that I have never read of yet, or have any knowledge of, but he hopes and expects to get an answer from me because I am the professor."

He turned his face to me and said, "My boy, a year, which is a part of life, is divided into four seasons: winter, which looks so calm and unproductive to the eyes of the world, is the season in which great things for the future are drawing to a head; spring, which has only beauty, is the time when tender vegetation and fruits are in blossom form only, and everything is mild to the eyes of the world; summer, when the blossoming trees are distinguished by their transformation into one kind of fruit or another; and finally autumn, which brings the harvest and is the only season to reap the benefits of the other three. Potatoes are gathered, fruits are picked in their maturity, grains are stored, grapes are gathered for wine, etc., etc. My poor boy, you are still in the winter, and you demand an answer of the autumn."

At this answer I looked at him and saw two big tears rolling from his eyes to his beard. I excused myself by saying, "Did I ask something wrong, Monsieur Draghui?"

"No, my little fellow, you have made me think of something that I have never thought of before. But I'm afraid you will never be entirely satisfied in this life that you ask me to explain to you."

I was only seven, and I realized later that we should remain for many, many years in the winter season, and by dreaming, enjoying, and living in the period of childhood we should not disturb the future knowledge which would come in its own time, as the fruit would ripen on the tree. I was very pleased that I had learned something that day.

It occurred to me also that if my name was Charpentier, and the name of the family I lived with was Camous, then I was exactly like the little duck in our village that was adopted by a mother hen. In fact, those most entertaining birds were our neighbors. Poor mother hen! The only time she ever screamed was the time that that little duck ran away from his brothers and sisters, the little chicks, and jumped into the pond, which was 150 feet long and about 100 feet wide and which had been placed there to irrigate the flowers and vegetables on our neighbor's property. By the screaming cackle and "ck-ck-ck" of the mother hen I knew that she wasn't laying an egg, but was in great trouble. I ran to the water and saw the little fellow swimming around with great unconcern for the trouble he was causing. His nine or ten brothers and sisters looked on, frozen with fear, while the mother hen rushed back and forth showing great anxiety. Her worried look seemed to say, "Of all my family, this little rascal always disobeys me." She could never believe and never understand that she had a champion swimmer in the family. I watched the return of that prodigal litttle fellow. Chicks and mother hen received him with enthusiasm as he ran quickly under the wing of his wonderful adopted mother. He never felt that he was an orphan, and just as he had the love of all in his foster-family, so had I in mine.

In the satisfaction of the answer given to me by Monsieur Draghui, I refrained from asking my question of the mayor. Later I was to be glad of it, because as I grew up and learned more, I discovered that although the mayor himself was a good man, he knew that Paris was in France but that was all.

RECIPES

✦

CANAPE, OLIVER EVANS

✦

SOUP, DAVID RITTENHOUSE

✦

OMELET, WILLIAM CLAIBORNE

✦

SCRAMBLED EGGS, THOMAS HOOKER

✦

BROILED FILLET OF SOLE, OLIVER PERRY

✦

PHEASANT, SAMUEL MORSE

✦

POTATOES, JOHN STEVENS

✦

BRAISED ENDIVE, HUGH ORR

✦

SALAD, RICHARD HOE

✦

STRAWBERRIES, ANNE BRADSTREET

✦

CANAPE, OLIVER EVANS

Prepare 2 slices of buttered toast. Cut 1 large tomato into 6 slices and place 3 slices on each piece of toast. Cut some green peppers julienne style and put them over the tomatoes. Then place 3 cooked shrimps on each slice. Mix 1 chopped hard-boiled egg with 1 finely chopped shallot, and sprinkle on top of the shrimps. To each slice carefully add 1 tablespoon of French Dressing. To finish, top each slice with 2 anchovy fillets.

SOUP, DAVID RITTENHOUSE

Chop: 1 onion, 1 raw peeled potato, and 1 stalk of celery. Cut up a few celery leaves. Let this simmer with a piece of butter in a covered pot. Then add 1 quart of water. Sprinkle with pepper and salt. Let it boil over a slow fire for 1 hour. Be sure the pot is covered. After boiling for 1 hour, pass water and all through a sieve into a double boiler. Add 2 tablespoons of cream, 1 tablespoon of butter, and the yolk of 1 egg. In case you wish to make the soup thicker dissolve ½ teaspoon of cornstarch in ½ glassful of milk, and add it, stirring constantly until it has become thick. Season to taste with pepper and salt. Place 2 tablespoons of finely chopped celery hearts into a tureen as well as 2 tablespoons of cream and a generous piece of butter. Pour the soup into the tureen.

OMELET, WILLIAM CLAIBORNE

Chop into very small pieces 1 thin slice of lean, cooked ham. Mix 2 finely chopped shallots as well as 2 finely chopped green onions, stems and all, with the ham.

Brown 1 tablespoon of butter in an omelet pan. Beat 6 eggs, just enough to break the yolks, and add the chopped ham, etc., to them. Pour into the omelet pan and cook in the usual way. Season to taste.

SCRAMBLED EGGS, THOMAS HOOKER

The day before you wish to prepare this recipe cook ¼ bunch of asparagus, pour off water, cool, and place in the refrigerator. The next day cut off and use the dry asparagus tips. Place 1 tablespoon of butter into a frying pan with 1 chopped shallot. Add at the same time the cut asparagus tips, 2 tablespoons of cream, and a sprinkle of salt and pepper. Slowly cook it until the first boil.

Scramble 6 eggs and place on a platter. Pour the asparagus, etc., over the scrambled eggs, and sprinkle with grated cheese.

BROILED FILLET OF SOLE, OLIVER PERRY

Place 4 fillets of sole into a baking platter with 2 tablespoons of melted butter. Turn from side to side until the fillets have become moistened with the melted butter. Salt, but do not pepper. Put the baking platter into the broiler, and then do not turn the fillets anymore. The broiler must be good and hot, but the flame must not be too high. Baste the fillets until they become brown. This will take 15 minutes. When they are nice and brown place 3 thin slices of fresh tomato over them, and sprinkle with a pinch of finely chopped shallots. Put them back under the broiler for 5 minutes. Season.

PHEASANT, SAMUEL MORSE

The feathers and the entrails of your pheasant should not be removed until the day you cook it. A pheasant, to be good, must, after shooting, be allowed to hang 4 or 5 days in a cool place where there are no flies, and no sun. It must not be skinned, but dry picked instead. And do not wash it. After it has been picked and cleaned, dry the inside with a cloth. Hold the pheasant over a flame and rotate in order to remove the remaining feathers and to give the skin a nice flavor. The flame must be permitted to penetrate the inside of the carcass for a moment or two, and the opening must be made a little larger for this to be accomplished. Place 3 pepper-corns inside the carcass as well as: 1 or 2 bay leaves, a few sprinkles of salt, a sprig or two of parsley, 2 unpeeled cloves of garlic, ¼ peeled raw onion, 2 or 3 juniper berries, a pinch of thyme, the tops of 1 stalk of celery (not the celery), and 2 strips of bacon which will moisten the carcass as well as oil the rest of the ingredients. Place 2 thin slices of raw ham on the breast of the pheasant and then truss the legs and breast properly to make the ham as well as the ingredients inside secure. Put the pheasant on its side in a casserole, and add a generous piece of butter. Baste it very often. A pheasant must remain juicy, but it must not be undercooked, and 25 to 30 minutes in a very hot oven should be sufficient. It should be turned as well as basted at least 10 times during this period. Before serving you must empty the carcass of its ingredients which are no longer necessary. Place the pheasant on a hot platter.

Add 1 finely chopped shallot to the casserole in which the bird has been cooked. Then, add 2 tablespoons of white or red port wine (it must be of good quality), and after wine and gravy begin to bubble stir in 1 tablespoon of butter.

Pour the gravy over the pheasant, and serve with the slices of ham. Season.

POTATOES, JOHN STEVENS

Peel, wash, and dry 3 or 4 potatoes. Place a generous piece of butter into a round baking dish, melt it, and then slice 2 layers of potatoes compactly into the dish. Add a little more melted butter and ½ clove of finely chopped garlic. Sprinkle with salt. Slice 2 more layers of potatoes, and again add a little more melted butter and a sprinkle of salt. Slice 1 more layer of potatoes, making 5 layers in all. Sprinkle some grated cheese over the top, add more melted butter, and a final sprinkle of salt. Put in a hot oven for 35 or 40 minutes. The success of these potatoes depends not only on the compactness of the layers, but on the way they are cooked. The finished product must look like a cake, the inside of which is soft and lovely.

BRAISED ENDIVE, HUGH ORR

Do not confuse the real endive with what is commonly known as salad endive. The real endive has the appearance of celery, is very compact, and is sold by the pound, and not by the head or by the dozen.

Wash 4 endives and place them into a baking dish. Add 1 tablespoon of butter, 1 chopped shallot, and season with pepper and salt. Pour 1 cupful of consommé and 1 tablespoon of meat extract into the baking dish. Place the dish in a hot oven for 1 hour until the endives are soft and brown. Serve hot.

SALAD, RICHARD HOE

Prepare the heart of 1 romaine salad by cutting it in half lengthwise. Peel 1 orange, 1 grapefruit and 1 alligator pear with a knife, and in doing so be sure to remove all the white pulp from the orange and the grapefruit. Cut them into sections. Arrange 1 section of orange, 1 section of grapefruit, and 1 slice of alligator pear on each half of the romaine salad. Do this alternately until the romaine has been covered.

Squeeze the juice of the remaining orange and grapefruit peelings into a separate dish, and add to it the juice of ½ lemon, 1 pinch of salt, 1 pinch of pepper, ½ teaspoon of sugar, and 2 tablespoons of olive oil. Mix together, pour over the salad.

STRAWBERRIES, ANNE BRADSTREET

Wash 1 pint of strawberries while they still retain their stems. If you do so after their stems have been removed you will wash away half their juice. Now, remove the stems. Put them into a bowl. Sprinkle with 3 tablespoons of sugar and add the juice of ½ lemon. Cover the bowl with a plate and shake the strawberries thoroughly for 3 or 4 minutes. Pour 1 glassful of claret over the strawberries. Mix and serve. These strawberries are usually accompanied by lady fingers.

Chapter II

THE THREE DEVILS

As LONG as Monsieur Draghui had said youth should be a time for happiness only, I used those precious days to become more proficient in running, jumping, and all the various athletic sports.

I liked the birds and imitated their songs and complaints. In no time at all I could converse with them. I felt sure they understood me, because they answered my calls. But when it came to what the birds were saying, even Monsieur Draghui could not help me.

Among the goats of the village was my own pet, Blanchette, who had only one horn. I presume that she lost one of them by defending her title in a fight with a stronger goat. She would not accept an insult, and so, although she survived the quarrel, she lost one horn. Blanchette felt badly about that, but, horn or no horn, she was still a very proud goat.

Bacci, the dog of the house of Camous, was my friend and companion. He was one of those mutts who might have had the respect of his mother, but he certainly had no pedigree. He, also, was a surprising animal.

At 4 P. M., after climbing the four steps, Blanchette, just as if she had a watch, pushed open the door of the schoolhouse with her horn. This movement made all the boys turn toward the sound. We had already heard her "ma-a-a," and one bark from Bacci, and by that Monsieur Draghui knew it was 4 o'clock.

"Class is dismissed," he said.

61

Charpentier carving a roast duck. In the background is a gaily-decorated parsley-and-flower platter. The dish in front is a hot fruit compote, served as an accompaniment.

Preparing shredded lettuce is an art in the hands of a master chef.

The entire room stood up, the little fellows filing out first, one by one, then the medium-sized, and finally the taller ones. Each kid saluted the professor on the way out. I was one of the very smallest, but I was in the advanced section of medium-sized boys. Bacci and Blanchette were anxiously waiting for me to come out, and many faces passed them by. They were not pleased that I was not the first to greet them. When I approached the door, Bacci pushed two or three other boys aside in order to jump to my face and lick me. This was a daily occurrence so the kids made room for me. Both animals were the friends of all the class. I scratched Blanchette on the place where her horn was missing and a little under her chin. With intelligent eyes, she looked at me, her continuous mastication moving her whiskers back and forth. If she had had a mustache she would have looked like Napoleon III, but without the title of "Majesty." Bacci ran around excitedly; he was ready to lead the parade which took place every day except Thursday and Sunday. There was no school in France on those days. I hung my books around my neck by the strap, grabbed Blanchette's horn, and with one foot hitting the ground every ten feet, we went like mad up the street with Bacci leading and clearing the way. We ran so fast and with such abandon it would have been too bad if anyone had been in the way. Old ladies stood on their steps or peeked through the windows when all that running through the street took place those five days a week. I was the only boy in Contes to cause such a disturbance, and the old people invariably said, "Don't they look like three devils, those three running there?" Bacci was proud to be the leader, and Blanchette did not regret having lost one horn because she was very popular among the other goats. Through those two I became the rascal of the village.

The Incorrigible Henri

In my childhood I sang quite well, but do not confuse my voice of then with my voice of today which has disappeared because of sampling too many good sauces and too much good food. But to return to the village and my good voice, which became quite evident at the tender age of seven. It was then that Père Don Albini chose me for an altar boy. He appreciated me very much except when I was up to some kind of mischief. The only thing I didn't like about being an altar boy was the hour I had to arise in order to be present at the early mass six days a week. I made Maman Camous laugh more than once by saying, "Maman, why does God want a mass so early in the morning? There is nobody there. Why doesn't the priest change the hour, anyway?" Only a few old people attended the early mass, those who were too old to sleep long and who were afraid they might die before they woke up. They were pleased to see another sunny day, never believing that one morning they would be absent from the church. I have always remembered the logic and wonderful spirit of Don Albini. He said that when the church was empty his imagination and memory pictured it as crowded, and that every seat was taken by all those he had baptized, those he had married, and those old, old ones whose only recreation was going to church. I understood his beautiful words later in life when I realized that my thoughts were similar to his and it was not necessary to be a priest to have them. By storing up in your memory moments which are crowded with happiness, the empty hours in life could be filled again. Then you would never be lonely.

Among the older people of the village there were about seventy who were past 100 years of age. If you saw one you saw them all. Folks with no teeth and no hair. The section on the right facing the altar was reserved for the men, and the section on the left for the ladies. All the old people sat in the first pews. Ladies, their hair covered with foulards, and men, who were nearly all deaf and who had been the babies of a century ago, had grown up together and had split good and bad days like one large family. One whispered to the other, "Who is going to be the first of the bald-heads to reach St. Peter?" The other fellow, because he was deaf, cupped his hand to his ear and screamed to the first one, who was deaf also, "What did you say?" Still it was not understood. Wonderful Don Albini continued his mass without paying any attention, since he was accustomed to those deaf old men. It was not the same among the younger ones, especially the children. All had respect for the church, but their youth was stronger, and some broke out laughing. Don Albini turned, not to say "Amen," but to look at them. I always managed to be in the middle of anything that was going on. It was my duty, as an altar boy, to attend to the censer which held burning incense, and to see that it was properly distributed by shaking it during the mass. By my laughing fit I almost put out the glowing incense. In the outburst I am afraid I gave the censer a bath. The priest, having remonstrated with me fifty times, and not being able to change my spirit and my laughing spells, counted me as one of the old men and paid no more attention to me. Very clever of him. Here was another mystery. How could one make an old fellow into a young one, or a young fellow into an old one? In mischief, I turned and shook the censer at the old people when Don Albini's back was turned. It was smoking like a chimney because I had added some extra incense. Again I was guilty. It smelled so grand those wonderful old bald-heads began to inhale it together, like annoyed elephants raising their trunks. Later I found out about elephants too, but right then the whole church was filled to the ceiling with smoke.

The old folks began to cough and sneeze, but all the time enjoying it. I was caught again doing something I should not be doing. After the Sunday mass Don Albini called me to the sacristy.

"Why do you burn so much incense?" he demanded.

"Monsieur le curé," I said, "if I hadn't put in that quantity there would have been none left for God, because those big noses would have taken it all before it reached the ceiling." I still believe today that He was there among those old people in the church, and inspired me to be generous with the incense, thereby making the poor priest still poorer by a few pennies. Each of the seventy old-timers smiled with contentment and happiness; even God Himself, I was sure, could see the thrill of the old people and the freckles on the incorrigible little Henri.

Giroumetta, my gentle grandmamman, was one of those who sat in the front row, and the very first to say to me later, "Your incense, Henri, smelled wonderful." She said that after the priest I was to be titled "owner of the church."

RECIPES

✤

HORS-D'OEUVRE, HENRY VAN DYKE

✤

CHICKEN SOUP, STEPHEN FOSTER

✤

OMELET, CHRISTOPHER SHOLES

✤

SCRAMBLED EGGS, ROBERT STEVENS

✤

POMPANO, JAMES BUCHANAN

✤

CREAMED CHICKEN, WILLIAM PENN

✤

POTATOES, ROBERT PEARY

✤

CARROTS, JOHN HAY

✤

DANDELION SALAD, BENJAMIN HOTCHKISS

✤

BAKED ALASKA, LOUISA MAY ALCOTT

✤

HORS-D'OEUVRE, HENRY VAN DYKE

Peel and slice 2 cold boiled potatoes that have been cooked in their jackets. Add ¼ pound of shredded, cold boiled salmon, pepper and salt, 1 small sliced tomato, and 1 finely cut raw onion. Mix together with 1 tablespoon of French Dressing. Place on plates and put 1 table-spoon of mayonnaise over the top of each. Cut 1 hard-boiled egg into quarters and arrange on top. Place ½ lemon on each plate, and garnish with parsley.

CHICKEN SOUP, STEPHEN FOSTER

Clean a 3 pound chicken and place it in 3 quarts of water. Add to the pot: 1 whole peeled onion into which 2 cloves have been stuck, 2 whole scraped carrots, a few celery leaves, and a little parsley. Boil for 40 minutes. Remove the chicken and put it aside. Take 1 quart of the broth and stand the rest aside to be used another time. Put 1 tablespoon of rice into the quart of broth, and boil until the rest of the recipe is ready.

Now take the fleshy part of one of the chicken legs, cut it into small pieces, and place it in a separate casserole. Add 1 peeled chopped tomato, 1 chopped onion, 4 okras which have been cut into small pieces, ½ finely chopped green pepper, 1 finely chopped stalk of celery, and 1 tablespoon of butter. Let it simmer for 10 minutes. Add the chicken broth and rice to the casserole, and let it boil for 10 more minutes. Season with salt and pepper.

OMELET, CHRISTOPHER SHOLES

Place 1 tablespoon of butter into a frying pan with 1 finely chopped shallot. After a moment add 1 peeled very ripe tomato, 3 chicken livers which have been cut into halves, 2 sliced mushrooms, ½ tablespoon of meat stock. Cook for 10 minutes. Make an omelet (see chapter on How to Make Omelets and Scrambled Eggs), and pour the sauce of chicken livers over it after the omelet has been properly rolled and is brown outside and soft inside. Salt and pepper to taste.

SCRAMBLED EGGS, ROBERT STEVENS

Scramble 6 eggs, using the chapter recommended in the preceding recipe as a guide.

Peel and cut into small pieces: 1 apple, 1 pear, and 1 peach. Place them in a pan and add the juice of 1 orange, 1 heaping tablespoon of sugar, and a generous piece of butter. Let it come to a boil, and pour over the scrambled eggs. Serve.

POMPANO, JAMES BUCHANAN

Clean 2 fresh pompanos that weigh about ½ pound each. Place them in a baking dish with a generous piece of butter, and sprinkle with 2 chopped shallots. Take a handful of ground hazelnuts and sprinkle them, also, over the top. Salt and pepper. Put in the oven at a temperature of 450° F. for 20 or 25 minutes. Baste the fish 2 or 3 times during the baking. Place them on a hot serving platter and squeeze the juice of ½ lemon over them. Measure 1 pony of brandy into a saucer, touch a flame to it and pour over the fish.

CREAMED CHICKEN, WILLIAM PENN

Place 1 tablespoon of butter, a few finely chopped chives, and 3 tablespoons of uncooked rice into a baking dish and stir for a few minutes over a fire to make them hot. Add 1 cupful of the chicken consommé that has already been prepared for the soup recipe in this menu. Put on top of the stove and stir constantly until the rice begins to swell. Place the baking dish into a hot oven. Add 1 tablespoon of consommé and stir. When it has been absorbed add another tablespoon of consommé and stir again. When the rice has swelled up still more add another tablespoon of consommé, stir it again, and proceed in this manner for 20 to 25 minutes until the rice is cooked soft, but firm, and does not stick together. Each grain is separate, even though it has been cooked.

Put 1 large tablespoon of butter into a frying pan with 2 finely chopped shallots. Cook for a moment, and then add 1 cup or more of cream. Mix ½ tablespoon of cornstarch in ½ glassful of cool liquid consommé, and then add 2 tablespoons of sherry to the dissolved cornstarch. Stir it into the shallots and cream and cook for a few moments until it becomes thick. It should not be too thick.

Warm up your chicken which has already been boiled for your soup recipe in this menu. Cut it into pieces, cover it with the rice, and pour over the above sauce. Season.

POTATOES, ROBERT PEARY

Peel and slice 3 cold boiled potatoes that have been cooked in their jackets. Put them into a pan with 2 sliced mushrooms and 1 clove of garlic which has been crushed into 1 tablespoon of chopped parsley. Add a generous piece of butter, and sauté for 10 minutes. Salt and pepper.

CARROTS, JOHN HAY

Scrape and wash 2 or more new carrots and cut them into small pieces. Put them into a pan that contains 1 pint of water, a pinch of salt, 1 teaspoon of sugar, and a few pepper-corns. Let them boil until they become tender. This usually takes from 35 to 40 minutes. Do not pour off the water. Add to the carrots and the remaining small quantity of water, a generous piece of butter, 2 tablespoons of cream, the juice of ½ lemon, and a little chopped parsley. Season.

DANDELION SALAD, BENJAMIN HOTCHKISS

Clean a handful of young dandelion greens. Wash and dry them well, and cut them. Chop 1 pickled beet and mix it with the dandelions.

Cut 2 strips of bacon into small pieces and put them into a frying pan. When the bacon is fried, add 1 tablespoon of wine vinegar, or any other kind that you may have, and 1 tablespoon of oil. Into this hot oil and vinegar break 1 egg and stir it.

Sprinkle the dandelions with salt and pepper, and pour the hot dressing over them.

BAKED ALASKA, LOUISA MAY ALCOTT

Have ready a sheet of sponge cake, and see that it is slightly bigger than your brick of ice cream.

Prepare the following meringue: Separate the whites of 6 eggs from the yolks. Beat them thoroughly, adding 3 tablespoons of sugar a little at a time.

71

Remove the brick of ice cream from the dry ice in which it has previously been packed. Place the ice cream in the center of the sponge cake. Completely cover the ice cream with the meringue, but do not cover the bottom of the cake. Put it on a board. Before browning the meringue in the oven indent the empty egg shells into the meringue. Put the whole thing into the oven, which has been made hot, until the meringue becomes brown. When it is ready to be served, pour a little curaçao into each egg shell, touch a flame to the liqueur, and serve at once.

Chapter III

THE EGGS ARE NOT ALL IN ONE BASKET

ONCE A YEAR, when Père Don Albini went around from home to home blessing each one, people gave their contributions to him and the Church. Four small boys were chosen to assist him. One kid carried a bucket of holy water, one carried the cross next to the priest, and the other two each carried a basket. I was one of the fellows with a basket. The priest held the aspergillum which was used to sprinkle the holy water. People who contributed put in *sous, dix-sous,* or francs. In those days there was no paper money of small denominations. The smallest was fifty francs and equivalent to ten dollars in American money. The *sous* were made of bronze and were as large as the United States quarter, but were equivalent to only a cent. The *dix-sous* were of silver, the size of, and equivalent to, the United States dime. The franc was a little smaller in size and denomination than the United States quarter, and it, also, was of silver. Sometimes someone would contribute two francs, a silver coin slightly smaller than the American half dollar. In the whole village we had only three or four millionaires, but I don't recall ever seeing anyone drop more than five francs in the bucket. I remember the kindness of Maman Camous, who, once a year, dropped her silver two francs in the bucket. Because of her poorness, she saved it, *sou* by *sou,* every day for a year, until she reached that contribution, which was considered large for her. God did bless her because she lived to be 100 years and two months of age and never was seriously ill. She repeated the same words every year. *"Dix-sous,*

73

Monsieur le curé," she said, "everything we can afford, and thirty *sous* more to repay what Henri has used in the church." This gave me the privilege, and almost the right, to take a few dozen eggs from the priest, because I had heard that Maman Camous had paid for them. I would help keep Don Albini in good health, then he wouldn't eat such large omelets and get sick from too much albumen. People who could not donate money gave a few eggs and other things as their contributions. When the priest was busy saying a prayer and sprinkling the holy water, my partner-friend with the other basket helped me hide the eggs. We tried to make some nests before the right season for such things. Not a sparrow's nest or any other bird's, but a chicken's nest, and without the hen. Among the parishioners there were many who were very generous with their eggs; they afforded us the opportunity my friend and I were waiting for. We could hide a few without fear of detection if there was a gift of many eggs. Whether Don Albini knew or not he never paid any attention to us; he found out later that when I came home with four or five dozen I was never allowed to keep them. Maman Camous never asked the why and wherefore, but always said, "Henri, take a few dozen over to Madame Marie," our neighbor who had a family but no chickens, "and tell her that Don Albini sent them." I felt that Maman Camous knew I was a young rascal but that I was not really a bad boy. I gave the eggs to the neighbor, but never mentioned that they came from the priest. Then how could Don Albini stop a charity which God Himself taught the world? "Never let the right hand know what the left one does" has always seemed very commendable to me.

RECIPES

✣

HORS-D'OEUVRE, PETER COOPER

✣

SOUP, DE WITT CLINTON

✣

POACHED EGGS, JOHN FITCH

✣

HAM AND EGGS, JOHN ADAMS

✣

CODFISH, PHILIP FRENEAU

✣

LAMB, GROVER CLEVELAND

✣

POTATOES, WILLIAM BRADFORD

✣

PEAS, JOHN CARVER

✣

GREEN SALAD, NATHANIEL MORTON

GREEN APPLE PIE, EMILY DICKINSON

✣

HORS-D'OEUVRE, PETER COOPER

Cook and strain a handful of green beans. Put on a serving platter. Place 2 herring fillets, which have been marinated, over the beans. Garnish with raw onions.

Mix, separately, 2 tablespoons of sour cream, the juice of ½ lemon, salt and pepper. Pour over the herring. Garnish the ends of the herring with cooked julienne beets. Sprinkle with chopped parsley and chopped shallots.

SOUP, DE WITT CLINTON

Chop 1 onion and let it simmer in a pot with 1 tablespoon of butter. When the onion is almost cooked, add 1 stalk of broccoli which has been cleaned and chopped very fine. Let the onion and the broccoli cook for a few minutes. Then, add 2 quarts of water, salt and pepper, and 2 strips of bacon which have been cut into small pieces. Let it boil from 45 minutes to 1 hour over a small flame. Break up ½ handful of very fine vermicelli, add it, and boil 15 more minutes. Before serving, add a piece of butter and 1 tablespoon of olive oil. Salt and pepper. In case you wish to make this soup using larger proportions it will improve by reheating.

POACHED EGGS, JOHN FITCH

Peel 2 potatoes and scrape 2 carrots and boil together. When they are done, pour off the water and mash them. Mix in 1 tablespoon of butter. Season with salt and pepper.

Poach 4 eggs, strain, and place them on top of the purée of potatoes and carrots.

Slice 2 uncooked pork sausages into a frying pan and add 2 chopped shallots, 1 large chopped tomato, 1 tablespoon of butter, 2 tablespoons of red claret, and ½ tablespoon of meat extract. Let it cook for 15 minutes. Prepare this garnish at the same time that you prepare your purée so that it will be ready to pour over the poached eggs. After pouring it over the eggs, sprinkle with a little chopped parsley that has been mixed with a few chopped, fresh tarragon leaves. Season with pepper and salt.

HAM AND EGGS, JOHN ADAMS

Put 2 small slices of boiled ham on a baking platter with 1 tablespoon of butter and place on top of the stove. Let the ham fry for a few minutes, and then turn it. Break 4 eggs into the platter on top of the ham. Then sprinkle bread crumbs on top of the eggs. Melt a piece of butter in a separate pan and when it is sizzling hot pour it over the eggs. Salt and pepper.

CODFISH, PHILIP FRENEAU

Use, in this recipe, 2 slices of fresh codfish which will usually weigh about ½ pound each. Dip them into flour and shake off the excess. Put 2 tablespoons of butter into an empty baking dish and place inside a hot oven. When the butter is hot put in the fish. Salt and pepper. After a few minutes on one side turn the fish and give it a few minutes on the other side. In a separate frying pan slice one large onion into 1 tablespoon of oil. Let it brown nicely on top of the stove. Cover the codfish, which has already baked for 40 minutes, with the browned onions and give it another 10 minutes in the oven. Salt and pepper.

LAMB, GROVER CLEVELAND

Take ½ rack of lamb and trim away the skin and fat that is usually found on top of the chops. Make the bones of the chops look like fingers. If you like, you might take a whole rack of lamb and serve it cold the next day.

Rub a clove of garlic on the bony side. Salt and pepper. Put the meat into a roasting pan. Peel one onion, cut into quarters, and add to the pan. Dip 2 unpeeled cloves of garlic into water and add them, also. Add 1 tablespoon of butter if it is ½ rack of lamb, and 2 tablespoons if it is a whole rack. The oven should be very hot before introducing the meat. Let it roast for 15 minutes before basting it. Turn the meat around so that the bony side is down and the meat side is up, and then baste it every once in awhile for 25 minutes. Generally, lamb should be roasted to a medium rare, but in case you want it to be very well done then leave it in the oven 55 minutes to an hour altogether instead of the usual 40 minutes. Remove the meat and place it on a very hot serving platter.

To the roasting pan, add a small piece of butter, 1 sherry-glassful of sherry and a pinch of pepper and salt. Place the pan on top of the stove over a large flame. When it begins to bubble pour it over the lamb.

Lamb must be eaten either very hot or entirely cold, because the fat is very disagreeable to the mouth of one who is refined. This rack of lamb must be carved and served like chops with the bones still attached to the meat.

POTATOES, WILLIAM BRADFORD

Peel, wash, and grate 3 potatoes. Squeeze the water from them. To these grated potatoes, add 1 tablespoon of milk, 1 finely chopped shallot, 1 raw egg. Mix together and add ½ tablespoon of flour. Shape and flatten into patties the size of a silver dollar, make them about ¼ inch thick. Dip the patties into flour and cook in boiling oil for 10 minutes. The oil should be deep enough to cover the patties. After 10 minutes on one side turn them over and cook for 5 minutes on the other side. Serve on a hot platter. Sprinkle with salt and pepper, and pour 1 tablespoon of melted butter over the finished dish.

PEAS, JOHN CARVER

Place in a pan 1 cupful of fresh green peas with just enough water to cover them. Salt the water. Add 1 teaspoon of sugar and a sprinkle of pepper. To reach the soft and tender stage fresh peas usually require 25 minutes of boiling in a pan which has been covered. Do not pour off the remaining water, which should be very little. Chop some parsley and add it to the peas with 1 generous tablespoon of butter. Let it remain on the fire for 1 minute. Mix separately a little salt, pepper, and sugar and when the peas are ready to be served sprinkle it over them.

GREEN SALAD, NATHANIEL MORTON

Mix a few leaves of lettuce, water-cress, and chicory. Add 1 chopped hard-boiled egg, 1 chopped tomato, and 2 tablespoons of French Dressing. Mix and serve.

GREEN APPLE PIE, EMILY DICKINSON

Peel, core, and slice enough tart apples for 1 pie into a mixing bowl. Sprinkle 4 tablespoons of sugar over the sliced apples, or if you prefer it more tart add only 2 tablespoons of sugar. Next, sprinkle on ¾ teaspoon of cinnamon and 1 level tablespoon of sifted flour. Add 2 tablespoons of water and 2 tablespoons of melted butter. Mix together. Place in a pie-tin which has been lined with pie-paste, and cover the top with a crust. Bake for 45 minutes. Your pie should be tasty and juicy.

Chapter IV

LIFE IN THE HOLY WATER

THE LITTLE VILLAGE OF CONTES is located in the Alps about one mile higher than the Paillon River and is approachable only by the main thoroughfare that winds up into the mountains. The world well knows the loveliness of the French Riviera, and its beauties were not wasted on little Henri. Those warm, carefree days after school were spent in the dazzling sunlight where I had for my teacher the most instructive one of all: Mother Nature. To me, she had not only great lessons of wisdom to teach, but also lessons of beauty which never failed to charm me. I was in love with her; she was the third of my lovely mothers.

On one of those happy afternoons I wandered down to the entrance of the village where I heard some little green frogs giving a serenade. Of course I found time to catch a dozen of them which I put into my beret. I was already thinking of the fun I would have with them that evening at benediction. I arrived at church twenty minutes earlier than anyone else in order to dispose of my captives. In the vestibule on either side were two holy water fonts.

I put half of the little frogs into one, and the remainder into the other. I then went to the sacristy where I dressed for the benediction. My censer was made ready with burning charcoal. I swung it in three sweeping circles to activate the charcoal and make it glow. The old people often said, "Thank goodness our church is made of stone instead of wood or Henri would have burned it down fifty times already." I was not too busy to watch the entrance of the church; I expected some very devout old lady to plunge her entire hand in the holy water and disturb the frogs. I waited for the sensation which would take place any moment. A young girl entered, but she must have been afraid to wet her hand because she only dipped her fingers before making the sign of the cross. Then some men came in and went through the same motions without touching the water at all. I was most disappointed until I heard the door being opened slowly, almost reverently, making the hinges squeak loudly. The slower the door was opened the more noise it made. My face felt warm, and I thought, "At last the show is on." I recognized the old lady as Pepina, the mother of my friend Pepi Straforello, chief flutist in the village. I said to myself, "Now, here it is." I was hardly through thinking this when a scream was heard throughout the church. The confusion, the effect of that shrill cry, was tremendous. Everyone ran out to the holy water font; I think God was there, too. The priest snapped his fingers which meant that one of the altar boys must get a chair. Don Albini was going to sit down in all the disorder and continue later when everything was quiet again. People yelled, "Frogs! Live frogs! In the holy water! How did they get there? They could never jump that high!" I laughed loudly, forgetting that I was one of the altar boys, and, when I couldn't stop laughing, passed my censer to one of the others and went into the sacristy until I could get over it. But I only laughed harder. The benediction that night was ruined; everyone else was laughing, too.

When Don Albini arrived in the sacristy he asked, "Who did that?"

I said, "Monsieur le curé, I didn't kill them, they're still alive. God's commandment says 'thou shalt not kill,' and they're still alive."

I thought I was exempt from that sin. I didn't know the trouble I gave that poor priest, who had to make a new benediction and change the holy water in the fonts. A half century later the village still talked about my little green frogs. I was punished to the extent that I had to pray 100 paternosters and 300 Avé Marias. I said one paternoster and three Avé Marias, and then asked someone nearby what time it was. I said two more paternosters and six more Avé Marias, and realized the church bell was ringing the quarter hour. Then I knew that to pray three paternosters and nine Avé Marias it would take a quarter of an hour. Therefore twelve paternosters and thirty-six Avé Marias would take me an hour. Consequently I was there two hours before benediction every day until my punishment was over. But I never said the prayers except for that first quarter of an hour. Monsieur Draghui found out about my green frogs, and said to me after school one day, "Where are you going now, Henri?"

I said, "To church, to pray two hours for my punishment until my 100 paternosters and 300 Avé Marias are finished."

The professor said, "Next time, Henri, let the frogs remain on the lily pads."

I didn't answer him since I couldn't swear that I wouldn't touch the frogs again.

A New Sherlock

I WENT TO ASSIST at the mass every morning and in the evening at benediction, and two days after my punishment was over I played another trick on Don Albini. I placed a big toad in my pocket; in France they weigh about one pound each. I put it on the bench underneath the priest's hat which just fit over it. Nobody saw me do it, and nobody heard me; I was not one of the boys who took care of the priest's hat. I was last in line at the opening of the benediction, and when the priest snapped his fingers for his hat, the boys made their genuflections and were ready to march. Poor Don Albini! He took his hat, and the toad jumped onto the floor. Faces paled, and this time I tried not to laugh. I bit my lips and thought of something sad, but my youth was stronger and I began to laugh when I looked at all those scared boys.

Don Albini said, "No one did it? The toad himself will find the guilty one." The animal began to move slowly. Instead of going to the front it went to the rear. One boy was white in the face before it passed, and red after; he wasn't guilty, only fearful. The second, third, and fourth kids trembled, and the fifth wished he could have been the first. Slowly the toad moved on, and the priest looked at the animal which stopped exactly in front of me, close to my feet. It wouldn't go any further but stood there like a soldier.

Don Albini said, "Now, you tell me if you did this, and why you did it?"

I didn't answer and I didn't laugh either, but when the other five boys began to snicker I joined in with them. I tried to push the toad with my foot, but it wouldn't move. I think it wanted to return to my pocket because it was nice and warm there. I was punished again; this time it was 200 paternosters and 600 Avé Marias. Maman Camous reprimanded me, saying, "Why did you do that, Henri?" And Papa Camous said to me, half smiling as he did so, "After those long hours of praying, you will make yourself into a priest, Henri."

The most disappointed of all were Bacci and Blanchette. Instead of going to the stable I went to the church, and neither one of them could understand it. Every old lady I met in the village, and each one liked me very much, asked, "Why do you do that in the house of God?"

"God created the frog and the toad, and they must be His friends also. I didn't do them any harm. I only made them swim, and they became Catholics."

One of the old ladies muttered, "You couldn't change that boy if you tried; he always has a good answer."

Monsieur Draghui repeated the words of Papa Camous, "My little fellow," he said, "at the end of your punishment you won't have to go to the seminary, you will know enough by then to be a priest." He caressed his beard and said, "Because of all your praying don't forget to do your school lessons."

That gave me an idea. Instead of praying I studied my lessons in church, and I think God helped me in His Own house and inspired me still further. The wonderful old Don Albini never found out about my doubling up on the prayers I knew and dreamed of. No one knew my school studies were learned in the temple of God, and that that was the reason my last fourteen months of school in Contes found me the proud possessor of the tricolor belt which was a mark of distinction given to the best student. This belt was similar to the one worn by only one other person in the village, the mayor. It was the same in every village in France. I wore it over my surplice on Sunday to high mass and was very proud and pleased, indeed. No matter how much of a rascal I was, and no matter how much mischief I invented, it was only because my warm blood was boiling over, and the energy which I displayed caused me to run and jump around like a little goat. I was the champion jumper, including all the frogs and goats. I never intended to harm anyone in my quest for excitement. I never intended, either, to confuse wonderful old Don Albini so that he made a mistake in front of all the Sunday school. On one side of the room were the boys, on the other the girls, and I was in the center because I was being punished again. Don Albini said, "Stand up, Henri." I did. He said, "I am sure that you possess in you both God and the Devil, and I don't know which is the worst of the two." At that slip he made the sign of the cross and said, "God forgive me." I could not impede my laugh, and all the Sunday school joined me. At that sublime moment I felt that God was with all children, and even played with them. For one moment, too, Don Albini was a boy again himself. It seemed to me that that kind old priest had blessed me by his indiscreet observation. He surveyed the class which was still laughing; because of it we all had to kneel down, the priest kneeling first. He said, "Henri, you lead with the paternoster in Latin, then the Avé Maria, and the Santa Maria, and give them in Latin also." The prayers were made very noisily by those 100 or more boys and girls, as they had been made many centuries before by other children and other priests. God must have been laughing at us noiselessly, as we kneeled there praying to

85

Him. He Himself inspired the great poet and writer Victor Hugo to say, "God does not like tears unless they are ones of joy and contentment. Tears of joy make the heart which is kind so happy it must share that happiness with the eyes. And because the heart cannot directly show contentment without shining eyes, then tears at such a moment represent priceless diamonds which are not for sale."

After our prayers, Sunday school was dismissed early, but I remained obediently on my knees. It was becoming the natural thing to do, and when the priest said, "You, too," I couldn't believe my ears. In one moment I was up, and in three leaps, out the door. I jumped quicker than the twelve frogs I had put in the holy water, and was in the street before the rest of the boys and girls who must leave by twos and genuflect before leaving the church. One child touched the holy water and then the fingers of his friend, both of them making the sign of the cross simultaneously. At this scene of contentment I forgot the holy water. I returned with the same quickness, plunged my hand into it, there were no frogs in it this time, made my cross, kneeled down, and jumped out again like a billy goat. Don Albini laughed and said, "The incorrigible."

On arriving outside I received the compliments of the girls and boys. Because of me the class at Sunday school had been shortened. I told the kids, "I think the priest wants to be alone to talk to God and ask Him to excuse the mistake he made about Him and the Devil. But don't tell anyone, because tomorrow I might be punished again." It is a fact that when you ask someone not to tell that is the moment he does tell. That wonderful old priest was only a man after all.

RECIPES

❦

HORS-D'OEUVRE, WILLIAM HOOPER

❦

SOUP, GEORGE WALTON

❦

EGGS, BUTTON GWINNETT

❦

EGGS, LYMAN HALL

❦

EELS, EDWARD LANGWORTHY

❦

BROILED LAMB CHOPS, WILLIAM HOUSTON

❦

POTATOES, EDWARD TELFAIR

❦

VEGETABLE MARROW, WILLIAM FEW

❦

SALAD, ABRAHAM BALDWIN

❦

TAPIOCA, MOLLY PITCHER

❦

HORS-D'OEUVRE, WILLIAM HOOPER

Thoroughly mix 1 tablespoon of blue cheese and 1 tablespoon of butter. Add 1 pinch of paprika, ½ tablespoon of Worcestershire sauce, 1 tablespoon of bread crumbs, and 1 tablespoon of sherry. Mix to a paste. Split 2 celery hearts and stuff them. Place the stuffed celery hearts in the refrigerator for 30 minutes. Sprinkle with paprika and serve with pumpernickel.

SOUP, GEORGE WALTON

Take ½ pound of very fresh mushrooms. Slice them very thin and place them in a dish with 1 glassful of milk.

Put 1 tablespoon of butter into a casserole and add 2 finely chopped shallots. Cover the casserole and let the shallots simmer until they become soft and white. Then pour in the mushrooms and milk. Add 1 glassful of cream. Salt and pepper and let it slowly boil on top of the stove for 25 or 30 minutes. Put a piece of butter, the yolk of 1 egg, and ½ sherry-glassful of sweet sherry into each of the soup plates. Pour the soup into the plates, and season to taste.

EGGS, BUTTON GWINNETT

Make an omelet in the usual manner, using 6 eggs. When you begin to roll it, place some diced cooked fruit in the center. Be generous with the butter in the omelet pan. Make it, as usual, brown outside and soft inside. The finished dish will be a surprise.

EGGS, LYMAN HALL

Scramble 6 eggs. Boil a few small pork sausages in water for 10 minutes. Drain. Place the sausages on top of the scrambled eggs and pour ½ glassful of boiling cream around them. Sprinkle 2 large tablespoons of grated Parmesan cheese over them. Season.

EELS, EDWARD LANGWORTHY

Clean, dry, and cut a 1 pound eel into 2 inch pieces. Put a generous piece of butter into a frying pan. Dip the pieces of eel into flour, shake off the excess, and put them into the hot frying pan.

When they are fried add: 3 sliced mushrooms, 1 crushed clove of garlic, 1 minced onion, a few sprigs of chopped parsley, salt and pepper, 1 bay leaf, 1 pinch of thyme, a few chopped mint leaves, and 1 glassful of claret. Place the frying pan in a hot oven for 15 minutes. Season to taste. Generally served with large croutons that have been rubbed with garlic.

BROILED LAMB CHOPS, WILLIAM HOUSTON

Take four lamb chops and scrape the skin from the top of the bones leaving them bare. Dip them in melted butter. Do not salt them at this time. Put them in a very hot broiler. After a few minutes on one side turn and broil them for a few minutes on the other side. After that turn them often so that the chops will be brown outside and juicy inside. The total length of time necessary for broiling is from 8 to 10 minutes. Arrange the chops on a hot serving platter in a standing position and place water-cress in the middle to support them. Sprinkle with salt. Add to each chop on your plate some of the melted butter in which you first dipped them. Have your plates also hot. Sprinkle the chops with a pinch of black pepper.

POTATOES, EDWARD TELFAIR

Peel, wash, and dry 2 medium-sized Idaho potatoes. Cut them lengthwise into pieces ¼ inch thick. Prepare a very hot fat and put the potatoes into it. It is necessary to have at least 2 quarts of fat so that the potatoes can swim in it. Or, if you wish, use 1 quart of lard and 1 quart of oil. Leave the potatoes in the fat for a few minutes, strain, and put them on a platter. Make the fat hot for a second time, and after your potatoes have spent 3 to 5 minutes out of the fat, place them back in it again. This time the potatoes will begin to swell like balloons. Let them swim, turning them over gently with a spatula so as not to break them. When they are nice and brown outside, and soft inside, strain, and place them on a pile on a platter that has been covered with a paper or cloth napkin. Sprinkle with salt, and pour 1 tablespoon of melted butter over them.

VEGETABLE MARROW, WILLIAM FEW

Wash carefully 2 vegetable marrows and slice them very thin. Add 2 sliced mushrooms, 1 chopped tomato, 1 peeled and crushed clove of garlic, a little chopped parsley, ½ finely chopped onion, 1 tablespoon of butter, salt and pepper. Stir and put into a baking dish. Place it in a hot oven for 40 minutes. Serve it either hot or cold.

SALAD, ABRAHAM BALDWIN

Cook separately some green peas, carrots, potatoes, beets, etc. In all, about 1½ pounds. Cool and dice them. Mix and garnish with slices of fresh tomato and a few strips of green pepper. Fry 4 slices of bacon, using a small flame to make them crisp. Chop and sprinkle over the salad. Put 2 tablespoons of French Dressing into a pan and let it come to a boil. Remove from the fire and add to it the juice of ½ lemon. Stir and pour over the salad. Serve with a few leaves of crisp romaine.

TAPIOCA, MOLLY PITCHER

Combine 1 tablespoon of quick-cooking tapioca, 1 tablespoon of sugar, a pinch of salt, and the yolk of 1 egg. Stir 1 cupful of scalded milk into the tapioca and cook it in a double boiler from 5 to 8 minutes, stirring it constantly until it thickens. Remove it from the heat and fold a small amount of the mixture into the stiffly beaten white of 1 egg. Then fold the egg white, in turn, into the remaining tapioca in the double boiler. Cool it slightly, add ½ teaspoon of vanilla, pour it into a mold and place it in the refrigerator.

Chapter V

WOODEN SHOES
FOR OUR CATS

ONE OF MY CHUMS, Humbert Ricolfi, became involved with me in another prank which was to afford the villagers more entertainment. Humbert later became one of the most prominent statesmen of the French Republic during the time of Poincaré, Joffre, Foch, Clemenceau, etc., last upholders of the great ideals of the French Republic before Laval, Darlan, Petain and Company—a company including too long a list of hideous French traitors who sold France for their own benefits. I praise Humbert Ricolfi as one of the great patriots of the first World War, the cleanest and finest of all the politicians. A true gentleman whose lovely wife, the daughter of André Mars, the French poet, bore him a large family of seven children. Ricolfi, as Minister of Finance, paid the fabulous sum of billions of francs for the building of the Maginot Line. He personally paid many government expenses from his own humble pocket even though he was far from wealthy. Ricolfi is to be compared with Colbert, the great Minister of the French Royalty during the time of Louis XIII and the grand King Louis XIV. Colbert said, "If I had ever done for the King of Heaven what I have done for both my kings here on earth, the gates of Heaven would be opened to me without any prayers or intercessions." My lovely friend, the great Humbert Ricolfi, acted for the Marianne, the old French Republic of 1914, in the same honest way that Colbert had acted a few centuries before.

But let me return to the happy days in Contes when Ricolfi occupied the same bench with me in the classroom of Monsieur Draghui, and in Sunday school shared the same lessons taught by Don Albini.

Humbert and I, and several other chums, decided to make another surprise for our little village. It was carnival time in Contes. Our choice of a surprise was very limited in our village where everyone knew everyone else, and all the animals were thoroughly acquainted, too. A dog was a companion and not a watch dog, because no one had anything to steal; and, anyway, if one of them recognized that you were from the village you could have stolen the whole house. And if he had had hands instead of paws he would have helped you, too; he would never have thought you were dishonest. The village cats were just as friendly; they lived and died in the same houses, as did their great grandmothers before them.

My chums and I felt the need of some new kind of excitement so we collected all the cats in the village and put them in the stable of an unoccupied house. Each of the kids took his own pet without telling his parents. My friend Ricolfi and I were the ringleaders of this enterprise. Another friend of ours, who later progressed and became a priest, brought some English walnuts which we carefully split open. As we ate the meats, we piled up the half shells. We enjoyed not only the inside of those nuts but the outside as well. Taking the empty shells we placed them on the four paws of each cat, as if they were wooden shoes. We tied them on in such a way that they wouldn't come off. In that stable we had 30 to 35 cats of various ages and descriptions.

There were a few complaints from the parents of our chums. One said, "We didn't see the cat last night." Another said, "Our pet is missing too. The gypsies are close to the village, but they don't like cats; they prefer chickens. I wonder what has happened."

We kept those poor animals in that stable all night, but fed them well, and when the other kids were at vespers the following day, we were over in the stable putting shoes on our captives. Ricolfi and I were supposed to let them loose at the right time, which was around 4 P. M. when everybody began their dancing at the Place de L'Église up the street. We had only one main street in our village and that was made of cobblestones which had been there for fourteen centuries. When the signal came from Ricolfi outside the stable I was on the inside with my newly made tigers.

He yelled, "Ready, Henri!"

I yanked open the door and clapped my hands loudly. The light from the door, and the noise, made the cats jump up from their soft spots in the stable and rush out the door like wild demons. Those nut shells clacked on the cobblestones like castanets; a new noise to their ears, never having heard anything like it before. It was terrible! Those poor animals scared each other. Some of them leaped furiously ten feet at a time, and all the jumping, frantic miaowing, and noisy clacking caused great confusion. The wooden shoes of Normandy were not as loud as the ones we had made. When that crazy gang reached the Place de L'Église it took one moment only to make the population crazy too. Women screamed and ran to get into a doorway, any doorway that was open. Some of the kids laughed, those who knew all about it. Even the musicians were scared, including Straforello, who claimed to be a good soldier. The surprise was a big success, animals and people were in an uproar. Away went the cats, jumping, and running up the mountain thoroughfare to the top of the village, where they jumped over the bushes and were gone, some of them, for eight days. On the way many of them lost their walnut shoes, but the strings, with some of the shells still attached, remained until they returned home. When I saw those frightened animals running like mad, and all the people running for cover, some of them screaming and some of them laughing, it was too much. I sat down in the middle of the street and laughed until I was red, blue, and black in the face. I rolled on the ground quite overcome. I didn't hear the approach of old Monsieur Faraut with his white beard and nickname of "St. Peter." And I didn't feel

the spanking he gave me with his cane; the enjoyment of my laugh
covered the customary sting. When he saw me so black and blue from
laughing, he said, "My goodness! He's choking to death!" By this time
old "St. Peter" was scared instead of me. My friend Ricolfi, leaning
against the wall with his arms covering his face, screamed with laughter
and made as much noise as the red hen of Maman Camous when she
laid an egg. Only this time the announcement to the world would
have been "here is an egg with two yolks," so great was the noise and
commotion. In the village of Contes that story will never die. Of course
there were repercussions. We expected to be punished by a serious
Monseiur Draghui that next Monday morning, and justly so, because
his cat was not home yet. He angrily bit his lips, which caused his
beard to move back and forth as if a wind were blowing it. Only this
time it wasn't the wind, and we saw no hand stroking his beard, which
was always a sign of contentment. The professor was angry.

He demanded, "Who did it?"

I was the first to go to his desk. I gave him my tricolor belt and
said, "I'm the guilty one." This time I didn't laugh. Ricolfi followed
in my steps, saying, "I'm the guilty one." The third kid was the son of
Monsieur Draghui himself, Auguste. He said, "Father, I'm the guilty
one." In one moment all the class came up, one by one, including the
little fellows four and five years old. One after the other said, "I
carried my cat," "I ate the walnuts," "I brought the string," "I brought
milk for them." The butcher's son said, "I brought some meat." By
that time all the class was guilty and wanted to be in on the story even
if some were a little late in joining in on it. The face of our teacher
changed. We saw one hand go slowly up to caress his beard, and the
other go up to scratch his head. That was the first time I noticed
evidence of a double kindness in the teacher.

He said, "Is that the way I taught you to become gentlemen?"

We should have been punished on account of the pets, but on the
contrary, Monsieur Draghui saw that his teachings and his confidence
in his pupils had created a unified classroom. All the good and bad
moments we had spent either in being chastised or complimented

The little - and quite grave - Henri is third from the left in the front row in
this classroom picture taken in Contes. The teacher is Professor Draghui.

by our professor tended to instill in us the spirit of "one for all, and all for one." I felt much better knowing that Auguste had been in on our deal. Our joke had almost turned into a panic. Monsieur Draghui wrote with chalk on the bottom of the blackboard, "A cat never wears wooden shoes," and this bit of information was left there for a full week. For the second full week we faced the admonition, "Be kind to animals."

Don Albini ignored the whole affair, but we did not escape altogether. Humbert and I were punished for having missed the vespers. Between the two of us we spent two hours each day for two weeks in praying. In completing that program I believe I was punished by God and every parishioner enough so I could excuse myself for not praying for the rest of my life.

For quite a time wonderful old Don Albini tried to reform me, but after all I could only be myself. How can you turn a lion into a mouse?

Don Albini said to me, "Henri, I think I must pray for you because all the prayers I give you for punishment do not change you."

A large smile appeared on my face, and he said, "You are smiling instead of crying." With that he began to mumble in Latin, which I couldn't understand. Maybe in that language he was saying I was right, but he wouldn't say so.

A New Christian

IN THE VILLAGE OF CONTES there was no running water, as we know it, but there were four fountains erected to supply us with the finest water imaginable, which ran profusely from a spring a few miles up the mountains. It was mysteriously beautiful to see that hard rock with its four holes from which the water poured limpidly, very cold in the summer, and pleasantly cold in the winter. It was made to run to the village by a pipeline. The first fountain was at the top of my village on the Rue Henri Charpentier, a street at that time unnamed. The second and main fountain was located in the Place de L'Église, and was 400 years old. It had a spout in the center with four mouths that permitted four pails of water to be taken at one time. The water surrounding the base made a very pleasant noise, and covered in circumference an area of about twenty yards. From there the overflow ran to a place 100 feet distant called the *lavoir,* where about fifteen women could wash clothes simultaneously. From the *lavoir* the water ran to the Paillon River a mile down the mountain.

The village animals left their stables twice a day to go to the main fountain for water, and returned again by themselves. Goats, sheep, donkeys, horses, etc., all had their rendezvous there a few steps from the church. All except the pigs which were locked in their pens. It looked to me like a big meeting by appointment, and I presumed by their language that they were glad to get together to gossip and tell their own stories.

One day, not long after the affair of the cats, I missed the Sunday class in catechism, which was held two other days a week also, on Monday and on Thursday. This class was one of preparation for the first Communion, and I was absent. I was outside getting a nice cold drink at the fountain, receiving more water on my head and shoulders than in my mouth. The shock of it in my face surprised me so that I didn't realize I had company. The donkey of Jacques, my neighbor, sauntering up, disturbed my drink. As long as he was hesitant I said, "Hello, Gris." Which meant in English that he was gray in color. I think he was the son of a white donkey and a black jackass. He had funny looking eyes, long ears, hair that was lustrous gray, and with all that a look that was very intelligent. I said again, "Hello, Gris, have you ever seen the inside of our church?"

He pointed both ears up and with an expression that was half laughing and half quizzical, with a *soupçon* of anger, he seemed to say, "What the devil are you talking about?"

I said, "Come on, you big jackass, I'm going to show you." I took him by the rope he had around his neck and led him up the four steps to the door of the church. I pushed him through the entrance, and with his head he nudged open the other door. When he saw that large marble bowl of holy water, and not having had time to drink at the fountain, he was greatly attracted. That poor gray donkey had never seen a holy water font before, nor had he ever made an entrance into a church; to him it was a new and pleasant experience. Everyone in the village agreed that our church had great beauty, and now the donkey of Jacques made it unanimous. He thought it was so wonderful he went to investigate further. There was a revolution among the children in the catechism classroom. When they saw Gris come in, several of them cried, "Look, the donkey of Jacques, how did he find the door?" And if I had not been snapping my fingers and laughing so much, Don Albini would not have known who it was. But he recognized me, because of all the kids I could snap my fingers the loudest. The sound of Chinese fire crackers came from the church entrance; I simply couldn't resist it. I was guilty without being seen. Don Albini came to push the donkey out, but Gris didn't want to retreat. The priest had to lead him around to the other door, and when he passed in front of the altar, poor Don Albini, for once, forgot to kneel. But Gris was not ready to leave; he very stubbornly recognized all the children, and I believe he regretted that he couldn't sit down on a bench and follow along with the catechism hour. When I saw the priest coming out I ran, and he ran after me. You can imagine the old gentleman with his robes and Henri with no encumbrances, as free as the air. But I laughed so much I couldn't run any further, and I had to sit down in the street, partly because I would have been punished anyhow, and partly because the old priest was so angry he would have suffocated if I hadn't given up. I knew the villagers would have forgiven the story of the donkey, but they would never have forgiven me if anything had happened to Don Albini. Completely overcome by laughter, I didn't realize he was close to me until I felt his warm hands clutching my ears. He raised me up and down several times much in the same manner that Maman Camous prepared the dough before cutting it to form her large loaves of bread. Don Albini asked, "What are you going to do next?" All the kids were outside of the church. The priest took me by one ear, and because his strides were long and my little legs were short, I almost hung by that one ear which seemed to be glued to his fingers. There in the center of the church, I kneeled while all the kids came inside again. Don Albini said, "You will recite the Act of Contrition." And when I was through he said, "Start over again." That afternoon there was no more catechism; everyone was listening to Henri.

Every time I met Gris, the donkey, he made a funny face at me; he probably found out the whole story of my punishment. Anyhow, Gris became very proud, and, as far as anyone knew, he was the very first donkey that could claim he had had a drink of holy water and had been to church. I believe God Himself was amused because a boy who lived in Contes had picked the same kind of animal that Jesus had chosen for His last journey on Palm Sunday. Who could tell, maybe Gris was a descendant of the donkey that carried our lovely Jesus to Jerusalem in those earlier days.

After being angry for many days, Don Albini said to me, "I forgive you because you chose a donkey instead of a horse; otherwise we would have remained enemies forever." Again he said a few words in Latin, words that I didn't understand and of which I never demanded the meaning. He often said much that was mysterious in that language, and I think he enjoyed it. In our village no one knew what he was saying when he talked in Latin.

That same evening I received a reprimand from Maman Camous when she said, "You know, Henri, the church is not made for donkeys."

I said, "Maman, what I did doesn't happen every day."

I guess she knew right then that there would be no getting the best of me.

She consoled herself by saying, "It's a good thing the donkey didn't break his leg. It would have cost us money to pay the damages if such a thing had happened." That made me see things more sensibly, and I resolved not to give any trouble to those two lovely people, Maman and Papa Camous, who had always given me nothing but kindness. I promised her I would never do it again.

I ate two plates of soup, a dozen fresh figs, drank my glass of claret, and all was forgiven, but not forgotten. Everybody in the village laughed and said to Jacques, "Jacques, you have a donkey who has become a Christian." And Jacques enjoyed the joke; he and Gris became famous when the story was passed around to the other villages.

Many years later Gris died in the stable of Jacques, but left behind this story which will never die.

RECIPES

⚜

HORS-D'OEUVRE, JOHN BROWN

⚜

SOUP, ELIPHALET REMINGTON

⚜

OMELET, JAMES WHISTLER

⚜

EGGS, NOAH WEBSTER

⚜

BROILED LOBSTER, CHARLES GOODYEAR

⚜

SCALLOPED VEAL, NATHAN HALE

⚜

POTATOES, GOUVERNEUR MORRIS

⚜

STRING BEANS, JOHN BROWNING

⚜

SALAD, C. FRANCIS JENKINS

⚜

MACEDOINE OF FRUIT, HARRIET BEECHER STOWE

⚜

HORS-D'OEUVRE, JOHN BROWN

Bake 1 pie shell. Separately chop 1 onion and place it in a casserole with 1 tablespoon of butter and 1 tablespoon of milk. Cover the casserole and let the onion cook to a white softness. Then add 4 tablespoons of cream, 2 tablespoons of grated cheese, 2 egg yolks, and a handful of cooked crabmeat. Mix, pour into the pie shell and place in a hot oven for 10 minutes. Season with salt, pepper, and paprika. Serve hot.

SOUP, ELIPHALET REMINGTON

Soak a handful of split peas overnight. The next day place them into 2 quarts of boiling water and add 1 chopped onion, 1 chopped stalk of celery, 1 chopped carrot, and 1 boiled chopped potato. Let it boil over a small fire, and watch it so that it doesn't all settle on the bottom of the pan, or it will burn. Or, to prevent burning, place it in a hot oven. Either way will take 1½ hours. When the split peas have been thoroughly cooked, pass the soup through a sieve. Add a generous piece of butter, 3 tablespoons of cream, and salt and pepper to taste. Croutons should be added to this sort of soup, as a final gesture.

OMELET, JAMES WHISTLER

Peel and dice 2 cold boiled potatoes that have been cooked in their jackets. Mix them with small croutons which have been fried in butter. Broil 2 thin slices of raw ham until crisp. Chop it. Mix the potatoes, croutons and ham together in a pan. Add a generous piece of butter and 2 chopped green onions. Place on the fire for 5 minutes.

In a separate dish break and stir 6 eggs. Add the potatoes, croutons, ham, etc., to the eggs. Make an omelet (see chapter on How to Make Omelets and Scrambled Eggs), making it brown, as usual, on the outside, and soft on the inside. Season.

EGGS, NOAH WEBSTER

Scoop out 2 large ripe tomatoes. Put the shells aside. Put 1 chopped shallot into a pan with a generous piece of butter and after it has cooked for a moment add the insides of the tomatoes. Add, also, ½ clove of garlic which has been crushed into a little chopped parsley, and 1 tablespoon of red wine. Cook for 8 minutes. Then sprinkle 1 tablespoon of bread crumbs over this preparation. Place 1 table-spoon of the mixture into each of the tomato shells that you have placed aside. Break 1 egg into each one and cover with the remainder of the mixture. Put the stuffed tomatoes into a baking dish with a piece of butter and place in a hot oven for a few minutes. Season.

BROILED LOBSTER, CHARLES GOODYEAR

For this recipe use 1 live lobster that weighs 1½ pounds. Split it in half. Remove the brain of the lobster and chop it. Add to it 2 finely chopped shallots, 1 finely chopped celery heart, 1 finely chopped hard-boiled egg, a few sprigs of chopped parsley, 1 tablespoon of oil, pepper and salt. Mix together and stuff into the hollow part of the split lobster. Sprinkle a little pepper and salt over the fleshy part of the lobster, as well as 1 tablespoon of melted butter. Make your broiler very hot, and then place the lobster under the flame which has been made small. Broil for 10 minutes, remove, and place it in a hot oven for 10 minutes more to finish cooking.

Put a generous piece of butter into a separate pan. Add 1 teaspoon of Worcestershire sauce, the juice of ½ lemon, 1 teaspoon of meat extract and a pinch each of paprika, salt, and pepper. Let it come to a boil.

Leave the stuffed part of the lobster as it is. Remove the rest of the meat from the shell, including the claws. Pour the sauce over the lobster meat. To have the full effect of this recipe one should eat a forkful of the stuffing and accompany it with a piece of lobster dipped in the sauce.

SCALLOPED VEAL, NATHAN HALE

Ask your butcher to cut 2 half inch slices from a leg of veal. Have them about 6 inches long. Hammer the meat to break down the tissues. Sprinkle both sides with salt and pepper. Beat two eggs thoroughly and dip the pieces of veal into the beaten eggs. Sprinkle 2 finely chopped shallots on the meat. Roll into bread crumbs. Put a large piece of butter on a baking platter, put the slices of breaded veal on it, and place in a hot oven. Baste every 5 minutes. If necessary, add more butter and let them cook from 35 to 40 minutes. Place on serving platter.

Mix some chopped parsley with 1 chopped hard-boiled egg and sprinkle it over the slices of veal.

Brown a generous piece of butter in a separate pan, squeeze the juice of ½ lemon into the brown butter, sprinkle with salt and pepper, and when it begins to bubble pour it over the meat.

POTATOES, GOUVERNEUR MORRIS

Peel, wash, and slice 6 raw potatoes. Sprinkle with salt. Into a separate pan put a piece of butter and 2 large chopped onions. When the onions are cooked stand them aside.

Place 1 tablespoon of butter into a baking dish and add a layer of sliced raw potatoes. Put a few of the cooked onions on top of this first layer, and then add another layer of potatoes. Add another thin layer of cooked onions, etc. Proceed until there are 3 or 4 layers of potatoes in the baking dish. Place in the oven and bake for 40 minutes.

STRING BEANS, JOHN BROWNING

Select ½ pound of tender, green string beans. Wash and clean. Boil in 2 quarts of water to which a little salt and the juice of ½ lemon have been added. Put the beans in the pan when the water starts to boil. Let them cook until they are tender, yet firm. Pour off the water. Place the beans in a serving dish, add a generous piece of butter, and season with pepper and salt. Chop a few sprigs of parsley and sprinkle over the beans.

SALAD, C. FRANCIS JENKINS

Dice some Swiss cheese and put it into a pan containing hot oil for 1 minute. Strain the diced cheese and let it cool.

Peel, core, and dice 1 pear and 1 celery heart. Sprinkle with salt and pepper. Add the juice of ½ lemon. Shred ½ head of lettuce, shaping it into a nest. Mix the diced cheese, pear, etc., together and place it in the nest. Cover the center with mayonnaise.

MACEDOINE OF FRUIT, HARRIET BEECHER STOWE

Cut into pieces: 1 slice of pineapple, 1 peeled peach, 1 pared and cored apple, 1 peeled and cored pear, 1 banana, and a few strawberries. Peel 1 orange with a knife, remove all the pulp and slice it into the bowl with the rest of the fruit. Add 3 chopped English walnuts or almonds. Stir together.

Make a dressing, using 2 tablespoons of sugar, 1 tablespoon of butter, the juice of the remaining oranges, 2 ponies of white curaçao, 2 ponies of rum, and 2 tablespoons of cream. Mix and pour over the fruit. Serve cold.

Chapter VI

THE FOREMAN OF
THE STABLE

OUR MENAGERIE consisted of Blanchette, the mule, donkey, cow, pig, the rabbits, and two chickens; just enough animals to fill our necessary needs. Bacci went in and out of that stable without ever sleeping in it; he felt he was too superior for such a thing. Halfway up the stairs he turned and looked down at each one as if he were saying, "You fellows stay down there; don't make too much noise and wake me up because I'm going to sleep with the boss." At that moment Blanchette looked at him with a face full of mockery which said, "I know you don't mean that for me, because if you did the only horn that remains in my head would make you change your mind." The donkey moved his long ears, looked at Bacci, and turned to the mule. The mule said to the donkey, "Father, see your mistake. I ought to be a horse, but because of you I'm a mule. If I were a horse I would at least have a pedigree and then I wouldn't mind the insults of that good for nothing dog with his patronizing attitude."

Our cow silently licked her nose. I believe Maman Camous had given her a little salt so that she would be more generous with her milk. Only Bismarck, the pig, locked in his pen, talked in German to Bacci, who barked a few times, letting everyone know he didn't like those remarks. After a last look, to see that all the stable was in order, he wagged his tail, looked once more at Blanchette, ran up to the second floor where he entered, and came over to the table to look into my plate. When he saw potatoes, string beans, cabbage and turnips he was

121

107

disappointed and gave me a look that said, "Hello, boss, when is there going to be meat in this place here?" I opened his mouth, put some potatoes into it, and closed it, nearly choking him by holding it shut. When he had swallowed it I let go. He sneezed for a quarter of an hour, but could not surrender the potatoes. A piece of bread spread with a little cheese made Bacci return. He loved that. His attitude was, "Gee whiz! Thank goodness it's not a potato!" Then he looked at Papa Camous and was ready to steal another piece of bread and cheese from his plate. He put his nose too close to it and Papa Camous could not support his boldness in coming so near his plate without being asked. So he gave him the bread and cheese and said, "Go away." Bacci didn't care, he had what he wanted. He looked at me triumphantly. We understood each other perfectly. He went over to his little water bowl and, in trying to lap up the water, bumped the small bell he had around his neck against it so that Maman Camous brought him some more. Then he lapped up a little at a time, and in doing that I think he washed himself and was ready to come to bed with me. He didn't want to bring the smell of the cheese with him. Bacci jumped on the bed and turned around and around, making his nest at the foot because he knew that Maman would not permit him to come inside with me. When he heard her say, "Is Bacci at the foot of your bed, Henri?" he moved one ear and opened one eye. When I answered, "Yes, Mom, goodnight," that dog knew it was meant for him, too. He crawled up and licked my ears, slowly making a place for himself inside. In no time little Henri looked almost like a small girl asleep with her doll. Bacci was in my arms; he was the doll.

But early in the morning he was always up ahead of me; he wanted to be one of the very first to see the fire that Maman had made and to see for himself if the coffee was being prepared. He wanted some with milk and a piece of bread in it. A few minutes later he jumped back on the bed and began to lick my face, and I could tell by the smell of coffee from him that breakfast was ready. From my earliest recollection of the days when I could not say much more than "maman" and "papa," my demand for three bowls of coffee predominated. Not one bowl after another, but three all at one time. I sat with one in front of me and one in each hand, and defied the neighbors who said, "Look at the little pig. Why don't you give him three slaps instead of three bowls of coffee?" The kindness of Maman Camous rebelled at that expression and she said, "Why shouldn't I give it to him if it makes him happy and does not displease me? It's none of your business. You raise your children the way you want to, I will not interfere." My real parents had offered thousands of cups of coffee to the peasants and had never cared whether one had three or not. I was spoiled and took advantage of all my opportunities. When I reached the church, after having had my breakfast, I joked with the priest, telling him I had had my three bowls of coffee and he, as yet, had had none because he must give the mass first. I tried to tempt him into asking for a cup of coffee and no mass. But that wonderful old gentleman only laughed and led the way to the altar. I opened his book and we continued with the ceremonies.

Café Henri Charpentier, 1

A New York at large

GREATEST NEWSPAPER — MONDAY, MARCH 8.

Henri Tells Of Monument To Dog That Saved His Life

...ted Memorial In France To A... Befriended Him

...the sunny slopes of a hill in... mongrel dog who saved the li... when the latter, a homeless an... death in London.

...who, after a kaleidoscopic... has settled down as the... and mellow host of the res... in Lynbrook bearing his... told the story at the month... meeting of the Men's asso... at the First...

Visitors Are Noted Company
During its distinguished career Henri's has been visited by the Prince of Wales, now King Edward VIII, Marshals Joffre and Foch, Georges Clemenceau, Sarah Bernhardt, Theodore Roosevelt, Woodrow Wilson, Willi... nixes Bryan, J. P... Smith, Jim... Perch...

Maison Francaise, Rockefeller Center New York City

By JAMES B. REST...
NEW YORK—Men of... able tonnage, gourmet... tors, guztlers, will tell you Charpentier, the town's... mous cook.

Henri claims to have invented crepes suzette among other things, and for this the town pays him homage. In he hommage, he in... be known by electric the telephone. He is known to the great men of the city, who... from one restau... past to another... HENRI

THE COOK OF KINGS and THE KING OF COOKS
Henri Charpentier
world-renowned French chef, will show you how he prepares his internationally famous Crepe Suzettes and other delicious uses of his new Liqueur Suzette.
Tuesday, Wednesday, Thursday, September 24, 25, and 26 at 2:30 P. M.
BLOOMINGDALE'S...th Floor

Restaurant Henri and Its Sun-lit Park Lure Patrons From Village, St... a Nation

...f Events Page of the New York

NOTES BY Robert Benchley

...the inventor of crêpes Suzette, ar... parcel post. His version of the ...ett is a simple and wholly cred...

..."Baths at Oxnard," he said, ...rd, then known to his in-

CAFE HENRI CHARPENTIER
AT MAISON FRANCAISE,
OF NEW YORK
Offers Simple Recipes for
Home Use

ANGOSTURA TON...
Toast slices of very fresh... crusts removed.: Butte... with and sprinkle with... slices and dry out over night. May be stored in a dry place for 2 or 3 weeks.

ANGOSTURA SUGAR
Mrs. 2. tablespoons ANGOS-TURA BITTERS with ½ cup granulated sugar. Spread thinly on a dish and dry out over night. May be stored in a dry place for 2 or 3 weeks.

DELICIOUS HOT CHOCOLATE...
ANGOSTURA...
Stir grated chocolate into... water, 1½ square per cu... add ... ANGOSTURA... Pot 2 ladies ANGOSTU... a novelty

RADIO Center NEWS

GASTRONOMY
By Betty Bachus

FOR 'ELEGANCE' there is no other restaurant in N... York quite like HENRI CHARPENTIER'S... Henri would rather spend h... a street vendor t... cafeteria. For ca... eat and die like a... service of royalty... coming from Henr... avec sherry. Petite... chablis...

NEW YORK HERALD TRIBU...
WEDNESDAY, DECEMBER 4,

Walter Winche...
Tells You
"Why to ...
Where

If you ate home last Thurz—or wherever yo... —we hope you did it well. If at all dissat... try these spots next time—or sooner.

ORIGINAL HENRI (Lynbrook, L. I.)
Orchids to Henri Carpentier, whose crepes suzett... sought by all the world—and that's no kidding. 'T... a rendezvous of epicures—and if you eat, you can... it, too.

World Famous Chef

POLICE DEPARTMENT
CITY OF NEW YORK
PASS Mr. Henri Charpentier
THROUGH ALL POLICE LINES
SPECIAL DEPUTY POLICE COMMISSIONER
107...

Lillian Roth makes chicken casserole under Henri Charpentier's tuition, at the House of Morgan.

Savory Secret... a Master Ch...

Henri Is Enlarging Noted Restaurant

Memorial Room, Dedicated
To Famous Visitors, Adds
Banquet Hall. T...

The great...
Charpenti...
closes for yo...
use some fro...
his w...
owned b...
magic...

At the Island Press Cooking School
TUESDAY, JUNE 2
2 P. M.

...er, who is the originator of crepes, Suzette, conducts an estab... Lynbrook and has been the subject of many articles in nation... d magazines and newspapers. He operated in Radio City where

...er will give an address on "Pleasing the Epicurean Fancies of ...and will reveal many of the secrets of cooking to the audience.

ALL ARE WELCOME
...ntary Tickets Now on Request to THE PRESS or at School Tuesday

LONG ISLAND DAILY PRESS COOKING SCHOOL
...estinghouse Electric Supply Co., Auditorium
AVENUE and 168TH STREET   JAMAICA

A Rendezvous For All People, Is Dream Of Noted Chef
(This is the second of a series of three articles on Original Henri restaurant, which will appear in...)

By Frank A. Culver
There are fo... acres of land in the leafy park where stands the Original Henri restaurant, on Scranton avenue, Lynbrook, where Henri Charpentie... sive society notables bea...

Monsieur Henri Charpentier
INVITES YOU TO ATTEND
HIS UNIQUE
Champagne-Suzette Dansant
SATURDAY AND SUNDAY AFTERNOONS
FOUR TO SIX

Canapé Niçoise
Crêpes Suzette   One Dollar
Coupe Champagne

MARIO BRAGGIOTTI
AND HIS ORCHESTRA
FOR DANCING

CASINO
Central Park
RESERVATIONS: RHINELANDER 4-3094

ED SULLIVAN SEES BROADWAY
(Copyright, 1932, New York Evening GRAPHIC)

A Veteran Speaks
He's one of the old-timers of the business, is Henri, and on the ledge above the fireplace, in his famous Long Island restaurant, is a plaque inscribed by Joffre when he was marshal of the victorious Army of France. Standing next to the plaque is the casing of a shell fired in the first French offensive.

I cite these things to indicate that Henri is rather unusual in his friendships. He is a cosmopolitan, and in his world travels he has seen a lot and experienced plenty. We were discussing present hard times.

"Depression," he shrugged his shoulders expressively. "Call it rather a magnificent lesson to the younger generation. To me and other older men hard times cannot teach a lesson. We have learned the lesson years ago, in other periods.

"So the present depression is for the younger generation, alone. It is a lesson to the homegrown youth to make sure slowly. Really, it is Godsend. Our young men have been reared in an amazing age, brought up to see the impossible achieved overnight. This is a lesson learned to see that the old laws of balance and average must work out. This is the finest thing that could have happened. The lessons learned by younger men in these times, will avert world panics of the future. Had the present slump not occurred, our young men, in years to come, would have rushed headlong into destruction because you young men no better.

As we were leaving, I asked him if he recognized one of the three attractive girls in our party. "I have seen the sky swimming in stars," he answered, the courtly old rascal, "why should I am not familiar with stars, and not recognize Mlle. Nancy Carroll?"

Let the man-about-town use that pretty speech. No wonder our... those Frenchmen.

RECIPES

✤

BEAUTY ON THE PLATE, MILES STANDISH

✤

CHICKEN CONSOMME, ROGER WILLIAMS

✤

PLAIN OMELET, PAUL REVERE

✤

POACHED EGGS, ALEXANDER HAMILTON

✤

BROILED MACKEREL, JOHN HANCOCK

✤

FILLET OF BEEF SAUTE, BENJAMIN FRANKLIN

✤

POTATOES, JOHN QUINCY ADAMS

✤

CAULIFLOWER, ELI WHITNEY

✤

ROMAINE SALAD, JOHN WINTHROP

✤

FRUIT COMPOTE, BETSY ROSS

✤

BEAUTY ON THE PLATE, MILES STANDISH

Radishes, scallions, sliced or quartered tomatoes, celery hearts, salt and pepper. The radishes and celery hearts should be cleaned and trimmed and a few leaves permitted to remain on them. The celery should be cut into quarters. The tomatoes must not be too ripe. A hard-boiled egg, cut in half, should be placed in the center. To make an hors-d'oeuvre for two, use: 1 tomato, 1 celery heart, 1 bunch of scallions, 1 bunch of radishes, and 1 hard-boiled egg.

CHICKEN CONSOMME, ROGER WILLIAMS

Boil some very thin vermicelli in clear water for 7 minutes. Strain it. Wash it with hot water and strain it again. The rewashed vermicelli will not cloud your consommé. Then pour on the desired amount of chicken consommé, and let it come to a boil. Salt and pepper to taste. Serves 2.

PLAIN OMELET, PAUL REVERE

Three eggs usually constitute a full portion for either the small appetite or the small purse. To make a plain omelet for 2, break 6 eggs and stir them gently to break the yolks. Season with salt and pepper. Put 1 tablespoon of butter into a very hot steel omelet pan. This is used as a foundation. When the butter has completely melted, add the eggs to the pan, stir gently, and when the eggs begin to thicken, add another ½ tablespoon of butter to keep them moist and soft. Raise your pan, tipping it so that only a corner of it will be in contact with the fire. With a spatula, begin to roll the omelet gently down from the top of the pan. Place another ½ tablespoon of butter between the omelet and the hot pan. The butter which has been put inside the omelet will keep it soft, and this last butter used at the right moment will make it brown and beautiful. A plain omelet will not take more than 5 minutes to complete on a good fire.

POACHED EGGS, ALEXANDER HAMILTON

Use two or more eggs, according to your desire. Add 1 tablespoonful of vinegar to the clear, boiling water as well as a few sprigs of parsley and a few pepper-corns. When the boiling water begin to roll, turn the fire down to a slow boil. Then break the eggs close to the water so that the yolks will be intact. Help the whites of the eggs to cover the yolks by using a wooden spoon. After 3 to 5 minutes in the slowly boiling water, remove the poached eggs with the help of a perforated spoon. Do not place them on your buttered toast until they are entirely free of water.

Fry a few strips of bacon and place them on top of the poached eggs on toast. Mix together some bread crumbs and grated cheese and sprinkle over the bacon.

Add to the bacon grease in the frying pan ½ tablespoon of butter, or more, according to the number of eggs used, and pour it, very hot, over the bread crumbs and cheese. A little parsley or fresh chives should be chopped and sprinkled on last. Pepper and salt to taste.

BROILED MACKEREL, JOHN HANCOCK

The only quality that a fish must possess is one of freshness. And that means fresh from the water and not fresh from the market.

A 1 pound mackerel is sufficient for 2. Clean, wash, and dry it. To free the fish oil during the broiling, make a few incisions on both sides of the fish with a knife. This will, at the same time, give the flame a chance to penetrate the fish without burning the skin to charcoal.

113

Place it in a very hot broiler for 4 minutes. Turn it on the other side, brush on some butter, and let it remain in the broiler for 4 more minutes. Do not brush on butter during the first 4 minutes of broiling. It will take 15 to 20 minutes to broil a fish this size.

Prepare in advance 1 or more tablespoons of butter, chopped parsley, chopped shallots, salt and pepper. Mix thoroughly in a bowl. Place the fish on a serving platter, and then put on the parsley and shallot butter. Serve hot.

FILLET OF BEEF SAUTE, BENJAMIN FRANKLIN

Cut into small pieces the tail-end of the fillet. About ½ pound will serve 2.

Cut up 1 green pepper, 2 mushrooms, 1 tomato, and 2 cold boiled potatoes. Place 1 tablespoon of butter into a frying pan and slice 1 onion into it. When the onion is brown, add the green pepper, mushrooms, tomato, and the cold boiled potatoes. This garnish will take 35 to 40 minutes to complete and may be cooked either on top of the stove or in the oven at a temperature of 450° F.

Fry the small pieces of fillet in a separate pan with a little butter, or, if you prefer, no butter at all. Use a spatula to turn the pieces so that they become brown. To completely sear the juice inside, use no butter and no condiments. This should take from 5 to 7 minutes, and no longer. Put the meat into the frying pan with the other ingredients. Salt and pepper to taste. Crush one clove of garlic into a few sprigs of chopped parsley and add it to the sauté. Mix well and serve.

POTATOES, JOHN QUINCY ADAMS

Peel 2 potatoes, large or small, as you wish, slice them thin and dry them. Place 1 tablespoon of oil into a pan and make it very hot. Then add the potatoes and cover them. When they are three-fourths cooked, drain off the oil and place them in a baking dish. Add a small piece of butter, sprinkle with a little grated cheese, and place in the oven for 10 or 15 minutes. Season to taste.

CAULIFLOWER, ELI WHITNEY

A cauliflower, to be at its best, must be fresh from the garden and its head must be very compact. The one which has grown loosely into a head is one which is hard to digest. One small head should suffice for two. Wash it thoroughly and leave it whole with a few green leaves on the bottom. Put it into boiling salted water to which a little pepper has been added. Squeeze the juice of ½ lemon into the water. Let it boil until it is done, about 35 to 40 minutes. Pour off the water.

Place the cauliflower on a serving dish and squeeze the juice of the remaining ½ lemon over the top. Salt and pepper.

Put 1 or more tablespoons of butter into a frying pan and brown. Pour it over the cauliflower and serve. You might add, if you wish, 1 teaspoon of wine vinegar.

ROMAINE SALAD, JOHN WINTHROP

Crisp, and not overgrown, romaine must be used. Chopped radishes as well as chopped scallions, tomatoes, celery, and chopped hard-boiled egg should be added to the French Dressing. Mix together and pour over the salad.

FRUIT COMPOTE, BETSY ROSS

Peel 1 apple, remove the core, and cut it into quarters. Prepare 1 pear in the same way. Peel 1 peach and cut it into quarters, removing the stone. Add a handful of blueberries, or any other kind, as you wish, and 2 quartered plums. In a separate pan put ½ glassful of claret, 1 glassful of wáter, 2 slices of lemon peel, and 3 tablespoons of sugar. Boil slowly for 10 minutes. Add 1 pony of cordial, any kind. Stir gently and pour over the fruit. The syrup may be used either hot or cold. Canned fruit may be used instead of fresh.

Chapter VII

HONESTY IS THE BEST POLICY

ONE DAY, which happened to be Thursday and therefore not a school day, I was busy playing with a few of my friends when Maman called out, "Henri!" I would have been deaf to anyone else, including Professor Draghui and Don Albini, but never to Maman Camous. I never disobeyed the voice of the lady who refused to listen to the neighbors when they complained about my three bowls of coffee. I ran to the voice and was greeted by the beautiful smile of Maman Camous. She said, "Run to Madame Christini and tell her to give you a nice big piece of meat, one pound." With that she extended her arms and mine also, and with the palms of her hands facing each other she measured off an imaginary piece of meat. I didn't pay any attention to the one pound, I looked only at the space between her hands, and forgot the final order. I ran from home to the butcher shop, which was almost half a mile away. I arrived there out of breath but happy with the thought of that big piece of meat. I scarcely had breath enough to say politely, *"Bonjour,* Madame Christini, Maman Camous told me to tell you that she wants a big piece of meat, *comme ça."* And I extended my arms as Maman Camous had shown me. But I added, like a parrot, "One pound."

I had six *sous* (six cents) in my pocket that Maman had given me for the purchase. Madame Christini took my hands and tried to push them closer together to make the imaginary piece smaller. I tried to resist, but she kept pushing and pushing them until finally she almost

117

reached the position Don Albini used when he was praying. She looked into my eyes which were dry because I was too ashamed to cry. But she cut me a nice piece of lean meat, and I paid her the six *sous*.

I didn't run back home, my exhilaration had vanished. Instead, I kicked every stone I met on the way without thinking that I might hurt my toes. I almost swore. I mumbled to myself, "Some big piece of meat, only two fingers, some big piece of meat, some big piece of meat."

At last I arrived home with my package which had been wrapped in thick brown paper. That sort of paper made a noise when you wrapped a parcel, and still more noise when you unwrapped it.

I said, "Look, Mom, Madame Christini gave me a small piece, not a big piece."

My lovely Maman Camous, God bless her, stood before me, her eyes shining; in her heart she wanted to offer me a large piece of meat, but her poor pocketbook could not stand it. She put my purchase on the scales, gave me four more *sous,* and said, "Take this money for Madame Christini, she gave you more meat than you paid for."

I almost disobeyed her, which would have been a big mistake. I was tempted to keep the money, and, if I had, then I would have cheated Maman Camous instead of Madame Christini. Realizing the sacrifices that Maman had made for me in trying to please my cannibalistic tendencies, I recalled that those same teeth of mine had crunched a lot of potatoes and vegetables, too. A strange thought came to me. My eyes had looked at cows, lambs, etc., but my teeth had never bitten them! They were my friends! This time I didn't run but walked back to the butcher shop. My friends yelled, "Hurry up, Henri, we must finish the game."

"I have to go back to Madame Christini's."

"Then why don't you go quickly?"

I said, "No." I was too disappointed.

When I arrived at the shop again I gave Madame Christini the four *sous* and said, "Madame, Maman Camous says you have made a mistake, you gave her more meat than she paid for."

I will always remember the red face of that kind old butcher woman.

She said, "Come on, Henri."

She took me back into the store-room, and my face changed from one of disappointment to one of surprise when I saw all those enormous pieces of meat. I smiled with contentment even though I had none. But Madame took my hands and stretched them across one of the large roasts of veal, and said, "Henri, was it like this, the size?"

I was paralyzed, I couldn't answer. My eyes were already picturing the roast, and, because my hands were still there stretched out measuring the meat and she didn't want to cut my fingers, she placed the knife three inches further along the veal and cut it off.

She said, "Take this to Maman Camous, Henri, with my compliments, and tell her she is the greatest and most honest woman, not in all the village, but in all of France."

I gave her no time to wrap it in her noisy brown paper, but quickly snatched it up, and with my precious cargo held tightly in my arms, I ran like a dog that was stealing. On the way I screamed over my shoulder, *"Merci, merci, merci,"* and continued running like mad. When I passed in front of my playmates every one of them called out, "Look out! The *gendarmes* are in back of you!"

"Ma foi," I yelled, "this is a present for Maman Camous." Hearing her name, Maman, back in the kitchen, called, "Yes?" She didn't recognize my voice and thought someone else was calling her. But when she saw me with that big piece of veal she said, "What did you do? Did you steal it?"

I said, "No, Mom, Madame Christini offers it to you with her compliments. She told me to tell you that you are the kindest, most honest, and the greatest woman in all of France." On my own hook I added the word "kindest." Maman Camous and Henri cried together that day. What a roast would be waiting for us on Sunday! On that day we saved the lives of two rabbits; they were replaced by the roast of veal.

I went out to finish the game with my friends who were almost ready to give up waiting for me. I thought of that big piece of meat which we were going to have in a couple of days, and, by anticipating, generated enough power to run and jump like a goat, thereby helping me to win the game. However, my friends objected; first I had made them wait, and then I ended up by winning, and they didn't like it. But I wasn't going to give in, and without intervention from Maman Camous I would have received a black eye and maybe given the other fellows a few as well.

In the process of running back and forth to the butcher shop I learned a lesson in honesty. I found that on the scales of life, honesty is the balance that should be maintained if there is to be a true civilization at all. The one who cheats merely cheats himself, because he has lost the scale by which right and wrong are the guides for the uncertain; in his confusion, for the moment, he has no more confidence in himself and in his ability to know right from wrong. Because of this, instead of just the Ten Commandments which are God's laws and Nature's, too, we have libraries full of law books that no lawyer in the world could live long enough to read, let alone have time to study.

It is so simple to stay with right; if you like sugar, others might like different forms of sweets. And if you don't like wine, don't prohibit those who love wine. Alcohol, we know, is very powerful. Use, but do not abuse it. And by no means condemn the totality. By doing that you deny God, since He has created all the things that should be enjoyed by human beings without excess. In drinking moderately, you taste, and know what it is. In drinking to the point of drunkenness, you revert and become uncivilized. If you don't drink at all you lose something from the earth. But if you impede this enjoyment you are just as criminal as the one who kills by taking the life of the individual. You take away pleasure and freedom, and this action I call criminal tyranny. You force the honest one to cheat, the truthful one to lie, and the sober one to become a drunkard. Quality disappears, cheap things come to the surface, the cream disappears from the milk, and honor leaves the human being. And that is the *chef-d'oeuvre* of a cheater. Common sense and sincerity are basic; with honesty there is also the complete obligation of "live and let live." Maman Camous' tranquil nature, the good logic of the lady butcher,

Madame Christini, and my fear of keeping the four sous for myself, all united to form the natural product of common sense, honesty.

The Two Nests

THAT SAME DAY after peace had been declared, the other boys and I decided to go looking for birds' nests. We ran around among the olive trees, contrary to the teachings of Monsieur Draghui, each boy trying to be the first to spy a nest. I found myself alone under one of the trees and thought of how lucky I was. Up in that olive tree was a mother bird with her babies which were just about ready to fly. Instead of being quiet as she should have been, so I wouldn't have noticed them, she began to call for the papa bird.

"Ch, ch, ch, ch," she screamed.

That gang of rascals, and my approach under the tree, terrified the mother bird. She thought two birds would give more protection to her babies, so she continued screaming, "ch, ch, ch, ch."

I called to my friends, "Here's a nest!"

Exclamations of happiness came from those young fools, including myself, as I started to climb the olive tree. Five little birds opened their beaks when I thrust my head and shoulders through the branches. They were expecting worms and didn't like the thief who had come to steal them when all they wanted was food and more food. I said to myself, "These fellows here never seem to get enough to eat." I put them, one by one, inside of my shirt. At that moment the papa bird arrived, and both he and the mother flew ferociously at my head. Later I couldn't understand how I, an orphan, could

121

have forgotten my kindness long enough to have also made orphans of those five baby birds. Now that I was ready to climb down the tree I couldn't do it fast enough, because those two fighting birds were still attacking my unprotected head. I needed my arms to descend; so I couldn't defend myself. They were screaming after me that they hoped I'd fall and break my neck. Well, I didn't fall or break my neck, but there was a tremendous surprise waiting for me when I neared the bottom of the tree. As I reached the last branch I looked down and saw another nest. It was the beard of Monsieur Draghui, and as I looked down and he looked up, that was just what it looked like to me. I saw there were no tears in his eyes, only a fierce light, and he said severely, "You climb up there again and return those birds to the nest, and count them!"

He didn't trust me. He thought I would put three back and keep two.

I said, "There are five here, sir."

I climbed the tree again branch by branch, like a monkey, until I reached the nest, while the professor yelled at me, "And don't hurt them!"

I had taken those little fellows from their home, and they were taking revenge on me by scratching around inside my shirt. I dared not do anything to hurt them with Monsieur Draghui watching from below. He saw the five motions I made as I returned each to the nest from the one I had improvised. Each was a handful so I could only put one back at a time. When the inhabitants of that olive tree were restored, the mother and father bird changed their tune and almost embraced each other in contentment at being reunited with their family. I would have liked to stay there longer, but Monsieur Draghui was waiting for me. After inspecting my blouse, he said, "I will talk to you about this tomorrow." He hadn't seen any of my friends, but he knew I wasn't alone.

On Friday when I reached the classroom I didn't go to my bench. Instead, I went to the front of the class and stood facing Monsieur Draghui.

He asked, "Who was with you yesterday?"

"Nobody," I replied.

He demanded again, "Who was with you yesterday?"

Again I said, "Nobody."

I was made to lie on the bench with my posterior upward, while the professor looked around for his switch. Then he proceeded to give me something to remember, something the parents of the birds I tried to steal would have loved to have seen and heard. He spanked me five times with all his strength, once for each baby I had taken from the nest. It was as hot as fire.

And he said, "Now another one for the father bird, and one for the mother bird!"

I think he would have counted up to the great great grandfather of those pesky birds if my friends had not come to my rescue. I was saved from that long line of the feathered family after number seven, but Monsieur Draghui was reluctant to quit. He was very angry and was ready to give me a good lesson in front of the class. The preceding day I had learned a lesson of honesty from Madame Christini and Maman Camous, and now I was learning that I must be kind as well as honest. That fact was now being impressed on me.

One boy jumped up with, "I was there, sir."

Another said, "I was there, too."

A third joined in with, "Me, too."

A fourth said, "Now we are all here, I'm the last one."

But the professor didn't spank the other four; he felt he had had enough with me. Maybe he was proud of the others because they had come to my rescue by admitting they were parties to my crime. We were made to sit on the bench which was reserved for punishment so that all the class could see us in our disgrace. In order not to look like a sissy I wore a small cushion in my pants for a week so I could sit down without making a face.

RECIPES

✠

HORS-D'OEUVRE, ELIAS HOWE

✠

SOUP, GEORGE BANCROFT

✠

EGGS, FRANCIS SCOTT KEY

✠

SHIRRED EGGS, RALPH BARBOUR

✠

BROILED SALMON, CHRISTOPHER GADSDEN

✠

ROAST PORK, JEFFERSON DAVIS

✠

BAKED POTATOES, ROGER SHERMAN

✠

ARTICHOKES, NICHOLAS ROOSEVELT

✠

ASPARAGUS TIP SALAD, FITZ-GREENE HALLECK

✠

FLOATING ISLAND, EMILY POST

✠

HORS-D'OEUVRE, ELIAS HOWE

Clean three large cups of dried lentils by placing them on the table and sorting them over one by one so that no impurities or little stones remain among them. Wash and put them into a pot with 2 quarts of water and a little salt. Finely cut 1 leek into the pot as well as 1 stalk of celery. Add 1 chopped onion and 2 whole cloves of peeled garlic. Let it boil from 45 minutes to 1 hour.

Strain, and place the broth aside for a soup recipe which is to follow later. Also put aside 1 cupful of the cooked lentils.

When the two remaining cups of lentils have become cold, place them in a serving dish. Chop 4 green onions and their stems and sprinkle them over the cold lentils. Season with salt and pepper; add the juice of ½ lemon and 2 tablespoons of olive oil and mix. Put 2 slices of cold boiled ham at the opposite sides of the dish of lentils. Garnish each of the other sides with a sprig of parsley.

When serving, place a piece of the ham on each plate and spread with a little English mustard. Then put the lentils over the ham. This hors-d'oeuvre will give you an excellent start.

SOUP, GEORGE BANCROFT

Take the cupful of cooked lentils which have been put aside from the preceding recipe and put them back in the broth which you have also put aside. Add 1 finely chopped onion, 1 finely chopped leek, 2 peeled, thinly sliced raw potatoes, and 2 whole cloves of peeled garlic. Place in a hot oven for about ½ hour, and then pass it through a sieve.

Place 4 tablespoons of cream, a generous piece of butter, salt and pepper into a hot tureen. Heat 1 glassful of claret in a separate pan and when it comes to a boil stir it into the seasoned cream and butter in the tureen. Then mix in the lentil purée which has been made very hot. Serve croutons separately, and sprinkle them over the soup as it is being served. Your croutons must be made in advance so that the soup will not have to wait for them. To make them, cut 1 slice of white sandwich bread into very small pieces and put them into a frying pan with a piece of butter. Keep turning with a spatula until they become brown.

EGGS, FRANCIS SCOTT KEY

Chop 1 onion, very fine, into a frying pan with 1 tablespoon of butter. Cover the pan until the onions become brown. Carefully wash and chop a handful of raw spinach. Put it into the frying pan. When the water of the spinach has become absorbed and cooked in with the onions, season with salt and pepper. Put the whole thing into a baking dish.

Poach 4 eggs and place them on top of the spinach.

Now, in a separate pan, prepare your sauce. Place 1 minced shallot into a pan with 1 tablespoon of butter. When it begins to cook, add 4 tablespoons of cream, and when that starts to boil add 2 tablespoons of sherry.

Dissolve 1 tablespoon of cornstarch in 2 tablespoons of milk. When the sauce of shallot, cream, and sherry begins to boil, mix in the dissolved cornstarch. Sprinkle with paprika, pepper, and salt. Stir in a teaspoon of meat stock.

Pour this sauce over the poached eggs and spinach. Sprinkle with grated cheese and place in a hot oven for a few minutes.

SHIRRED EGGS, RALPH BARBOUR

Place 1 finely chopped shallot into a frying pan with 1 tablespoon of butter for 2 minutes. Take 2 lamb kidneys, cut them into small pieces and add to the frying pan. Slice 2 mushrooms into the pan, and add as well: 1 teaspoon of meat stock, 1 sherry-glassful of dry white wine. The whole thing should be cooked no longer than 12 minutes.

Melt a piece of butter in a baking dish and break 4 eggs carefully into it. Arrange the cooked kidneys, etc., between the yolks, covering only the whites of the eggs. Put in the oven for 3 or 4 minutes. Sprinkle with chopped parsley, salt and pepper.

BROILED SALMON, CHRISTOPHER GADSDEN

Place 1 pound of sliced fresh salmon on a baking platter. Sprinkle with a little salt, no pepper. When it has been broiled on one side for 4 minutes turn it and broil it for 4 minutes on the other side. Then, place a generous piece of butter on top of the salmon, and when it melts begin to baste it. Have the flame of your broiler turned low so that the fish will broil without burning.

Mash 4 anchovy fillets into 1 clove of garlic, chopped parsley, and 1 large tablespoon of butter.

Put the broiled salmon on a serving platter and place the crushed anchovies, garlic, etc., over the top.

Pour the remaining hot butter of the baking platter into a saucer and mix it with 1 or 2 ponies of good whiskey or brandy. Touch a flame to it and pour it over the anchovy butter on the broiled salmon. Do not forget to garnish both ends of the platter with parsley and both sides with slices of lemon.

ROAST PORK, JEFFERSON DAVIS

Use a 2 pound loin of pork (with the bones). Do not have your meat boned. Rub the pork with salt, pepper, and a clove of garlic. Put it into a roasting pan with 1 tablespoon of butter and place it in a hot oven of 450° to 500° F. When it begins to roast, stick a fork into the fat part to give the meat a chance to tenderize and to get the fat into the gravy. Add 1 whole onion to the roasting pan as well as 2 or 3 unpeeled cloves of garlic which have first been dipped into water. Every 15 minutes add 1 tablespoon of sherry and a small piece of butter. Baste the pork with this. To recognize when the pork is done stick a fork all the way into the meat and then touch the prongs of the fork to your cheek. If the prongs are very hot your pork is well done, but if the prongs are only warm then it must be cooked longer. It is very important that pork be cooked until it is well done. It will generally take 1½ hours to thoroughly cook a 2 pound roast. After ¾ of an hour in the oven turn the temperature down to 350° F.

Chop 2 shallots into a separate pan with some butter. Peel, wash, and cut 3 potatoes into quarters and add them to the chopped shallots in the pan. Place in the oven for 15 minutes. Peel, core, and cut 2 apples into quarters and add them to the potatoes with a small piece of butter. Add a handful of seedless grapes, and let it all cook together in the oven for 15 more minutes. Then place this preparation of potatoes, apples, etc., into the roasting pan with the pork. Baste it and place it in the oven again for 5 more minutes. Put the roast on a serving platter and arrange the other ingredients around it. Cut and serve the pork with a bone as you would a chop, and pour a spoonful of gravy over the meat.

BAKED POTATOES, ROGER SHERMAN

Select 2 large Idaho potatoes and see that the skins are intact. Wash them and place in the oven. If you wish to prepare these potatoes with the above pork roast then your oven will cook three things simultaneously: the roast, the garniture, and the potatoes. By the time your meat is roasted your potatoes will be ready.

When the potatoes have been baked, cut a cross into the center of each and remove a little. Sprinkle the potato remaining in the shells with pepper, salt and paprika. Add a piece of butter, and with a fork work it in so that it penetrates. Mix the part that was removed with a little grated cheese and place back in the shells.

ARTICHOKES, NICHOLAS ROOSEVELT

Trim and clean 2 artichokes and place them upside down in a quart of boiling salted water. Add 1 slice of lemon. It usually takes 35 to 40 minutes of boiling before they are done. To test an artichoke, pull off a leaf and bite into it. If it is soft and tender it is done. If the leaf does not come off readily the artichoke has not been cooked enough. When they are done, drain off the water, dry the artichokes and remove a few of the leaves from the center. Let the remaining leaves stay attached to the heart. With a teaspoon, remove the hairy-looking part that covers the heart inside the remaining leaves. Open the leaves.

Squeeze the juice of ½ lemon into a pan, add a piece of butter, salt and pepper, and 1 tablespoon of white vinegar. Let it come to a boil and pour over the middle of each artichoke so that it reaches down into the center. Take leaf by leaf from the center, which possesses the sauce, and eat only the tender part of the end that has been pulled from the heart, about ⅛ of an inch. When you come to the heart, add a little more sauce and finish it using a fork. The leaves are to be eaten with your fingers.

ASPARAGUS TIP SALAD, FITZ-GREENE HALLECK

Boil ½ bunch of asparagus in salted water. Let it cook until it is soft and tender, yet firm. Pour off the water. When it is cold, serve on top of lettuce leaves. Sprinkle with salt and pepper and pour 1 tablespoon of French Dressing over each salad.

FLOATING ISLAND, EMILY POST

Break 4 eggs and separate the yolks from the whites. Beat the whites until they become stiff.

Boil 2 quarts of water in a casserole and add: 1 bay leaf, 1 clove, 1 small piece of stick cinnamon, and 2 tablespoons of white wine. When it is all boiling, take large spoons of the egg white and place them on the boiling water. Turn them over once or twice until the boiling water has made the egg white firm. Do this with all the egg white, and remove from the water.

Prepare the sauce for this dessert in advance. Pour into a pan: ½ glassful of milk, ½ glassful of cream, 2 heaping tablespoons of sugar, 1 teaspoon of vanilla extract or 1 vanilla bean. If you have used a vanilla bean remove it after the ingredients begin to boil. In a separate dish beat the 4 egg yolks with 3 tablespoons of sugar and 1 tablespoon of cream. Pour the boiling milk and cream over the egg yolks, stirring it quickly. Let it become cold and serve it over the egg whites.

Chapter VIII

A STRANGER IN THE CHICKEN'S NEST

DON ALBINI had a good laugh out of my escapade. The news travelled fast, and he asked me if I didn't want a cushion to sit down on. That made me half angry, but still I had to laugh.

Just the same I wanted to give the priest an answer since he had laughed at me, and as I looked at him I already had an idea. For several days I had been hiding a duck egg at home, and since I didn't like the taste of them I planned to exchange it for two chicken eggs from the coop of Don Albini.

The priest's sister was an elderly lady, and I had the freedom of their house so that I might run in and out daily with a few pails of water; that great servant and soldier of God had no more privileges than the other villagers. The comfort of running water was not known in those days.

I entered the house, calling out as I did so, "Mademoiselle Lena, it's Henri, I've come to bring you some water so you'll have a reserve supply." I made three round trips, running like a billy goat with my pail. I had the duck egg tucked safely inside my shirt, and it was a miracle that I didn't hatch a duckling with the warmth of my body, or make a raw omelet on my nude belly, because I never wore any underwear when I was a boy.

On my third trip I stopped at the chicken coop and chased away the hens so that none of them would be on top of the nests making new productions and a new income for the priest. Don Albini, who was praying in the church a quarter of a mile away, would have known that he had a new egg in his possession if he had heard any cackling. In fact, I caught one big, plump red hen just in time. Walking like a princess on the way to the nest, she was getting ready to lay an egg. She talked to me in her own language and stopped to look at me.

I said, "Reddy, ten seconds, and then after that you can stay on the nest twenty-one days, if you want to, and make a big surprise for the priest. It'll be a big surprise, too, because Don Albini will think you've hatched a duckling from one of your own eggs."

It looked to me as if that chicken understood. Instead of running away she stood there eyeing me curiously. I weighed the big greenish-gray duck egg in my right hand like a grocer trying to decide if it was equal to two or maybe three chicken eggs. My conscience told me two, so I followed its advice.

There were five eggs in one of the nests, and every finger on my hand had a temptation of its own to steal. Thank goodness those fingers had no stomachs! I reached into it with my left hand, because I had the duck egg in my right, and grabbed two. It was impossible to capture any more, my hand was full. Thank goodness, again, it was not big enough or I might have taken one more. Very gently with my right hand I placed the duck egg in the nest in the spot made vacant by the two chicken eggs. That was the first time in my life that I applied the adage, "Never let the right hand know what the left hand is doing." My conscience was not guilty; by carrying in the water and exchanging the big one for the two smaller ones I still had the idea that maybe my duck egg was worth three chicken eggs.

I said, "Au revoir, Mademoiselle Lena." She was surprised at how quickly I had supplied her with a water reserve.

I was not 300 feet away when I heard Reddy scream and cackle so loud and so long that in one moment all the roosters in the village began to answer her. They were annoyed and crowed, "All right, Reddy, we know you laid an egg, now, shut up!" But the screaming continued.

Reddy had seen me take two and leave only one in exchange, and in doing that I made her feel inferior. In my mind one duck egg was equal to two chicken eggs, but she was offended. No one should ever say or think that she was inferior to a duck. That day she laid two more, one after another, and made such a commotion that I hardly got away in time.

The common sense of the chicken was far greater than the judgment of little Henri, and the proudness of Reddy saved me from making a mistake. I learned from her that an egg was an egg whether it was that of an ostrich or that of a pigeon. She was willing to accept the duck as her equal, but as to its being a better bird, no. Now that she had evened the score she was satisfied, and I still had two for one.

Don Albini never found more than five eggs in his chicken coop, and I thought I had been saved by that champion layer of them all, Reddy. But three days later, Sunday, the priest chose me to assist him as his water boy. It was my duty to carry a decanter of water on a tray with a glass and stand very close to him, because as he preached his sermon from the pulpit its lengthiness might necessitate a refreshing drink. I was not very tall and I could just see over the railing. After preaching at great length, and after giving plenty of advice and comments, I heard him say something that was certainly directed at me.

Don Albini said, "My children, I want to tell you how even a duck can be kind. Down at the entrance to our village there lives a fowl who succeeded in recognizing my house, I don't know how, since she couldn't ask anyone for the address and I have no ducks there to attract her. But she came in, found a nest that contained five chicken eggs, and there laid hers. Now, my children, God has given this larger bird the kindness to make her own production without destroying that of other birds. But what intrigues me most," and at that moment he looked at me instead of the people, "is the question: Who was it, among you, who opened the door to the chicken coop for that bird, thereby permitting her to present me with an egg?"

I understood by the look he gave me that he knew I was the duck, and one without feathers. But he never knew that two eggs were missing. My friend Reddy had rectified my mistake by laying two extra ones that day. If she hadn't I would have been caught again. As it was I didn't have to tell my story, but I had one ready for the priest. I was going to say that my egg was equivalent to two of his and so it was an even exchange. I learned that still another adage, "God helps those who help themselves," worked for me, too.

I found my duck egg in the sacristy where Don Albini was waiting for me.

He said, "Next time, Henri, bring the water to my sister, but don't try to fool the hens, because it's wrong to bring them a duck egg to hatch."

So I took my prodigal egg back home to Maman Camous who mixed it with flour, water, chives, and a pinch of salt, and made an omelet enough for five. It should have been named "omelet poor home style" and, if it must be made known, it was a form of German pancake which was light enough for a German stomach but not quite for one that was French.

RECIPES

❦

HORS-D'OEUVRE, FRANCIS MARION
❦

SOUP, THOMAS HEYWARD, JR.
❦

EGGS, ARTHUR MIDDLETON
❦

EGGS, THOMAS LYNCH, JR.
❦

SOLE, EDWARD RUTLEDGE
❦

STEAK, CHARLES PINCKNEY
❦

POTATOES, JOHN MATHEWS
❦

LIMA BEANS, HENRY MIDDLETON
❦

SALAD, RICHARD HUTSON
❦

PEACHES, BARBARA FRITCHIE
❦

HORS-D'OEUVRE, FRANCIS MARION

Soak 1 cup of dry white beans overnight. The next day put them into 2 quarts of salted cold water. Add 1 chopped leek, 1 chopped onion, 2 whole cloves of peeled garlic, and 1 chopped stalk of celery. Season with pepper and add a generous piece of butter. Cover the pan and place it in a hot oven for 1½ hours, after which time the beans should be tender. Remove the pan from the oven and let the whole thing cool. When it is cold, strain, and stand the juice aside. Let ¼ of the beans remain in the juice.

Place the other ¾ in a bowl. Make a dressing, using: 1 clove of garlic which has been crushed in a little chopped parsley, the juice of ½ lemon, salt and pepper, 3 tablespoons of olive oil, and ½ tablespoon of red wine vinegar. Pour it over the beans.

SOUP, THOMAS HEYWARD, JR.

Take the remaining juice and beans which have been set aside from the above hors-d'oeuvre and add: ½ finely chopped Savoy cabbage, ¼ pound of salt pork (in one piece), 1 chopped leek, 1 turnip that has been cut into quarters, 1 chopped onion, and 1 pint of water. Let this boil in a pot for 1 hour over a small flame on top of the stove, or, if you prefer, in a hot oven. After it is cooked, season with salt and pepper, and add 1 tablespoon of olive oil. A little more pepper must be sprinkled on this kind of soup to give it sharpness.

EGGS, ARTHUR MIDDLETON

Break 6 eggs into a baking platter, add a piece of butter, and place over a small flame. Put a generous piece of butter into a separate frying pan, melt it, and add ½ tablespoon of red wine vinegar. Let the butter and vinegar become brown. Chop: 1 shallot, a little parsley, and a few fresh tarragon leaves. Sprinkle (uncooked) over the eggs. Pepper and salt. Pour the hot, browned butter and vinegar over the eggs.

EGGS, THOMAS LYNCH, JR.

Boil together: 1 scraped carrot, 2 peeled potatoes, ½ handful of fresh green peas, ½ handful of fresh lima beans. When they are cooked, strain and dice. Put them into a baking dish with a piece of butter, salt, and pepper. Arrange 6 eggs, which have been poached, on top of the vegetables. Put ½ tablespoon of cream over the top of each egg. Mix 1 tablespoon of bread crumbs with 2 tablespoons of grated cheese and sprinkle over the eggs which are wet from the cream. Put in a hot oven for 4 minutes.

SOLE, EDWARD RUTLEDGE

Purchase 1 large whole sole and clean it, cutting off the head. Remove the black skin and leave the roe intact in the fish. Put a generous piece of butter on a baking platter, melt it, and lay the sole in the butter. Season with salt only. Place in a preheated oven, 450° F., for 15 minutes without looking at it. Then baste it with the melted butter. Bake the sole for 10 more minutes, and baste it 2 or 3 times during that period. When it is ready to serve, sprinkle it with a little more salt, and, this time, a little pepper, too. The bones baked with the fish give it greater taste and more softness.

STEAK, CHARLES PINCKNEY

Cut 1 pound of sirloin steak in half and hammer it to make it thin. Sprinkle with salt and pepper. Put a generous piece of butter into a frying pan and make it hot. Place the steak in the pan and let it fry on one side for 1 minute. Turn, and let it fry on the other side for 2 minutes. Lay the thin 3 minute steak on a hot serving platter. Sprinkle 2 finely chopped shallots, a little chopped parsley, and a little freshly ground black pepper over the meat. Put another generous piece of butter into the frying pan that was used to fry the steak. When it has melted and begins to bubble, pour over the steak on the hot platter.

POTATOES, JOHN MATHEWS

Peel 3 large potatoes. Cut them into 6 pieces each, shaping them like olives. Put them into a baking dish with a generous piece of butter. Add 6 whole mushrooms and 6 green pitted olives. Sprinkle with 2 chopped shallots. Place in a preheated hot oven and bake from 20 to 25 minutes. Season to taste with salt and pepper.

LIMA BEANS, HENRY MIDDLETON

Boil 2 handfuls of fresh lima beans in enough salted water to just cover them.

Put a generous piece of butter into a frying pan and add 2 chopped shallots, 1 large peeled and mashed ripe tomato, 1 clove of garlic which has been crushed into a little chopped parsley. Cook it for 15 minutes.

When the lima beans become tender there should be very little water left in the pot. Do not strain them. Pour the cooked shallots, tomato, etc., over the lima beans, and stir.

SALAD, RICHARD HUTSON

Chop: 1 celery heart, 1 peeled and cored apple, and 2 cold boiled potatoes. Add a pinch of salt and pepper, 2 tablespoons of cream, and the juice of 1 lemon. Serve with water-cress.

PEACHES, BARBARA FRITCHIE

Peel and slice 1 large peach. Crush a handful of very ripe, washed and cleaned strawberries. Add 1 tablespoon of sugar and 1 pony of either kirsch or cherry brandy. Mix and serve with vanilla ice cream.

Chapter IX

BADOU LIVED UP TO HIS TITLE

BADOU, THE COACHMAN of the diligence which carried passengers from Nice to Contes and back again, was a great friend of Papa Camous. In the early part of October each year he took a week off to come and visit with us and watch the *vendange*, the cutting of the grapes. He didn't come to help, but to eat all kinds of grapes; in doing so he titled it "a week of my own cure."

I was present one day and heard a conversation between Papa Camous and the old fellow. Badou kept looking at the old mule of Papa Camous until the latter said, "You can look at Fannie all you like, she was born a mule and has been with me for thirty-four years and still she is a mule, but I would not exchange her for your fine horses even if they are fifteen years younger."

Both men were good friends, and both loved their own animals.

Badou made the crack, "The lions in the zoological gardens at Nice would refuse to bite the best piece of that mule, including the filet."

Papa Camous said, hotly, "Badou, don't make me angry. If you like me, please respect my mule."

To which the coachman retorted, "I like you, I like your mule, too, but why the Devil do you pick on my horses?"

He stood there eating a huge bunch of grapes, which were the color of golden honey. The conversation, with its slightly angry tone, was calmed by the fruit which didn't have a chance to ferment and become wine. Badou ate them for one full week every year in memory

Theodore Roosevelt often stopped at the Original Henri Restaurant for his favorite onion soup when driving between his Oyster Bay home and New York City. The photograph is inscribed, "To my friend, Henri. 1914."

of his mother who always appreciated their sweet wine. I wondered at the capacity of that old fellow who would say between bunches, "By eating this fruit I keep the memory of my mother green as well as the tradition she held that one week of eating them would cure one of any ailment."

When the week was over old Badou said to Papa Camous, "Tomorrow we'll drink the wine which has been bottled for three years."

And for eleven months and three weeks you couldn't put one more grape into his mouth. His mother, in the other world, believed that her Badou was a good boy for one week.

As the conversation always turned to the mother of Badou, Papa Camous made everyone laugh, including myself, when he turned to the old coachman and said, "I bet you if the old lady were here she would spank you yet."

Badou, in my small boy's estimation, was the essence of adventure and a great and wonderful coachman. He had never married and had sacrificed his personal life in order to support his mother, to whom he was more than devoted. He couldn't bear the thought of marrying some girl who might have had an argument with the old lady. I was very small when his poor mother died, but I remember his tears; his grief was inconsolable.

After Papa Camous made the remark about the spanking, Badou repeated the story that he told very often to anyone who would listen, including his two fine horses, that he had lived seventy-two years with his mother and there had not been one single night in all that time that he had not slept under the same roof with her.

At that last expression the laughing stopped, and more eyes than just Badou's were wet and shining from the effect of his words. Mine were misty, too. There was a true affection among those people who had always loved him and the old lady who had brought him into the world.

At the *vendange* Papa Camous and six other men helped to cut the luscious grapes that hung in enormous bunches on the vines. He very proudly informed our village, and all the surrounding villages, that his land produced the finest of grapes, which in turn made the finest wine in

141

all of France. He was very stingy in offering the fruit, but very generous
with his bottled treasure. He was angry with the birds; those little
fellows loved his grapes, but refused to drink his wine.

Included among the *vendangeurs* were Maman Camous, her children
Celestin and Césarina, and old Giroumetta, who was in her last year of
life. Not so far from the group were two boulders on top of which was
a large copper pot that had been in the family for centuries and was
still in good condition. This arrangement for cooking our "farmer soup"
was every bit as good as the range in Maman's kitchen. After the fire
was lit underneath that big pot it was my duty to find the wood with
which to keep it burning. The aroma of the soup delighted the countryside for half a mile around. Even a fox would have been fooled into
thinking that nothing so tempting could have been prepared in such a
simple manner. Badou, the great and wonderful coachman, assumed
the rôle of cook and presided over our copper pot like a king.

The ingredients consisted, first, of a large cup of olive oil and three
huge onions, finely chopped. This first combination was seasoned with
pepper and salt. As soon as the oil was almost absorbed by the golden
brown onions, some tomatoes were cut up and added. Three cloves of
garlic were crushed with parsley, celery leaves and more pepper and
salt. This preparation was sprinkled over the tomatoes that were slowly
fusing into the melody which was known to everyone as "farmer soup."
Then a large bucket of water was added, a small quantity at a time,
to give it a chance to slowly become blended, as had the olive oil. Then
some green string beans, some potatoes, celery, cauliflower, and onions,
were all cut into small pieces; some lima beans, peas, some green cabbage finely chopped, some more crushed garlic, more onions, tomatoes,
etc., etc., were added until all the vegetables that were on hand slowly
disappeared into the volcano which had a fire underneath and was boiling inside.

Papa Camous looked into the pot and said to Badou, "A nice piece of
beef would turn this "farmer soup" into "king soup"; kings prefer meat
to the greens with which Nature has garnished our land. I believe that
if the old king of France Henri IV of Navarre were still alive and pass-

ing by here today, he would chase all of his cooks from the palace and take you, Badou, to be his master chef, because of this *chef-d'oeuvre* that you are preparing for us today."

This flattering speech stopped Badou from saying to Papa Camous, "One leg of that old mule of yours would take the place of the beef."

The coachman bit his tongue, and by his twinkling eyes, which looked at the mule who was not far away, everyone understood without his having to say it, and everyone knew also why Badou, for once, was mute. Now he was worried about his soup and how he could find a piece of meat for it. Whether beef, mule, horse or anything else, it didn't matter to him. After having been declared a master chef by Papa Camous and fit to be in the palace of the great king Henri IV of Navarre, had he been alive, Badou felt that he simply had to produce meat for the soup. It was this king of France who had declared and promised that every Sunday, for every French family in the kingdom, there should be a chicken in the pot. After changing from Huguenot to Catholic, he issued an order to every priest in France to preach and spread his kind words: "A chicken in the pot makes a soothing broth for the throat, one that will warm the stomach and make the heart gay so that the spirit of intelligence will emanate from everyone."

Papa Camous, after admonishing the coachman that he must watch the soup so it wouldn't spoil or be unworthy of him, the master chef, returned to work with Giroumetta and the others. Each carried his own basket for the grapes which were cut and assembled according to quality. It was up to Maman and Papa Camous to sort and grade them so they would produce, as usual every year, the same wonderful wine that Papa Camous was so proud of and which was so highly approved of by hundreds of others. Everyone called him the best wine maker in that region. Over fifty years have passed since those carefree days, and now, after having spent those fifty years as a restaurateur, I also agree with all those people, who are now dead but not forgotten, that Papa Camous truly was a maker of wonderful wine.

I went in search of dry wood so our volcano would not become extinct. Badou was left there alone with his pot of soup and his two titles:

143

that of "best coachman in France," and the new one of "master chef of Henri IV of Navarre."

I gathered one armful of wood and wandered off in quest for more. Badou kept feeding the hungry flames. I had to go further in my search since I had already scoured the immediate neighborhood and left it barren. I was bending down to pick up a stick when I saw a snake asleep in the warm sun. My eyes opened wide with horror and I stood rooted to the spot, paralyzed with fear. To my small self it looked so big I thought it was a boa from Africa. When finally I could move I didn't turn, but backed up slowly in retreat, my arms holding tightly to the wood. After retreating for about 200 feet, with my eyes glued to the reptile all that time, I turned and began running wildly. When I reached Badou I was wet with perspiration and gasping for breath. I wanted to say so much, but my tongue refused, and I could only exclaim, "Badou! Badou! Badou!"

He said, "What's the matter, Henri?"

I yelled, "Whew! There's a snake back there bigger than your leg!"

Then it was Badou who was paralyzed, and Badou whose eyes opened wide with incredulity.

"Where?" he asked.

I said, "About half a mile from here."

He took my load, placed it under the copper pot, and then said, "Show me where it is."

The snake was still sleeping when we arrived, its belly big with food which it had engulfed. This caused Badou to say that he had never seen such a large one in his life, and I was happy at having been the one to find it and show it off. I was only seven, and I had discovered the largest snake in that locality!

Now what were we going to do with it? In less than five seconds Badou jumped in and grabbed its head with one hand and its body, a little farther down, with the other. He pulled so quickly and vigorously that he killed it instantly. Then he skinned and cleaned it, and that was when we saw that our big snake had swallowed a rabbit. Not only that, but the rabbit was half alive yet! I believe Badou would have skinned that animal, too, but he saw me looking at him; it was a good thing I was there.

Poor Papa Camous! If he had ever found out about that story he would never have been able to eat again.

When the snake was skinned and cleaned Badou put it into a bag, the same kind of sack that carried the bran for his horses. He tied the top and put the whole thing in the soup, bag and all. That was the first time I learned how to turn a water bouillon into a meat bouillon, and also how to camouflage it in such a way that no bones could be found. That method may have been invented by old Badou himself. He skimmed off the fat which had formed on the soup and threw it on top of the wood underneath. The fire, accelerated by the fat, flared up, and the contents of the big pot bubbled. I was to be reminded of all this later when I saw and heard the volcano Vesuvius. Then, too, I thought of the day Badou had put the snake into the pot.

Ten minutes before it was ready he threw three handfuls of vermicelli into the pot. He removed the bag with the boiled snake in it and hid it.

The *vendangeurs* were busy with their grapes, and no one came until Badou yelled that the soup was ready. He served everybody, and while all those wonderful, famished people were busy eating, I pretended to swallow mine but couldn't bring myself to do so. I spilled it on the ground, leaving a little in the plate to make everyone think I had eaten. Then I excused myself so I wouldn't have to be present while it was being consumed. Badou had made me promise not to tell, and when everybody exclaimed, "Never has there been such a wonderful soup!" I felt sick.

Papa Camous declared, "Only Christ could turn water into wine, and only Badou can turn water into consommé."

Had he known that a few yards away there was a boiled snake with only the bones remaining, and that that was why the water had turned to consommé and not because of any magic on the part of Badou, his digestion would never have been the same. Papa Camous, the man who refused to eat his soup if a fly went to someone else's plate! What would he have said to Badou if he had known about that snake? I never told the story to him, or to anyone else, even after many years had passed. I was afraid I would provoke some feeling of repugnance and destroy the memory of those wonderful days we had spent during the *vendange*.

When Badou and I met after that soup episode he gave me extra packages to carry so I could make a few more *sous*. He didn't want me to say anything to anyone. Poor old fellow! He, too, didn't want to play that joke on Papa Camous. He only wanted to find any kind of meat just so he could live up to what was expected of him and be like King Henry IV and his "chicken in the pot." When Badou died he must have met the spirit of that lovely king in the other world. If he did he must have said, "Your Majesty, I couldn't exactly comply with your wishes that there should be a chicken in the pot. One day I found a snake, and it was much easier to skin that snake than it would have been to take the feathers from a chicken. I know you will excuse me and say that the intelligence and ingenuity of the French people will always enable them to make a successful broth that is rich and soothing. But, your Majesty, if that little fellow Henri had denounced me I believe there would have been a lot of seasickness even if we were nine miles away from the sea."

But before this conversation could take place Badou would have had to pass St. Peter himself who would have stopped him from going further into Paradise by saying, "You must stay here and await the arrival of Papa Camous to tell him the truth, because Henri has never told on you. Then I will let you both go further."

Papa Camous, bless him, died some thirty years after this story.

RECIPES

✤

TOMATO, DANIEL WEBSTER

✤

SOUP, HORACE GREELEY

✤

SHIRRED EGGS, FRANKLIN PIERCE

✤

EGGS, JAMES MONROE

✤

FLOUNDER, WILLIAM H. HARRISON

✤

SQUAB, DANIEL MORGAN

✤

POTATOES, JOHN TYLER

✤

ASPARAGUS, PETER MINUIT

✤

SALAD, GEORGE H. THOMAS

✤

CUSTARD, MARY BAKER EDDY

✤

TOMATO, DANIEL WEBSTER

Scoop out the insides of 2 fair-sized ripe tomatoes. Do not throw it away because it is to be used later. Chop very fine: 1 celery heart and ½ green pepper. Chop 1 hard-boiled egg. Add to this 1 tablespoon of cooked crabmeat and 2 tablespoons of French Dressing; then the insides of the tomatoes. Mix it well and stuff it into the tomato shells. Garnish with water-cress.

SOUP, HORACE GREELEY

Chop ½ green pepper as well as ½ onion and a few stalks of celery. To this, add ½ tablespoon of butter. Place in a covered pot over a small fire for 5 minutes. Then add 1 quart of water. Boil for 10 minutes and then add 1 tablespoon of uncooked rice. Boil 20 minutes more. Put a small piece of butter on each soup plate and pour the soup over it. Sprinkle with grated cheese and a little chopped parsley. Salt and pepper to taste, and serve.

SHIRRED EGGS, FRANKLIN PIERCE

Break 6 eggs gently into a baking platter which contains 1 tablespoon or more of melted butter. Prepare on top of the stove. Place 1 anchovy fillet on each yolk.

Finely chop 3 small sour pickles and mix them with a sprig of finely chopped parsley and a finely chopped clove of garlic. Salt and pepper. Sprinkle this over the 6 eggs.

Into a separate pan put 1 large tablespoon of butter, 1 teaspoon of Worcestershire sauce, 1 tablespoon of pickled capers, and the juice of ½ lemon. When it comes to a boil, pour over eggs and serve.

EGGS, JAMES MONROE

Cut the tops off 2 baked potatoes, remove ½ the insides of the potatoes, and, with a fork, loosen the remainder. Place a small piece of butter and a pinch of salt inside each loosened, half-filled potato shell.

To the potato which has been removed, add a small piece of butter and enough cream so that when it is mixed it will have the consistency of heavy cream. Replace it in the half-emptied potato shells and leave enough room on top of each to hold a raw egg. Pour ½ tablespoon of cream on top of each yolk. Be sure it does not run over. Put into a hot oven for 3 minutes. These potatoes should be eaten with a spoon.

FLOUNDER, WILLIAM H. HARRISON

Take a 1 pound flounder, clean it properly, and do not remove the bones; but skin the black side. Place the fish in a baking dish with 1 tablespoon of butter. Sprinkle over it 1 finely chopped shallot, a little finely chopped celery, a little chopped parsley, and 1 thinly sliced carrot. Season with salt and pepper. Give it 5 minutes in a very hot oven. The oven must be very hot before introducing the fish. Add ¼ glassful of water to the baking dish, and as soon as it boils, which will take about 5 minutes, add ½ sherry-glass of white domestic wine and a small piece of butter. Ten minutes later add another ¼ sherry-glass of the same wine. Let it remain in the oven for 5 minutes. Before serving, sprinkle with a little chopped parsley.

SQUAB, DANIEL MORGAN

A squab, to be good, must not weigh less than three-fourths of a pound. It is a tender young pigeon which has not yet flown from the nest. A jumbo squab weighs as much as 1¼ pounds.

Clean 1 or 2 squabs, whichever you desire. After cleaning, dry them with a cloth. Do not wash them. Take each one by the beak and the legs and hold it over a flame, slowly rotating it. This will free the bird of any remaining feathers and give it a wonderful taste and aroma which the oven cannot produce. Cut off the head and feet. The head, feet, and gizzard of any fowl may be put aside to be used with a veal or beef bone to make a good consommé. It is a great mistake to throw away the feet and heads of fowls; they are necessary to make the perfect consommé.

A pinch of salt and pepper, the liver, and a piece of raw onion should be placed inside the carcass of each squab. Put them into a baking dish with 1 tablespoon of butter. Your oven should be very hot before placing the baking dish inside, 450° to 500° F.

Roast in a separate baking dish: 2 potatoes which have each been cut into quarters, 1 chopped onion, ½ dozen whole green or black olives, 1 sliced tomato, 4 medium-sized whole mushrooms, 1 crushed clove of garlic, 1 tablespoon of butter, salt and pepper. Put this in the oven 15 to 20 minutes before the squabs. A squab demands a roasting period of 30 to 35 minutes, and the garniture demands 45 minutes.

Add more butter to the squabs from time to time as they are being basted. Five minutes before removing from the oven, add 1 sherry-glass of sherry to the baking dish containing the squabs. Then place the squabs in the baking dish with the vegetables, and pour over the gravy in which they have been cooked. Leave them in the oven for 3 minutes; salt and pepper to taste. Serve.

POTATOES, JOHN TYLER

Place in a baking dish: 1 tablespoon of butter, 4 potatoes which have been peeled, washed, dried, and cut into squares, 1 chopped red pepper, and 1 chopped leek. Be sure that the leek has been properly washed. Make the oven hot and put it in for 40 minutes. Salt and pepper to taste, and add a little butter when served.

ASPARAGUS, PETER MINUIT

Never peel asparagus. Merely cut the bottom part and scrape. Put into boiling salted water. It should be cooked to a firm tenderness rather than to a state of mushiness. Boil it 18 to 20 minutes. Pour off the water.

Mix together 1 tablespoon of bread crumbs, 1 tablespoon of grated cheese, the yolk of 1 hard-boiled egg, salt and pepper. Sprinkle over the top of the hot asparagus. Pour melted butter over that, place in a hot oven for 5 minutes, and serve.

SALAD, GEORGE H. THOMAS

Cut 1 boiled potato into small pieces. Add a few tablespoons of cooked green peas as well as a few tablespoons of green beans, and a few of chopped celery. Add several slices of raw onion and 2 or more tablespoons of French Dressing. Mix well Serve on lettuce leaves.

CUSTARD, MARY BAKER EDDY

Boil 2 cups of milk with 1 vanilla bean and 2 large tablespoons of sugar. When it begins to boil, remove and wash the vanilla bean and place it in a jar with some sugar that you will use at some future date. Put the yolks of 4 eggs into a baking dish and mix. Then pour the boiling milk over them. Stir together. Place the baking dish into another dish which contains water, but not so much water that it will boil over, in order to make the custard firm. Place both dishes into a hot oven. Sprinkle a little sugar over the top a few minutes before taking it from the oven, let it become brown, and serve.

151

Pvt. Henri Charpentier, age 21, in the uniform of the French
Army of the Republic.

Chapter X

THE MAGIC OF A
SWEET OLD LADY

For many centuries the family of Papa Camous lived in close association with the extremely kind and wealthy family of Madame Gasiglia which consisted mainly of doctors and lawyers. When I was seven that wonderfully gracious lady was eighty. Alert and intelligent, she still danced about like a young girl. She sang like a bird all day long in her large mansion, where she lived alone with her maid and companion, Françoise. Of her three sons only one was still alive on Madame Gasiglia's eightieth birthday. He was a doctor in Paris; his two brothers, one of whom had been a banker in Nice and the other a gentleman farmer, had died several years before. The widowed daughters-in-law and their children often came to visit the old lady, who kept open house for them. The grandchildren of Madame Gasiglia were each several years my senior. Sometimes when they were there, visiting in the big house, the doctor from Paris would arrive by surprise, and then his mother would invite many guests from the village to come in. On such special occasions the first to be summoned by the kind-hearted old lady would be Giroumetta, Maman and Papa Camous, and their children. Her house was large enough to take care of us all in great comfort.

But almost every evening in the wintertime Madame Gasiglia would come to visit Maman Camous and Giroumetta. There she would sit under the chimney of our fireplace and tell stories of her younger days. Her chair, which was a very comfortable one, was called "the chair of Madame Gasiglia" by the Camous family. The old lady, in the course of the conversation, would flatter Papa by telling him that there was no other man in all the village who could keep a fire burning with such beautiful flames. Papa Camous, two hours before her evening call, had busily fed the flames with the dried branches that he had trimmed from our olive trees. The flames produced from those burning branches were very beautiful. The vines of our grape arbor were also trimmed every year by the expert hands of Papa Camous. This gave them new vitality, slowed down their growth and produced, as a result, more grapes. These dried vines also had their uses. Papa put them on the fire to delight the heart of old Madame Gasiglia.

I, too, had my little place under that large chimney with our three cats and Bacci. They were always present. Bacci, after half roasting his nose with the flames, would put his head on my knees. Very often the fur of the cats would start to burn, and those darn, lazy animals would begin to yowl without moving.

Then Giroumetta would say, "Old ladies are like cats, the fire doesn't burn them anymore."

I sat there looking at those two old people. Madame Gasiglia, who between them was always called "the baby," was eighty years old, and Giroumetta, who was twenty-seven years older, was 107. That eighty-year-old "baby" had the most respectful reverence for the lady twenty-seven years older. When Madame Gasiglia had been a baby, Giroumetta had changed her diapers daily, and when she had grown into a young woman, Giroumetta was still unmarried. She only married at the age of forty-seven, and after that became the mother of five children, of whom Papa Camous was the fourth.

Many times while visiting at Madame Gasiglia's I had to laugh at her when she addressed her companion. She always called her "young lady," and Françoise was past 70!

The companion often said, "Madame, why do you always go to see Giroumetta?"

The answer was, "Françoise, you don't know how to make a nice fire. Here we have enough wood, branches, and leaves to make a fire three nights a week that would embrace the whole village in its illumination, but you are too economical. Is it because you are afraid to burn the wood, or yourself? I feel as if I am really an old woman when we are both here together with our cheap little fire burning without any pep to it. And besides that, you don't like a glass of wine, and I don't like to drink alone. If our cats and dogs would only drink it, I would invite them to keep me company. But, Françoise, at the home of Papa Camous everyone from Giroumetta to little Henri, to whom no one would say "no," has a glass of wine. Leaving them at night I feel great pleasure at having lived and added another day to the many years which our Lord has given me. I have accepted smiles and tears, and every time I feel like crying I start to sing. The tears, instead of forming in my eyes, go to my throat, which needs the humidity. I have never told this secret to anyone, Françoise, and when people hear me sing, and compliment me on my voice, not one of them would believe that Madame Gasiglia who felt like crying chose to sing instead."

The kindness of Madame was shown in many different ways. Maman, who had only two chickens in her possession, and no rooster, collected two dozen eggs a week from those two hens. And all because Madame, who lived next door, had several dozen chickens and many roosters. I loosened a picket on the fence and let one of her nice roosters into our yard to pay his compliments to the chickens of Maman Camous. Some of Madame Gasiglia's hens, which were close friends of his, ran through the hole and into our yard. Some came in for curiosity's sake, some because of jealousy, some because they wanted to displease the rooster, and some because they wanted to make our own chickens jealous. To do so they came over and disturbed the nests by laying a few eggs in them—eggs which were no property at all of our two hens. Only myself, and possibly Madame, ever knew the secret of how the two Camous chickens managed to become the best laying hens in all of France. They laid twenty-four eggs in a week, or 1,248 in a year, and a few more on every leap year because of the extra day.

Until one day everything was explained to Maman. That day, very late in the afternoon, she heard an extra loud cackle and went out to investigate. She found a beautiful black hen, the pet of Madame Gasiglia, announcing to the world that she had laid an egg on a foreign nest. She was really a beautiful bird with her black lustrous feathers, red comb and golden legs, the queen of all the chickens next door.

I almost had tears in my eyes when I thought that now my large omelets would be coming to an end.

Maman Camous called, "Henri, take this egg to Madame and tell her that her black hen is not faithful to her."

I walked, very reluctantly, to the house next door, and, when I was greeted, said, "Madame Gasiglia, Maman sent me over with this egg because it doesn't belong to us. It belongs to your pet chicken, the black one which is like you, Madame, too generous."

She bent down and kissed me, and I saw tears in her eyes. This time, instead of singing, she began to cry. She felt that here was a little fellow, an orphan, and he had discovered what she thought was a deep secret. She could see that I was disappointed; I felt guilty at having acquainted her rooster with our chickens and for creating jealousy among her forsaken hens.

Madame stroked my hair and said, "Henri, I'll put this egg to be hatched. Tomorrow you come back and I'll give you the chickens that come from it." And then she added, "Don't forget."

I didn't know whether I should keep the appointment or not because I didn't think it could be possible.

Then she said, "Run to the fountain and get me two pails of water, Henri, Françoise is too old to do it anymore." From that day forward I carried water every day for those two old ladies as well as for the sister of Don Albini.

I couldn't sleep that night. The metamorphosis of that egg kept me awake as I wondered and wondered if such a thing could be possible. My movements in the bed kept Bacci awake and he spent most of the night licking my face. That was the first time, in my recollection, that night seemed so much longer than day. My days were filled with people, and I was occupied with working, playing and fighting. At night I could only wait for another day.

The next morning neither Maman Camous nor Bacci had to awaken me to drink my coffee and go to serve at the early mass. Bacci and I got up at the same time, which was before the coffee was ready. Maman was surprised into saying, "Why do you get up so early, you who complain that God should make the early mass later in the morning?"

"Maman, I still think it's too early for the early mass, but this morning I'm hungry."

What I said pleased my wonderful Maman Camous; even if she had no money she always had plenty of food. She placed the three bowls of coffee, with milk from Blanchette, on the table, as usual, against the wishes of the neighbors. She accepted the challenge and stoutly maintained that as long as coffee existed in Contes, and Blanchette gave milk, she would line up those three bowlfuls like three soldiers presenting arms to their general.

Bacci looked at those three receptacles and then at me, and I could feel that he envied me. When each of them was almost empty he got the remaining bit with a little bread. The sugar that stuck to the inside caused him to make a distinct lapping noise, and Maman said, "I think some day Bacci will take the enamel off your bowls. It's a good thing you are not stingy and leave a little for him; otherwise he would break one of them, and then you could not blame me for not giving you three if he broke one."

Those three bowls are still intact, as is the memory and kindness of that grand woman. In later years, after I had departed from the village, she put them on top of the cupboard as exhibitions. When she looked at them every morning she saw the little orphan whom she had taken care of so wonderfully, and to whom she had been a mother twice over.

I ran to church that morning half fearful of what Madame Gasiglia would tell me when I saw her. She always attended the early mass, and as I poured the wine into the chalice for Don Albini I turned to look for her, causing some of it to be spilled on his hand. This excitement, I thought, was the fault of God Himself for putting my mind on the chickens instead of on serving the mass with devotion. I repeat again that God likes little children and often joins them in their play. If I had been the priest, instead of Henri the altar boy, I would have made that short mass still shorter so that Madame could have received the full pleasure of her surprise much sooner. During the mass I had seen her nod her head, which meant that the appointment was to be kept after church was over.

The moment it ended I hurried to the sacristy to take off my surplice. I did it so fast that Don Albini must still be guessing what new mischief I was up to.

I thought Madame would be gone, but there she was outside the door waiting for me. We walked together up the street, and I'll never forget the lovely and kind face of that old lady when she said to me, "Henri, your egg surprised me this morning. I looked in the sack, and the egg was broken, and there were six nice chickens all grown up!"

I looked at her, bit my lips, moved my ears, and said, "Madame Gasiglia, you'll have to tell Don Albini the next time you go to confession."

She said, "Come on, you'll see."

When we arrived at her home, sure enough, there in a sack was a broken egg shell with no evidence of the inside of the egg, only the shell and six beautiful hens which I recognized as the deserters from her chicken coop.

Madame said, "Maman Camous will still have two dozen eggs a week. And Henri, you had better put the picket back in the fence the way you discovered it; don't let the rooster come over any more. And let's keep it a secret between you and me."

And so we always had our two dozen eggs a week, thanks to the generosity of our close neighbor, that wonderful eighty-year-old "baby," Madame Gasiglia.

Too Many Pears

THE SMALL TWENTY FRANC GOLD PIECES that Monsieur Draghui presented to me from the State involved a problem in mathematics that was not so easy to solve. This problem was given to every boy in the Paillon River Valley section and included about twenty-five small villages. It concerned a mother who had three boys and a basket of pears which she wanted to divide among them in a certain way. They must be divided so that the first boy, Pierre, would receive half the basket of fruit plus ½ pear. The second boy, Jean, would receive half of the remaining half basket of fruit plus ½ pear. The third, Charles, would receive the remainder. Now, we were to find out how many pears there were in the basket and what share each of the boys, Pierre, Jean, and Charles would receive. And all this was to be done without cutting any of them in half.

This puzzling problem in mathematics gave me not only a headache but a bellyache as well. On that memorable afternoon Bacci and Blanchette were disappointed in me because class was dismissed half an hour earlier. It was no fun for them to see me arriving at the stable when I was supposed to wait in school until they called for me. They looked at me in surprise and thought the world was coming to an end. I scratched Blanchette where her horn was missing and also under her chin. I pulled her whiskers a little, and she said, "M-a-a-a," which meant, "Don't bother me." I spanked Bacci on the back and said to them both, "Now, no noise from you two. Bacci, don't you bark, and

159

Blanchette, don't you say, 'm-a-a-a,' and don't bother me. I'm going to be so darn busy counting and cutting pears that I won't have time for you. You, Blanchette, can have the remains of my problem." I was totally confused that evening because I shouldn't have cut any pears at all.

Those little gold pieces were very desirable, but the prospect of losing my tricolor belt made me sick, and I perspired just by thinking of it. My proudness kept me so busy I didn't even notice that the sun had already set. I sat down on the attic floor and put pears into three different sized baskets, beginning with the largest, a bushel basket. I counted, divided, added, subtracted, and the more I counted the less it seemed that I would ever arrive at a solution.

Maman Camous called up, "The soup is ready, Henri, are you coming?"

And I replied, "No, Mom, I must finish this problem."

"But, Henri, it's already nine o'clock."

I said, with determination, "Mom, I won't eat or go to bed until I have the answer to this basket of pears."

I could hear her mumbling, "It's a good thing I never had the good Monsieur Draghui in school; I'm sure he would have made me crazy as well as the rest of the kids, too."

She didn't know that there were hundreds and hundreds of other little boys working and despairing over those pears in their attics. The third basket, which was the smallest, gave me an idea. I began eating its fruit, and the juice, running down my chin, dripped onto my paper and pencil. I was so mad I regretted that Blanchette didn't have Bacci's legs so that she could run up the stairs and eat the whole darn mess of fruit, including the baskets. I was so furious I began talking to myself; then I began to swear. It was a good thing Don Albini didn't hear me; otherwise he would have had me in church praying again.

At that moment of despair something came to my mind. It was the expression, "God helps those who help themselves." My mouth was full of pear, a part of which my small teeth let drop into the basket of those I was counting. In the process of retrieving that half-eaten pear, which had accidentally become mixed with the others, I picked up seven of them and put them aside. At that moment I stopped to look at those seven pears and thought that half of seven was $3\frac{1}{2}$. Then in a flash it came to me that $3\frac{1}{2}$ pears plus $\frac{1}{2}$ pear would equal 4. The remainder was 3. My eyes were big with surprise, and the remaining three looked as large as pumpkins to me. I thought half of 3 was $1\frac{1}{2}$, plus $\frac{1}{2}$ pear would give the answer of 2. Then there was only one pear left.

I jumped up and down excitedly, and, not realizing that everyone was asleep, I awakened the whole house. Bacci, downstairs, helped me. He didn't know what time it was either and began barking. It was almost midnight.

In my elation I yelled, "I found it! I found it! I found it!"

But at the same moment I thought maybe the number was too small, so I began to worry again. I didn't want to lose my first solution, so, holding my breath for fear I would be wrong, I tried out all the numbers up to fifteen, and found out that fifteen was all right, too. Half of fifteen was $7\frac{1}{2}$, plus $\frac{1}{2}$ pear would be 8. The remainder was 7. Half of 7 was $3\frac{1}{2}$, plus $\frac{1}{2}$ pear would be 4. The remainder was 3.

When I finally solved my problem, reaching the conclusion that 7 and 15 were the only two possible answers, it was already one o'clock in the morning. Everything was quiet in the house, and this time I went out on tiptoe to post my answer in the envelope that had been given to me and which I was to send to the judges at Nice.

Only four boys out of all the hundreds reached a correct solution. Two of them had the number 15 for an answer, and one had the number 7. But freckle-faced Henri was the winner because he alone had the only two possible numbers, which proved that the other boys were either too tired or too lazy to go further.

I received two twenty franc gold pieces as a gift from the State and one ten franc gold piece as a gift from the mayor. This, in American money, was a total of ten dollars. The other three boys each received a ten franc gold piece from the State. Monsieur Draghui was so pleased that he added a five franc silver *écu* from his own pocket, which I kept as a souvenir and later gave to my son as a memento.

Our school had a one day vacation because one of its boys had won the first prize of merit among the twenty-five schools.

I was very pleased and very proud, and, because of all the pears I had eaten in solving my problem, I had a bellyache that lasted for three days. Blanchette had a banquet from the remaining pears. And no bellyache. When Bismarck, our pig, saw the goat eating that fruit he couldn't bear it. He grunted and squealed, "Oink, oink, oink," but Blanchette was stingy and refused to give up even a single core.

Poor pig! When Papa Camous was a sergeant in the French army in 1870 he hated the Germans so much that he named every pig he ever had after that "Bismarck," in honor of the "Iron Chancellor," who ruled at that time.

Bismarck snorted and carried on until he didn't have the power to squeal any more and all he could feebly produce was, "Wee, wee, wee, wee."

All the animals assembled in our stable were tied up except the hens, and they assisted at that unfair splitting of the pears. Bacci didn't give a darn, he wasn't a pear eater; however, he was offended and was sulking because he hadn't been invited up to the attic. Only Bismarck didn't like it, and objected, but he was too fat to jump over his pen.

Maman received a great surprise when she looked for her bushel basket of fruit and found that there was none left.

She said to Papa Camous, "No wonder Henri is sick, Monsieur Draghui has made him eat the whole basket of pears."

When that story became known the entire village said, "Never invite Henri over to eat pears because he'll eat the tree, too."

That made me so mad that I had a hundred fights with the other boys, and, as a result, there were many black eyes, including my own. Then Maman mixed some raw spinach and garlic, put it on my eye, and tied it in place with a strip of cloth. Every time I served a poached egg on spinach, later in my life, it always reminded me of my problematical pear story and the spinach and garlic that Maman put on my eye.

162

RECIPES

✤

HORS-D'OEUVRE, PATRICK HENRY

✤

SOUP, JOHN SMITH

✤

SCRAMBLED EGGS, ROBERT E. LEE

✤

EGGS, DANIEL BOONE

✤

SEA BASS, GEORGE WASHINGTON

ROAST CHICKEN, THOMAS JEFFERSON

✤

POTATOES, JOHN PAUL JONES

✤

GREEN BEANS, ANDREW JACKSON

✤

CUCUMBER SALAD, JAMES MADISON

✤

BAKED APPLES, MARTHA WASHINGTON

✤

HORS-D'OEUVRE, PATRICK HENRY

Remove the skins from 3 or more hot, boiled potatoes, and slice them.

In a separate saucepan prepare: 1 tablespoon of red wine vinegar, salt and pepper, and 2 tablespoons of oil. Let it come to a boil.

Place the sliced potatoes on a serving platter and sprinkle 2 finely chopped scallions over the top. Break 1 egg into the pan with the hot vinegar and oil. Stir, and leave on fire for 1 minute. Pour it over the potatoes.

SOUP, JOHN SMITH

Boil together in salted water 1 leek which has been washed and peeled, 1 peeled potato, and ½ chopped onion. When it has been cooked to softness, pass it through a colander, and return it to the water in which it has been cooked. Place it in a double boiler and add 1 tablespoon of butter, 1 glassful of milk, 1 tablespoon of cream. Season it to taste with pepper and salt. Serve hot.

SCRAMBLED EGGS, ROBERT E. LEE

For your table for 2 take 6 eggs and scramble them, following the directions given in the chapter, How to Make Omelets and Scrambled Eggs.

Boil thoroughly 6 or more large shrimps in a pepper and salt water. Clean the shrimps and cut them into small pieces. Add a small piece of butter, 1 tomato (or two tablespoons of canned tomatoes), 1 small minced onion, and a little parsley into which ½ clove of garlic has been crushed. Sprinkle pepper and salt onto the parsley and crushed garlic before adding to the shrimps. Cook for 25 minutes.

Place your scrambled eggs into a dish and garnish them with the shrimp sauce by pouring it around as a border. Sprinkle 1 tablespoon of grated cheese over the finished scrambled eggs. Serve hot.

EGGS, DANIEL BOONE

Slice 6 hot hard-boiled eggs into a serving dish. Place 1 tablespoon of butter in a pan with 1 small chopped onion. Cook for 5 minutes. Add 2 tablespoons of cooked chopped spinach, 1 glassful of milk and 2 tablespoons of cream. Let it all come to a boil, pour over the sliced hard-boiled eggs, salt and pepper to taste, and serve hot.

SEA BASS, GEORGE WASHINGTON

Clean a 1 pound sea bass thoroughly and dry it. Place it on a baking platter. Mix together 3 sliced mushrooms, a little chopped parsley, and 2 finely chopped shallots. Season with pepper and salt and sprinkle over the fish. Put 2 tablespoons of butter on the baking platter and place it into a preheated oven whose temperature is 450° to 500° F. Bake for ½ hour. Serve it with plain boiled potatoes and a cucumber salad.

ROAST CHICKEN, THOMAS JEFFERSON

Clean your chicken thoroughly and wipe it out with a clean cloth. Do not wash the fowl. Put salt and pepper and ½ onion, in one piece, inside the carcass. Lay the chicken on its side. Place 2 tablespoons of butter in the roasting pan, and be sure to have the oven hot before putting in your chicken. Turn the temperature to 450° to 500° F.

A chicken for 2 usually should weigh from 2 to 3 pounds. During the roasting it should be turned very often and basted at the same time. After a short time in the oven add a little more butter. A chicken of this size demands 30 to 35 minutes in the oven. When it is well browned, but not dried up, serve it after sprinkling it with salt. Pour over the butter which was used in basting. Serve it accompanied by a crisp green salad.

POTATOES, JOHN PAUL JONES

Boil 4 potatoes which have been peeled and seasoned with salt. Pour off water and mash them. Add 1 tablespoon of butter, a pinch of salt and pepper, the yolk of 1 egg, and 1 tablespoon of cream. Stir together thoroughly. Put the potatoes in a small baking dish and place 1 tablespoon of cream and a small piece of butter on top. Place in a hot oven for 10 minutes, and then serve.

GREEN BEANS, ANDREW JACKSON

Beans should be used as soon as possible after picking. Take 1 pint of green beans, clean them, and, if they are small in size, do not cut them into pieces and they will retain more flavor. Salt the water, and when it is boiling, put in your beans. Let them cook until they are tender. Strain them. Chop a little parsley and sprinkle it over the beans. Salt to taste. Add a few sprinkles of freshly ground whole pepper and 1 tablespoon of butter. Do not cook the butter in with the beans but add it after the water has been poured off and the beans have been taken off the fire. Mix together and serve.

CUCUMBER SALAD, JAMES MADISON

Cucumbers should be placed in the refrigerator the day before you want to use them. Be sure they are not too ripe but are a dark green in color. Peel 1 cucumber and slice it very thin. Add 1 chopped shallot, the juice of 1 lemon, 3 tablespoons of oil, salt and pepper, a little chopped parsley, and a few chopped chives, if you have them. Mix and serve cold and crisp.

BAKED APPLES, MARTHA WASHINGTON

Place 2 apples into a baking dish after they have been cored. Put a piece of butter in their hollowed centers. Add 1 cup of water to which has been added 2 tablespoons of sugar and 1 tablespoon of currant jelly. Add a pinch or two of cinnamon to the butter in the center of the apples, but don't sprinkle it over them. This will make them more tasty. Place in a preheated oven whose temperature is 450° to 500° F. Baste them 3 or 4 times during the baking which will take 30 to 35 minutes. Sprinkle 1 tablespoon of sugar over the apples 5 minutes before removing them from the oven,. and don't baste them any more after that. This gives them a varnish which makes them, truly, apples with finesse.

Sitting on the steps of his intimate restaurant in Redondo Beach, California.

Chapter XI

A HAT FOR FANNIE, THE MULE

TODAY, because my legs are almost a complication to my body, I blame those early days in Contes when every holiday was an occasion for competing in the races, and I could not resist them since I could run as swiftly as a deer. Then, too, it was a matter of pride with me. It gave me great satisfaction, even a thrill, to know that I was the champion of all the boys my age and, of some, even older. At the age of seven I had a determination and an ability to apply myself that amounted to tenacity itself.

All the suburban hamlets of Contes from two to four miles around, some of them close to the Paillon and some perched like eagle's nests on top of the mountains higher up, participated in celebrating each other's holidays. Each hamlet and village had a patron saint about whom stories and great events were related with much enthusiasm. The patron saint of Contes was Marie Madeleine, and we extended the celebration of her day, July 22, to three days. The number of days celebrated depended upon the size of the village. During these holidays everyone came to Contes, including many people from Nice who wanted to look at and enjoy the wonderful peasants. At the festivities the peasants and the rich alike drank, ate, and danced together, because each one owed something to the patron saint of his forefathers. The day Contes had selected Marie Madeleine as its patron saint the whole village had been in need of a miracle. And Saint Marie Madeleine had not chosen to confer her miracles on anyone in particular. Rather, she

169

treated all as one, and one as all, and everyone shared in her protection.

A group of young men, those who were about to enter into military duty, were assigned to escort a small carriage which was pulled by a donkey and on which there was a barrel that would hold forty or fifty gallons of wine. In the center of the barrel was a big funnel. Several of the young men played serenades on musical instruments and one with a good voice was chosen to call rich and poor alike to the wine barrel with contributions to fill it. This young fellow entreated with a half singing and half talking voice, and without discrimination sang out the name of each villager as the wine barrel stopped in front of his house. In variable ways he sang, "If your wine is good, and your cellar is full, then bring to the barrel the most your heart wishes to offer. But, in case your wine is poor, or if you yourself are poor, bring only one glass and pour it into the funnel; then when the donkey begins to move he'll shake up the good and poor wine and they'll become one. Tomorrow, on our saint's day, rich and poor men will be mixed like the wine. Tomorrow our saint wants no one to be poor, and, above all, there must be no tears. Marie Madeleine demands that our village be united in dancing and singing. Everyone must smile and be happy. The two or three barrels of mixed wine, which we are now collecting, will be placed in the Place de L'Église, where strangers, rich and poor alike from other villages, will be offered a drink. A mixed wine which represents a mixed people! And, as one, we will serve it to them with the same *beau geste*, welcome to our village."

Each stranger, before spending any money in the cafés, had a glass of wine from one of those barrels—a drink which we might say served as an apéritif. There were always some old-timers who felt and criticized the hot July sun which made them thirsty and, therefore, caused them to drink more frequently. Those old babies very often visited, not the udder of the cow, but the spigot of the wine barrel. So that no wine would be lost by opening and closing the spigot, a wooden bucket was placed underneath. That bucketful of wine was a prize which all those old fellows tried to get in on. Every evening when the barrel was closed for the night, the wine remaining in the bucket, and I always remember

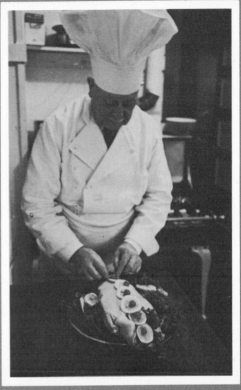

Above left, Henri Charpentier preparing a hot fruit compote to serve with roast duck.

Above, garnishing the duck by placing pieces of thinly sliced oranges, a maraschino cherry in each, down the center of the breast.

Left, preparing a salad, with careful attention to appearance as well as taste.

seeing that bucket full, was drunk by five old fellows who were selected at random. Only five were permitted to participate. An empty sack was placed on the floor, and each one, in turn, laid on it with his hands palms down to support his body. Then, without touching his nose to the wine, he must suck in a mouthful and swallow it. The one who took the most swallows without removing his head from the bucket received a five franc piece as a prize. In American money, at that time, one silver dollar. No one ever really lost since all five of them got some good wine in their bellies. The winner of the five franc piece could not compete again on the two following evenings. The old fellow who won on the first night was almost mad because he had no right to put his face in the bucket again. It was generally the one who started first who was the winner, and he drank enough to satisfy himself for those other two days when he would not be permitted to drink. That bit of competition was only for the very, very old ones.

For the fellows forty to sixty years old we had a race wherein each one had his legs tied in a sack and had to jump the entire length of the field. The first prize in that contest was another five francs. The second was two francs, and the third was one franc. There were always ten or twelve ready to jump in that race, and watching those fellows was enough to make your belly ache for a week from too much laughing.

For those twenty to forty years old there was a contest for the sharp-shooters. The gun held five small buckshot and a fellow had to make only one bull's-eye to win. The young men who competed were almost all rich boys; each shot cost ten *sous*. Sometimes it took any number of shots before a bull's-eye finally could be made. It often took all three holidays to produce the lucky winner. The prizes of a pig and a lamb, if they were not won in that three-day period, had a chance to grow into bigger mutton and pork roasts because they were kept until carnival time the following March when both of them were killed and roasted for the community. The villagers said, "The sharpshooters are not so sharp, and we're glad; now we have a reserve of 400 francs for the benefit of the poor and needy in our community. And by next March we will have a bigger feast with our pig and lamb."

172

I always felt that the sharpshooters were happy to lose the pig, the lamb, and their francs, too, and were contented with just making a noise with their shooting.

Until March, then, the two animals were given to the richest farmer in the village to be fed and taken care of. When it came time to butcher them the rich farmer's only return would be the skin of the lamb and one ham from the pig. But generally the whole pig was roasted and another lamb was added to the feast; our rich farmer didn't want to look like a piker. Instead of taking he was giving, and the fertilizer of the pig and lamb was his only profit.

The little fellows from 7 to 16 years of age ran a foot race of 1 kilometer, about 1000 yards. The first prize for this race was always a hat, which hung on a wooden cross along with the other prizes which consisted of a beret, some ties, etc. I won so many hats that Papa Camous, on my return from America many years later, still wore one. I was the champion runner of anyone my age or double my age in the village and all the surrounding villages. Very often there were many young fellows who were poor sports and who refused to run when they saw me in line. This only made my freckled face more brown by my tenacious determination. Then I regretted that my legs were not the legs of Gris, the donkey of Jacques, so that I could give those fellows a good kick.

One strange young fellow from Nice said to me before the race, "I'll give you a head start of twenty paces and when I pass you the wind will blow you down."

I said, "Oh, yes? I don't want one inch from you, and you can keep the wind for yourself because you'll never pass me."

He was ready for a fight, but realized that I was much smaller than himself. He saw my clenched fists. One of my feet was ready to give him a kick, and he would have received both kick and punch at the same time if the starter had not yelled, "Attention!" Then the gun went off. In my madness at the stranger I felt my legs were made of rubber, they had such elasticity; in one moment I had wings and no legs. I thought I was flying, and that was long before the airplane had

173

Bacci waits for a bone, instead of a lion, on the Rue St. Martin.

A small picnic gathering in Contes. Maman Camous, aged 98, is knitting.

been invented. I grabbed the wooden cross with the hat that was twice my size! I was the winner, and the out of town boy was mad and disillusioned. Because of the remark he had made about passing me up, he wanted to make a quick exit. Some of my schoolmates were ready to run him out of the village faster than he had run in the race to get the prize. But Monsieur Draghui was there with us once more to remind us of our manners with a few of his famous words, "You must salute a stranger three times, young or old, rich or poor, it makes no difference. And when you ask me why we must salute him three times, I will tell you. First, because he is the one who came to visit you and he is entitled to the hospitality bestowed on a newcomer. You must salute him the second time because you recognize him as a stranger. And the third time so that your politeness and respect will make him want to come again."

Professor Draghui looked at me and my funny looking hat that was still hanging on the wooden cross. I didn't have time to give my tongue and lips the pleasure of expressing to the stranger the fact that I was not entirely in accord with Monsieur Draghui's ideals. I had to swallow my words because the teacher stopped the unpleasant quarrel short when he shook my hand to compliment me on winning the race.

He said, "Try on your hat, Henri." He placed it on my head, and everybody laughed. He looked around at everyone and made them laugh still more when he remarked, "If you were taller, Henri, you would look like Don Albini, even though you are not a priest."

The strange boy from Nice finished the day by dancing instead of by running away in anger.

Papa Camous put a few pieces of thick wrapping paper in between the lining of the hat so he could wear it, but still it was too big. He looked so funny in it that one day he decided to make two holes in it and put it on our mule Fannie, to protect her from the sun. Of all the hats that I had won that one became famous; it was known for a long time after that as the "mule's hat."

In every village of the sixteen closest to Contes I was called "the hare." I never had one defeat in a race. When I look at my legs today, over fifty-five years later, I am sorry for the wear and tear I gave them and the energy I expended in order to win so many funny hats that invariably adorned those wooden crosses, including the famous one known as the "mule's hat."

RECIPES

✤

CANOE, JAMES FENIMORE COOPER

✤

CREAM OF TOMATO SOUP, HENRY HALLECK

✤

OMELET, WASHINGTON IRVING

✤

SCRAMBLED EGGS, WALT WHITMAN

✤

SMELTS, PHILIP H. SHERIDAN

✤

SIRLOIN STEAK, "STONEWALL" JACKSON

✤

POTATOES, ZACHARY TAYLOR

✤

BRUSSELS SPROUTS, MILLARD FILLMORE

✤

ENDIVE, SAMUEL ADAMS

✤

RICE PUDDING, ANNA ELEANOR ROOSEVELT

✤

CANOE, JAMES FENIMORE COOPER

Peel 1 cucumber, cut it in half lengthwise, and scoop out each half. Place into a bowl: 1 chopped tomato, 1 chopped shallot, 2 chopped sardines (canned), 1 chopped hard-boiled egg, salt and pepper, and 1 tablespoon of French Dressing. Mix and stuff into each half of the cucumber. A slice of tomato should be placed on each end of the cucumber so that it overlaps. Cut 2 strips of ribbonlike green pepper for each half cucumber and place them, across the cucumber, equal distances from the center. Leave enough room in the middle to put a tablespoon of mayonnaise.

CREAM OF TOMATO SOUP, HENRY HALLECK

Place one tablespoon of butter into a casserole with 1 finely chopped onion. Cover and let it simmer until it is soft, but not brown. Cut up 3 tomatoes, mix together, and let simmer for 15 minutes. Then add 2 teaspoons of sugar and 1 glassful of milk, and continue simmering it for 10 more minutes. Place a small piece of butter and 1 tablespoon of cream into each of the 2 cups, and pour the soup over. Salt and pepper.

OMELET, WASHINGTON IRVING

Break 6 eggs and stir gently. Chop finely and mix together: chives, parsley, and fresh tarragon leaves. Stir into eggs. Salt and pepper. Put a piece of butter into your omelet pan and follow the directions for making an omelet as set forth under the chapter, How to Make Omelets and Scrambled Eggs. The finished omelet should be soft inside and brown outside.

SCRAMBLED EGGS, WALT WHITMAN

Scramble 6 eggs, using the principles given for scrambling eggs. Slice 4 mushrooms into a separate frying pan and add: 1 tablespoon of butter, 2 shallots that have been chopped very fine, 4 chicken livers cut into halves, 1 tablespoon of meat extract, and ½ tablespoon of Worcestershire sauce. Cook for 7 minutes. The chicken livers should not be cooked longer than that. Arrange the scrambled eggs into a nest and place the mushroom sauce in the middle. Sprinkle with grated cheese and a little chopped parsley. Salt and pepper.

SMELTS, PHILIP H. SHERIDAN

Clean and dry 1 pound of smelts. Sift flour onto a plate and dip the smelts into it. Shake off the extra flour. Put enough oil into a frying pan to make the fish swim. Make it very hot, and carefully put in the smelts. Fry them no longer than 7 or 8 minutes after which time they should be nice and brown. Remove them from the hot oil. Place ½ bunch of parsley into the oil until the sprigs become crisp. Arrange the parsley around the fried smelts, salt and pepper, and serve on a plate with ½ lemon.

SIRLOIN STEAK, "STONEWALL" JACKSON

Use 1½ pounds of thick, choice sirloin of beef. Place on a hot broiler without salt, without pepper, and without butter. Absolutely alone. Broil one side for 3 minutes and then broil the other side for 3 minutes. After that brush some butter on the top only and let it broil 4 more minutes. Turn it over and do the same to the other side. Altogether, it should take only 14 minutes to broil the steak. Place the meat on a hot serving platter and add salt and pepper and a generous piece of butter. Put it back under the broiler for 1½ minutes to facilitate the melting of the butter without actually cooking it. You might slice your sirloin steak into 4 pieces, each about 2 fingers wide. By carving it the juice of the steak will mix with the melted butter and condiments, giving you more refinement at your table for two. The serving of a whole, unsliced sirloin steak makes it appear that either cannibals or lions are dining at that table.

POTATOES, ZACHARY TAYLOR

Scrape 6 or more small new potatoes, do not peel. Wash and dry, and put them in a frying pan with 1 tablespoon of butter. Cover the pan and place over a small flame for 20 minutes. Stir every 5 minutes until they become soft inside and brown outside. Sprinkle 2 finely chopped shallots over the potatoes and let them remain on the fire for 5 more minutes. Salt and pepper.

BRUSSELS SPROUTS, MILLARD FILLMORE

The day before you want to serve the Brussels sprouts take 1 boxful, wash, and then boil in salted water for 15 minutes. Strain, and when they are cool place them in the refrigerator to be used the next day. They must be cooked 24 hours in advance to bring out their full flavor in the second cooking. Put 2 tablespoons of butter into a pan, make it hot, and add the Brussels sprouts. Cover the pan and place over a small flame, or in a hot oven until they become brown. This usually takes 25 to 30 minutes. Salt and pepper. Before serving, add a piece of butter which has only been melted and not cooked. The Brussels sprouts will be dried, brown and wonderful, instead of watery, mushy, and no good.

ENDIVE, SAMUEL ADAMS

The endive must be crisp. Wash it. Cut it in half, or into quarters, depending on its size. For the dressing use: 1 small piece of American Blue cheese, Roquefort style, 2 pinches of paprika, 1 teaspoon of Worcestershire sauce, ½ tablespoon of red wine vinegar, or any other kind, the juice of ½ lemon, 2 tablespoons of oil, 1 chopped hard-boiled egg, 1 or 2 finely chopped scallions, a few sprigs of chopped parsley, 1 teaspoon of mustard. Pepper and salt. Mix well, pour over endive, and serve.

RICE PUDDING, ANNA ELEANOR ROOSEVELT

Stir 2 tablespoons of sugar and 1 teaspoon of vanilla extract into 2 cups of milk. Let it boil and put it aside.

Put 2 tablespoons of rice into 1 quart of boiling water and let it cook for 15 minutes. Strain it. Mix it into the boiled milk. Add the yolks of 2 eggs, a little more sugar, 2 pinches of cinnamon, and 2 tablespoons of any kind of fruit jelly. Stir, and pour into a baking dish. At the last moment, before baking, pour 2 tablespoons of cream over the top. Bake it under the same principle used for thickening custard, that is, in a separate water bath for 5 minutes. Serve either hot or cold.

The Buffet Froid which Henri Charpentier offered at Maison Française, Rockefeller Center, in 1934.

Chapter XII

THE LION TAMER

OUTSIDE OF THE DOMESTIC ANIMALS of my village I had little knowledge of the others. At seven, my small vision had seen only a few dead foxes and wild pigs that had been shot by *lou garde* Pierre, the game warden of the forest. As far as the rest were concerned, I didn't know they existed. In that respect I was like Christopher Columbus. He had felt that somewhere there was a new land, but before he could reach it he had had his doubts; when finally he did reach our beautiful America, whence I am writing these lines, he knew that at last he had been compensated. The trouble and the honor were his; the wealth and the happiness were for others. The beautiful and adventurous spirit of that great sailor must have encountered the spirits of many of my old friends, and I am pleased to think that Don Albini may have made a new acquaintance—one to whom he could relate those little stories of which he alone knew the secret. Who can tell? Maybe, at that moment of story-telling, the great Christopher Columbus and the humble priest, Don Albini, together selected these lines which you are now reading, even before they were printed; if so, another discovery has been made.

To return to Monsieur Draghui in the classroom and my limited knowledge of wild animals. Actually none of the other boys had ever seen any of them either; not even those in the zoo at Nice, because it was too far away. Monsieur showed us pictures of a ferocious-looking tiger with its snarling face and sharp teeth, an elephant with its long nose, and all the other animals of the five continents.

Not many years after my schooling I accompanied the Russian Prince Alexandre Pariasdensky in his travels to the jungles of Africa and India, and was pleasantly surprised and unsure of myself when I saw some of Monsieur Draghui's wild animals in their original settings. I had the greatest admiration for the Prince who was a prince twice over; once, because he was born to the title; and twice, because he had such great kindness and intelligence. He said that he had not come to the forest to shoot and destroy the wild inhabitants, but had come rather as their guest, to visit them. He seemed very confident and gave the appearance of being as acclimatized as the jungle animals; neither the Prince nor the animals felt the need of a higher protection. Not one of those ferocious beasts padding about near us made any sign of a bad welcome. I sweated more from fear than from the heat, and not so much for myself but just from thinking that something might happen to the Prince, who was so good to everyone.

My ventures into the jungle with him, when I was 16, bring to mind the classroom in Contes where Monsieur Draghui never stopped, even for a single day, his teachings which developed patience, kindness, honesty, decency, friendship, sincerity, and courage. The day we had our African geography lesson the king of beasts was represented by a misguiding picture which was tacked on the wall of the classroom. The lion had a crown on his head and closely resembled His Majesty the great King Louis XIV of France. In my great curiosity I always tried to find the answer to too many questions, against the logic of the good Don Albini, who so often said, "There is a great deal of mystery that cannot be divulged." So I said to myself, "Who the devil put that crown on the lion's head? Who gave it to him, anyhow?"

Monsieur seemed to read my thoughts because he said to the class, "My boys, here, of all the animals of the forest, is the king. He is so named because he is audacious and courageous. The lion's direct look, there is no smile on his face, his short ears and beautiful mane all give him such prestige and great nobility that every other animal fears him. He doesn't provoke, but neither does he retreat. The tiger, elephant, and all the rest try to avoid him; never have they succeeded in ending their fights in a draw. The lion is always ninety-nine per cent victorious. The instinct of those other animals shows that they have more common sense than man, since not one of them will try to get ninety-nine lickings in order to prove he can win once. And that is why the lion is called the king of the forest."

Our village, which I have previously described, has a one-way street that winds its way up into the mountains. It has only one entrance and that entrance is also the only exit. Professor Draghui had his own way of giving us knowledge and, at the same time, courage. "Sometimes," he said, "when there is nothing he can do about it, a man is greater if he can face death with courage instead of running away, because then he must die twice—once from fear, and a second time because it is inevitable."

Then to each boy in the classroom, one after another, Monsieur Draghui said, "Suppose a lion came through the entrance to our village and you came from the opposite direction, now, what would you do? You, Paul?"

Paul, the first boy on the bench, stood up and said, "I would run away, sir, and fast too."

"Sit down," said Monsieur Draghui. "You, Jacques, what would you do?"

Jacques jumped up and said, "I would run also, sir."

"You, Louis, what about you?"

"I would follow the advice of my friends, sir."

Monsieur Draghui made a face, not one of contentment or even displeasure, since this problem was one concerning great audacity and none of the kids could have been compared with the king of the forest for fearlessness. After calling on Jean, Auguste, Charles, and a few others, he received the same answer. So he said, "All those in the class who would do the same because they are afraid of the lion, please stand up."

The whole class, except myself, stood up like one soldier, so straight and so promptly that some of the pens, pencils, and ink bottles rolled onto the floor, as if the lion were already there. There was only a few cents damage, but a lot of work, for someone, to remove the spots from the floor. I don't know why I remained seated.

Some of the kids said to me, "Did you hear what Monsieur Draghui said?"

I said, "Yes," but still I wouldn't stand up.

One kid said, "Do you want another licking, Henri?"

"Maybe."

This little conversation drew attention to my hidden position among the standing boys, and in less than ten seconds the whole class forgot the strict etiquette of facing the teacher and turned their eyes on me.

I saw the most predominant pair of all, Monsieur Draghui's, as he stood there, now, stroking his beard. His eyes were shining, and he smilingly said, "Come here, you."

When I was close to him I turned and faced all my school chums, large and small, and asked, "Monsieur Draghui, is the lion in front of Madame Trapenat's gate?"

On that street the only place that had an iron grilled door belonged to Madame Trepenat, and it could be opened and closed readily. In my imagination it would have afforded a chance to escape without running backwards. Maybe then I could tease that king and get the best of him without his scratching me.

"No," said Monsieur Draghui, "the lion is in the San Martin section and there is no escape for you unless you retreat."

As long as I was licked in advance by not being at Madame Trapenat's gate, I bit my lips and made a mad face. I clenched my fists in the air and declared, "Then I would fight him!"

A hundred voices echoed what I said; they made a noise that was fifty times louder than the crack of Badou's whip.

Only Monsieur Draghui was calm. He said, "Explain why you would do that, Henri."

"Well, sir," I said, "a lion has four legs and I have only two, consequently he can run faster. We are always talking about miracles. Just the other day you read us the story of the man whom the Romans threw into the arena with the famished lions and who wasn't even hurt. Caesar then gave that man his freedom. So, why couldn't that happen to Henri? The lion, because of my insignificance, would turn tail and go in the other direction, and I certainly wouldn't run after him. Instead, I would go inside Madame Trapenat's gate and stay there overnight. I would eat some fresh figs from the trees and forget to go home to Maman Camous so I wouldn't have to meet the king of the forest; this time he might change his mind, and, instead of my first movement of courage, I might just turn into a big meal for him."

Monsieur Draghui said, "My boys, I am proud that one of you in this class has solved the problem. Don't look for trouble, and don't look for a fight, but when you are in a battle, fight! Have the courage to die facing the enemy, and have dry eyes, because tears will not stop the flow when you are bleeding to death."

He put his hand in his pocket, took out a silver two franc piece, and gave it to me, saying, "I'm proud and pleased to offer my salary of one day to a little fellow who has saved the honor of the school. I know that none of you would run away when you saw that one of you had the courage to fight; with the help of all, you would become masters of the situation. The lion might vanquish a few, but he couldn't conquer all. Remember, boys, that the unity of all means force, and if you think deeply at all you will know that intelligence is stronger than force. Common sense will always be the master."

Since those early days I have found out, and agree, that the lion is not the most ferocious and the most difficult to fight. I have learned that to fight a man, or men, is even more difficult, because then you must contend with treachery, cowardice, sneakiness, and a thousand other things which go toward making him *mesquin*. Courage loses its magic spell when treachery is the foundation of the individual. When a man's honor is lost, his pride and all his virtues gone, time, courage, and patience, with intelligence included, will win out over his cheap, sneaking, false arrogance. It is only the individual, the family or the nation that is upright and honorable which can survive and proceed to a happy destiny.

That episode of fighting the lion caused all the kids in my village to nickname me "the lion-tamer." Then again, I became so mad I returned home more than once with a tricolor face of red, white, and blue. Red, because I was bleeding; white, because my face was pale from anger; and blue, because I had discolored eyes. All these patriotic colors gave me distinction.

The silver two franc piece in his pocket became a good luck piece to the incorrigible Henri. It was not a coin that could be spent. Before fighting with my chums I took it out and looked at it so I could fight better. But often it was only a battle to a draw, and both of us quit with my adversary and I looking like twin brothers because of the battle's effect. I kept the two francs for several years and then one day put it in the contribution box of St. Antoine of Padou, who helps people recover that which has been lost. I said a short prayer to that saint and thought that as long as I gave him two francs he ought to pray for me and not me for him.

That was before I left home to go to the Cap Martin. If Don Albini had known it he would have framed that coin and put it in the church as a relic from a little devil who gave up his good luck piece and prayed that Monsieur Draghui and himself might have a long life so they could continue teaching their ideals.

I still think that Monsieur Draghui's salary for that one day is worth the erection of a monument to that great gentleman for the knowledge he dispensed in the many, many years of his career. He gave too many of those little silver coins from his own humble pocket. He had no fortune, and, on his small salary, he could not afford it.

It was a good thing, too, that he never found out that I put the coin into St. Antoine's box, or he would have demanded a refund of Don Albini. That would have made enemies out of those two friends. Monsieur Draghui would have said, "I gave it to Henri to spend and not to give to St. Antoine."

Then Don Albini would have answered, "St. Antoine collects for me, and I collect for God." The discussion would certainly have ended very unpleasantly with Professor Draghui adding, "And God tells me to tell you to refund my two francs." So the secret was kept by St.

Antoine and myself, and the two franc piece became mixed with the sous in the contribution box that helped to spread the kindness for which Don Albini was famous.

After Prince Pariasdensky and I left the African jungles we journeyed to India, where there are no imaginary lions such as the one in Contes. There the sublime courage that Monsieur Draghui gave to his pupils would have a chance to be exercised. Even as I thought of the professor I realized that the forest seemed to have no beginning and no end, had no streets at all, and was brimful of wild animals. There was no thought of running away, because I had no fear—I was in safety on top of a tame elephant.

I watched the rabbits as they hopped along unmindful of our huge, lumbering animals. The legs of those great beasts were almost as large as the pillars of the temple of Solomon, which were noted for their great strength. A little rabbit hopped onto the right front foot of my elephant; to me, he looked about as large as a fly on the toe of a human being. Only there was a difference. The human's first thought is to kill the fly that bothers him. I closed my eyes because I thought the elephant would have the same thought. After a few seconds I opened them and saw his big ears moving back and forth, like the rudders of two small boats. He looked down his long nose, and, instead of rudely and brutally pushing the little fellow from his foot, waited patiently for him to hop off. But the rabbit would not oblige. He looked up impertinently, as if he were defying a great and powerful general. The next few seconds seemed like hours, and I thought that now, surely, there would be a very sad and disastrous finale. I thought, "Here's the end of that little rabbit with his great insolence," and pictured him flattened out on the ground like a pancake, and not a Crêpe-Suzette either.

The Prince and I were surprised when we saw my elephant put his long nose down and blow a few times as if to say, "Get off, and I mean it!"

The rabbit leisurely placed his front paws on the ground and turned around to give the big fellow another impudent look, which seemed to say, "All right, all right. Don't be in such a hurry. Just a minute, and I'll be off."

189

And off he hopped. The smiling face and eyes of the large animal met those of the courageous little one, and in that farewell look each seemed to say, "So long, I'll see you again some time."

RECIPES

✤

HORS-D'OEUVRE, WILLIAM DODD

✤

CONSOMME, THOMAS PAINE

✤

EGGS, WILLIAM STRACHEY

✤

SCRAMBLED EGGS, EDWIN BOOTH

✤

TROUT, ANDREW JOHNSON

✤

ROAST DUCK, JAMES K. POLK

✤

POTATOES, EDWARD WINSLOW

✤

SPINACH, ISAAC BABBITT

✤

SALAD, SAMUEL LANGLEY

✤

BAKED ORANGES, MARY MAPES DODGE

✤

191

HORS-D'OEUVRE, WILLIAM DODD

Arrange 4 slices of salami and 2 slices of Virginia ham on a plate with a few green onions, green and black olives, 1 celery heart, 1 finochio, 1 green pepper, 1 tomato, 1 Bermuda onion, a few radishes, and water-cress. Use salt and pepper, or a very sharp *vinaigrette* dressing. This hors-d'oeuvre will beautify the table as well as tempt your appetite.

CONSOMME, THOMAS PAINE

Use 2 consommé cups. Place the yolk of 1 egg into each cup. Pour hot consommé over the yolk. Salt and pepper. Croutons with cheese may be added. Sprinkle a few raw chopped chives on top.

EGGS, WILLIAM STRACHEY

Boil 2 artichokes in salted water and when they become tender remove the leaves. The leaves are not used in this recipe. Remove the hairy-looking part that covers the heart. Broil 2 slices of ham and have 2 poached eggs ready as well. Put the 2 remaining artichoke buttons into a frying pan with 1 tablespoon of butter. Brown both sides, and put each artichoke button on a hot plate. Place a slice of broiled ham over each, and 1 poached egg on top of the ham. Cover each with 1 large tablespoon of hollandaise sauce, and sprinkle with a few drops of meat stock.

SCRAMBLED EGGS, EDWIN BOOTH

Chop the meat from the tail of 1 boiled lobster. Put a piece of butter and 2 finely chopped shallots into a frying pan. Add 2 chopped chicken livers, 3 tablespoons of white port wine, 1 teaspoon of Worcestershire sauce, a pinch of salt, a pinch of sugar, 2 pinches of curry powder, and 2 tablespoons of cream. Then add the chopped lobster, and stir. Be sure the lobster is added last. Boil for 5 minutes.

Scramble 6 eggs, place them on a serving platter, and arrange the garniture as a border.

TROUT, ANDREW JOHNSON

Put 2 quarts of water into a pot and add: 1 slice of lemon, a sprig of parsley, ½ onion, 1 whole clove of garlic, a pinch of thyme, 1 bay leaf, a slice of carrot, 4 pepper-corns, a pinch of salt, and 2 tablespoons of vinegar. Let it come to a boil.

Clean 2 brook trout and have them as fresh as possible. Put them into the boiling water for 10 minutes. Remove the fish, place them on a serving platter, and sprinkle them with a little salt and pepper. Squeeze the juice of ½ lemon over the fish. Melt a generous piece of butter and pour it over also. This is generally accompanied by plain boiled potatoes.

ROAST DUCK, JAMES K. POLK

Purchase a 5 pound Long Island duck. Clean and dry it with a cloth. Do not wash. Sprinkle salt and pepper inside the carcass. Put the duck into a roasting pan with ½ glassful of water and place it in a preheated hot oven of 500° F. for 30 minutes. By this time some of the fat of the duck will have been released and added to the water in the pan. Turn the duck upside down. Add 1 tablespoon of water to cool the fat and let it continue roasting for 20 minutes longer, basting it every 5 minutes. After a total of 50 minutes in the hot oven, pour off the water and fat. Turn the oven to 450° F. Then add a generous piece of butter to the roasting pan, and baste the duck every 4 minutes for another 20 or 25 minutes, making a total of 1¼ hours of roasting.

When it has become a nice, crispy brown, place it on a serving platter. Put another generous piece of butter in the roasting pan and place it over the flame on top of the stove. Add 2 tablespoons of sweet sherry or port wine and a sprinkle of salt. Stir it thoroughly with a wooden spoon, and pour it over the duck.

POTATOES, EDWARD WINSLOW

Dice 4 cold boiled potatoes and mix them with 1 cooked red pepper cut julienne style. Add 1 chopped shallot and a few sprigs of chopped parsley. Mix. Sprinkle with flour and add 2 tablespoons of melted butter. Place 3 tablespoons of oil into an omelet pan, and put in the above mixed ingredients. Push them down so that they are compact, and begin to roll like an omelet. Let it become brown. Season.

SPINACH, ISAAC BABBITT

Clean and boil 2 handfuls of spinach. When it is cooked, pour off the water and chop it very fine. Put it back into the pan and add: 1 tablespoon of butter, 2 tablespoons of cream, salt and pepper. Let it come to a boil. Place it on a serving platter and garnish it with 1 hard-boiled egg which has been cut into quarters. A few small croutons which have been fried in butter may be sprinkled over the finished dish.

SALAD, SAMUEL LANGLEY

Cut up 1 crisp, white escarole salad. Take 2 crusts of French bread about the size of a silver dollar and rub garlic on them. Put them into the salad bowl with the escarole. Salt and pepper. Add 2 tablespoons of olive oil and ½ tablespoon of wine vinegar. Mix and serve.

BAKED ORANGES, MARY MAPES DODGE

Boil 2 whole seedless oranges until they are tender. To determine this, prick them with a fork. Remove them from the water, cut them in halves, and place them into a baking dish.

Now, add 1 cup of sugar to the water the oranges were boiled in, 1 tablespoon of butter, 1 teaspoon of orange blossom water, and 1 pony of white curaçao. Cook for several minutes. Pour it over the oranges and bake them for 30 minutes. This hot dessert is very delicious when served on a menu which also includes roast duck.

Chapter XIII

PAPA CAMOUS KEEPS HIS PROMISE

THE GREAT PROMISE of Papa Camous to take me to Nice "some other day," "tomorrow," "next week," or "next month" was finally kept one day in March. Only it was not Papa Camous who took me; it was Maman Camous.

One Thursday, when there was no school, Maman awakened me early so that we could take the first coach with the greatest coachman in the world, Badou! A basket had been filled with bottles of Papa Camous' best wine and two bottles of olive oil that had been freshly made the day before. It was called "virgin green oil" and was, even though amateurly made, a very delicious one for gourmets.

I had known on Wednesday that on Thursday I would, at last, have my first thrilling trip to the big city I had dreamed of for so long. The adventure of a few months before, when my friends and I had collected black eyes and had created such a disturbance by our unfinished trip to Nice, was finally to be completed. This time I was certain it would not be postponed, for I had heard Papa Camous say to Maman Camous, "You will tell me how Monsieur Escoffier likes my wine."

I was so excited and anxious that Bacci complained because I kept him awake almost all night. I was afraid we might miss the first coach and that Badou and his two old horses would suddenly become young again and be off too early, and without us.

All the kids, and some of the grown-ups, scared me almost to death by saying, "Henri, don't go too close to the sea; if you do, you'll drown."

I had no idea what they meant by "the sea" and thought that whatever it was it would be at the bottom of a precipice. Instead of which the sea met the land on a level. I was anxious to see it and afraid of it at the same time.

Badou conducted his diligence with great dignity and much conversation, which was directed, a greater part of the time, to his beloved horses. When we finally reached Nice it was only 7:30, and I was consumed with curiosity. The shops, the long streets, the fine carriages that had one and sometimes two horses, and those multiple noises that are found in the city were almost too much for me. The sights were too many for just my two eyes that wanted to see everything all at once, and I turned around and around on my little feet, like a wheel, so that I wouldn't lose anything that was either in front of or in back of me.

The landscaped flower gardens of Nice in the Jardin Massena were breath-takingly beautiful and pleased and excited me so much that I lost Maman Camous for a moment. Then, from a distance, I saw her with her basket, worried because she thought she had lost me and talking aloud to herself, "Where's Henri? Where's Henri?" She must have thought we were in Contes and not in Nice where there were a thousand Henris. Maman asked a man if he had seen me, and he replied in patois, her language, "I see a little fellow over there looking at the flowers, and I'm almost sure he's the one you are looking for." My freckled face and funny looking shoes were noticed by all the Niçois, and I knew that Maman Camous could never lose me because there was only one boy with such shoes, and only one boy with such a face full of freckles. I was that one.

When I saw her worried face I knew she was in trouble, and I asked, "What's the matter, Mom?"

"You ask me what's the matter? Why, I lost you!"

"No, I'm here."

But from that moment Maman had two packs, the basket full of wine and oil in one hand, and, in the other, myself. I was chained to my wonderful Maman Camous whose strong hand held mine tightly.

She said, "You want to look at the sea, then come on, because after that we are going to Monte Carlo."

It was only a five minute walk from the artistically arranged flowers in the park to the sea. As we approached, my eyes opened wide with astonishment, and my legs refused to go one step further. Maman pulled me, saying, "What's the matter with you?"

I had remembered what the other kids had said about drowning, and, like a young donkey, balked at taking one step more. Maman Camous, poor woman, explained that there was no danger and that we could not be drowned because of the barrier at the end of the promenade. From the barricade to the water itself there was a beach as wide as the Paillon, 300 feet, and just as dry. She put her basket down and asked several people who went by to help her in her trouble, and to tell me, either in patois or in French, that the sea was exactly as she had said.

At last one kind woman, who felt the distress of Maman Camous, came to our rescue. She gave me a bar of chocolate for which she had paid two *sous;* it was the biggest piece of candy I had ever had in my mouth. Each lady took a hand and pulled me until, finally, I saw the barricade. Then and then only did I believe that Maman was right. We proceeded. The roaring of the surf, as it foamed on the stony beach, was a new and strange noise to me. I remembered how Don Albini had talked about Satan, and thought, "Here, surely, is the Devil."

At that moment my courage returned to its full strength, and I detached myself from the ladies. I didn't want Maman Camous to tell everyone in Contes that I was scared. Intrepidly, I ran the 150 *mètres* to reach the balustrade. Thank goodness in those days there were no automobiles, only horses, because in my excitement I raced across the Promenade des Anglais, a very large boulevard with plenty of traffic.

In thinking that Nice was like Contes, I created confusion among the coachmen who saw a wild animal, myself, streaking across without thought of danger. Both ladies ran after me screaming, "Stop! Stop! You'll be killed!"

But I was already on the other side, and as long as the traffic had stopped for me it remained that way for another moment until my wonderful Maman Camous and that strange, kind lady had crossed too.

Maman yelled, "I think he's dead!"

People asked, "Who's dead?"

Poor Maman tearfully cried, "My little boy."

One man asked, "Do you mean the fellow with the million freckles on his face and the funny shoes on his feet? The one who ran across here a moment ago?"

"Yes!"

The strange man continued, "Why, he's at the balustrade looking at the sea."

At that answer Maman Camous thanked God in a very loud voice.

When she caught up with me the two *sou's* worth of chocolate were gone. I had telltale brown marks on my mouth and nose and I was licking my lips with my tongue, like Bacci. Both my hands tightly grasped the balustrade, and, through the bars, I gazed in fascination at the sea. The reflection of the sun on the water's surface made it shine like crystal. I was so filled with emotion I was ready to remain there and forget Monte Carlo, the basket, and even Escoffier.

Maman had pulled me to look at the sea, and now she had a new worry. How could she get me away from the sea?

She said, "Come on, Henri, let's go to Monte Carlo now."

"We can't walk there, Mom."

"No," she replied, "first we'll take a horse-car, and then we'll take a train."

The thought of this new excitement caused me to relinquish the balustrade.

Maman bought me another chocolate bar for one *sou* that was a big piece anyway; in Contes one *sou's* worth of chocolate was cut up into five small pieces. I already had had two *sou's* worth, and now I had one more. If Don Albini had known that, he would have punished me for being greedy. That last bit of candy was to induce me to board the horse-car. My only fear then was that I would be left behind on the car.

Maman said, "Get on, Henri."

"No, you go first."

We were both afraid, I for fear that she would not follow me, and she for fear that I would not follow her. A gentleman got off the tram, helped her on with the basket, and then hoisted me on. In all that commotion Maman paid the conductor two *sous* for her fare, which he took without even asking how old I was. He had lost too much time already in getting us on. The horse-car company would never thank us, or ever become millionaires because of us. Everybody on the car laughed at the farmer lady, the funny kid, and the large basket—we were three curiosities.

At last we arrived at the station where we could take a train to Monte Carlo, fifteen miles distant. Maman Camous bought a round trip ticket for twenty-two *sous*. The basket and I travelled complimentary.

When we got inside the depot, and I saw the big chimney on the train puffing black smoke, it was too much for me. I thought, "Now, I'm *positive* this is the Devil." I started to run, and if the *chef de gare* had not been there to grab me, I don't think I would be here to tell this story.

Poor Maman Camous! In the many years that have since passed by, and the innumerable times that I have taken the train on that same trip, I have never failed to think of my first journey when I paid no fare. And I can still visualize the great worry I gave that wonderful woman whom I called "mother," and who loved me, I think, more than a real mother.

But in the depot that day her troubles were not over. The train left five minutes late because of me. Maman got on and the *chef de gare* pushed me in behind her. We were imprisoned in a compartment that had ten seats. The people who travelled with us on third-class tickets were poor; there were so many we were packed in like sardines.

The following little scene was not the first to have been enacted on that train, but to the people accompanying us it was quite a surprise. Before we had even started I was ready to jump from it, but the door and

199

windows were closed. When I heard the noise of the engine starting up, I regretted that I had ever left Contes. I almost said, "Papa Camous was right to postpone the trip to 'tomorrow,' 'next week,' or 'next month.' "

When we reached the first tunnel in the mountain, the Mont Boron, I screamed because the sun was shut out and everything went black. I grabbed Maman by the skirt and yelled, "Let's get out of here!" Everybody laughed. They knew there were four more tunnels to go through before reaching Monte Carlo. You can imagine the surprise and the feelings of that freckle-faced kid who had only left Contes a few hours before.

I screamed and made so much noise in that compartment that a man gave me a *sou* to shut me up. Another did the same, and when I had collected five in the same way, I felt like the sacristan in the church, and thought, "Why don't the other three give me something?" Maybe they were poor fellows, but my telepathy must have reached them and opened their hearts because I succeeded in getting three more before we reached our destination. Maman Camous gave me one, too.

She said, "Now, you be a good boy and don't scream any more."

We arrived at Monte Carlo and got into the elevator which we had to take in order to reach the street level. When the darn thing started to go up I was so afraid I nearly punched the elevator boy.

I demanded, "Where are you taking me?"

Again everyone laughed. I saw ten or twelve pairs of eyes, including those of Maman, looking at my freckled face. It was the first time in my life that I had ever seen an elevator going up without anyone pulling it, and I was surprised. It made me think again of Don Albini and what he had said about going up to paradise. But that was when you were dead, not alive. It was a good thing I didn't see the empty space beneath the elevator. As we approached the top the seaside came into view. I looked at Maman and said, "It's a good thing this darn thing didn't tip over, otherwise we would all be in the sea."

Everyone roared. The elevator at Monte Carlo is hydraulic, about

the only one in the world that is not inside of a building but is outside in the open. I was more disgusted when I remembered that
Maman Camous had had to pay one sou to ride in it, and I remarked,
"What! You paid one *sou* to break your neck, Mom?" There was
more laughter. Everybody, including the elevator boy, seemed to be
having so much fun.

We stopped not far from the famous Casino where millions of
dollars were gambled away every day. Millions of dollars to me might
as well have been millions of *sous*. My knowledge of money, at that
early age, was limited only to the few *sous* I had earned by carrying
packages for Badou, a few silver francs of compensation from Monsieur Draghui, and the prize of the ten franc gold piece. To me, the
bank of England or the bank of France had no more significance
than the box of St. Antoine where donations were placed. They
were the same. I was so young I thought St. Antoine, St. John,
St. Joseph, and all the rest, were bankers.

The worries of Maman Camous were temporarily over when
we found that we were only a few steps away from the Grand
Hotel, where the great master chef Auguste Escoffier was in charge.
He was related to the family of Maman Camous. My foster-brother
Jean Camous, who was then sixteen, was his apprentice. On that exciting day I had the privilege of meeting Monsieur Escoffier for the first
time. The master of them all was a little man with a grand and noble
spirit who wanted nothing more than to live another day so that he
could learn more and bring greater satisfaction to a larger number of
palates by his wonderful food.

When Maman Camous and I walked into the kitchen and saw the
great number of white jackets and caps I could not restrain my laughter.
Only Maman understood why I laughed with such great enjoyment.
The place seemed like a monastery to me; every one of those cooks
looked like a white monk. But it returned to being merely a kitchen
when I saw the several dozen huge pots and pans that were being used.
The aromas were tantalizing. From some of the pots and pans came the
sound of sizzling butter; from others, the bubbling of water. One,

Edward G. Robinson is one of the many celebrities who visited Charpentier's small Southern California restaurant in the late 1940s and '50s.

In 1919 the village of Contes named a street after him. Here, he shows the "Rue Henri Charpentier" to his friend, Pepi Straforello.

instead of emanating a bouquet, gavè off smoke, and that was the fault of some apprentice who, as yet, didn't have the secret knowledge and finesse to create a sublime dish. Some of them were only twelve years old.

At that moment ten cooks yelled in unison, "Hey, you! Who told you to let it burn?"

With those words three or four wooden shoes sailed through the air close to the ears of the apprentice. In those days wooden shoes were worn in the kitchen, and certainly none of them were ever aimed at the boys to hurt them but were merely thrown to scare them. They were a tradition and were worn so that one would not slip while handling the hot bouillon; thus diminishing the danger of accidents. Those flying wooden shoes interested me very much. To me and my vivid imagination, they looked like angry birds without feathers that were attacking the small apprentice who was armed only with a ladle. It was intriguing; all the rest was too dull. I waited for another pot to burn so the wooden shoes would start flying again.

My expectation turned to surprise when I heard, *"Voilà le patron, le chef!"* Maman Camous and Papa Escoffier greeted each other with a kiss and then started talking patois together.

Maman said, "I bring you the wine and the oil that you like so much."

In no time at all Auguste Escoffier, Maman, and I were lunching in the private office of the great chef, a room enclosed in glass so that he could keep an eye on the business in the kitchen. When Rose, the woman who peeled vegetables, served us, Papa Escoffier said to her, "Bring us two plates of soup," and added, "one for Maman Camous and one for me." My eyes shone with happiness. I didn't want any. The great Escoffier knew that in Contes everyone was always full of soup, that we grew from soup, and that I didn't like soup. Besides that, we were not in Contes, we were in Monte Carlo.

The great man said, "Rose, bring some chicken for the little fellow, and don't bring any dogs in here; Henri will be the dog, and there won't be any bones left."

I looked at him and wondered how he knew all those things. I imagined that in his little village, Ville Neuve Loubet, the people were no different than those in Contes, since it was in the same locality and not far from Nice. I imagined also that the great chef Escoffier had often heard the cackling of his mother's hens when they laid eggs, but had seldom heard the bubbling of the chicken itself as it was being cooked in a pot. In his family, as in my own, the hens were there to lay eggs and were not to be eaten, because they were too scarce.

When their servings of chicken were placed in front of Maman Camous and Papa Escoffier, I had already finished mine. They were so busy talking that no attention was paid to me. But Papa Escoffier must have been watching me because I saw him take my empty plate and replace it with his full one. This went unnoticed by Maman who was so engrossed in the interesting conversation that she said to Monsieur, "You are a fast eater, you are already finished."

She was not aware that he had had none when he said, "I eat very fast," I felt that that was an order to proceed with my second portion. He had saved me from the reproach that Maman might have given me about my bad manners and impoliteness. The great master and little Henri understood each other without any need for words. Monsieur Escoffier had so many chickens that he could partake of them every day if he wished, but I had only a few to take care of and could not eat them.

That day in Monte Carlo was certainly my day. After the coffee, Papa Escoffier took us to the *pâtisserie* shop where French pastries of all shapes and colors were on display. There were creamy vanilla, light and dark chocolate, pink, blue, vermillion, etc.; at the sight of them my eyes became as large as those of Fannie, our mule. My little hands were too small to grab them all, my tongue was drowning in saliva, and I could only stand rigid like the statue Don Albini had told us about. The one that had turned into salt. I wouldn't have cared if I had been turned into a candy statue because I was in the middle of the *pâtisserie* shop. Blanchette would have preferred the salt, but Bacci would have licked me until I disappeared in his belly, and then Don Albini who might have had a new story would have been fooled because he would have had no statue to show the world.

Papa Escoffier said, "Help yourself, Henri."

But didn't I say I was like a statue? I couldn't budge. How could I move, and how could I help myself when my hands were so small, there was so much pastry, and I had only one mouth with which to eat? I won out by my silence because the *pâtissier* brought me a tray with twenty-four French pastries on it, every one different in form and color. The anticipation was so great that I put all of the first one in my mouth at one time. I opened that cavity wide enough so that not only the French pastry but the whole of France could have followed as well. My eyes alone showed that the taste was sublime. Papa Escoffier laughed, and Maman Camous was ashamed. The *pâtissier* cried out because he had never seen such a pastry eater. When I reached my sixteenth cake I asked Papa Escoffier if the whole trayful was for me. I was getting crowded for space, and by the movement of my eyes he could tell that I would have liked to put the remainder in my pocket to take home to Contes.

He asked, "So you want to be a cook, eh?"

"Yes, sir."

"Then," he said, "swallow the rest."

Papa Escoffier had never seen any mastication on my part, just one swallow and it was down. He looked at Maman Camous and said, "Alesandrina, it's a good thing you never learned how to make *pâtisseries*. You would have lost your ten fingers because that young fellow would have bitten them off before the cakes were ready."

When I turned around I saw that the whole kitchen had assembled to look at the little fellow who had such an enormous appetite. A very large basket, the same one that had contained the wine and oil for Papa Escoffier, was packed with all kinds of *pâtisseries, petits fours, massepains,* etc.

Papa Escoffier said, "Take these home to Papa Camous and the rest of the family."

I looked at him and nodded, "Yes."

Then he raised me up and put me on top of the table which was in the center of the kitchen, put his large cap on my head and said, "I crown you king of the cooks."

By the time he had finished saying that, my head had disappeared beneath his bonnet.

I said to him, "Don't smother me, I'd like to eat some more cakes."

It was hot underneath that chef's cap, and, when he pulled it off my head, my face looked like a strawberry, even to the little marks that were duplicated by my freckles. When I began to laugh my little white teeth were a noticeable contrast to those brown spots which covered my face and even my lips.

That caused the great chef to remark, "I think Henri must have taken a bite out of the sun to get such freckles. He didn't get them from just being exposed to it. If the sun had been a cake and he had swallowed it we would have been in the dark for forty days, and maybe we would have had another deluge."

We were ready to leave for Contes, but with reluctance on my part. I thought our trip had been too short. I embraced Jean, and this time I kissed Papa Escoffier.

I said, "Thanks for the cakes, sir, and also for the chickens."

Maman Camous was too busy talking to her son Jean to notice what I had said. So she was never to know that I had had more than one serving of chicken.

She said to them both, "This little fellow wants to be a cook, but he is too small. One of you take him by the head and the other by the feet, and stretch him."

I was not so sure of them and was half afraid they would really do it.

My fears vanished when I heard Maman say, "In a few years he'll be big enough to come and be an apprentice with you."

We left for the station with our basket of goodies. This time I refused to get into the elevator, and no amount of money could have induced me to do so. I took her by the hand and said, "We'll make a big detour to get to the station. I don't want to go down on that old thing."

What a difference there is between the days of long ago and those of the present. Compare the elevator at Monte Carlo, and its drop of sixty feet, with the elevator in our present day Empire State building! That little fellow, Henri, has grown up since his first trip to Nice and Monte Carlo, but all those beautiful memories and original emotions have remained the same throughout the years and will always be with him. The lovely people whom I have mentioned have all passed on, but that fearful elevator at Monte Carlo is there yet; and every time I took it up and down, later in my life, I was reminded of that first trip and my twenty-four delectable *pâtisseries*.

Color Photo, Opposite page:
Crêpes Suzette
(Recipe, Page 407)

Color Photo, Opposite page:
How To Make Omelets and Scrambled Eggs
(Instructions, Page 29)

Color Photo, Opposite page:
Advice For a Lady With a Market Basket
(Page 34)

Color Photo, Opposite page:
Rack of Lamb, Grover Cleveland
(Recipe, Page 78)

Color Photo, Opposite page:
Roast Duck, James K. Polk
(Recipe, Page 193)

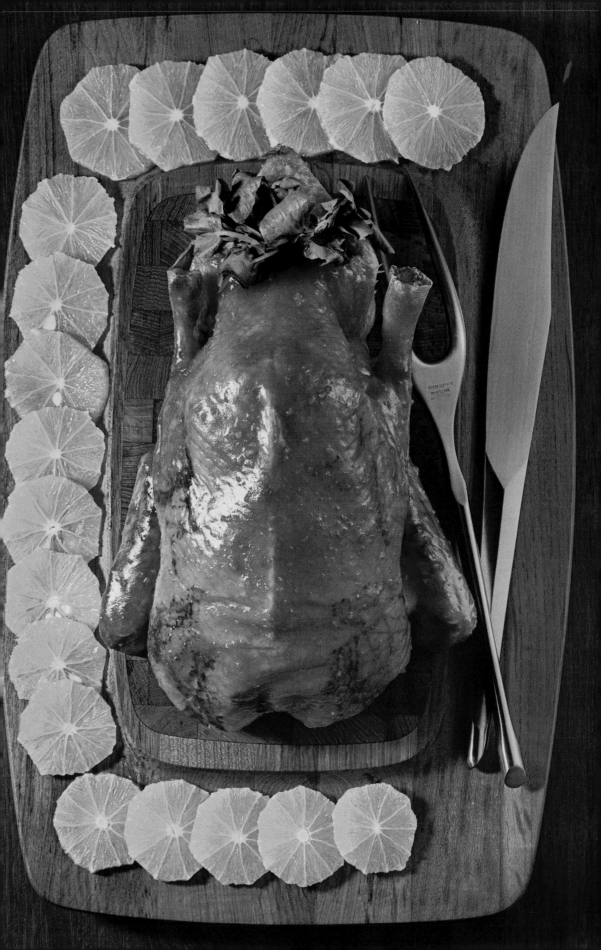

Color Photo, Opposite page:
Pudding, Anna Shaw — Garnished with cherries
(Recipe, Page 288)

Color Photo, Opposite page:
Soup, William Kelly
(Recipe, Page 378)

Color Photo, Opposite page:
Lobster, Charles Dillingham
(Recipe, Page 391)

RECIPES

✣

HORS-D'OEUVRE, JAMES FENNER

✣

SOUP, GEORGE ROGERS CLARK

✣

EGGS, NATHANAEL GREENE

✣

SCRAMBLED EGGS, JAMES OGLETHORPE

✣

BROILED SHAD, ROBERT FULTON

✣

GUINEA HEN, ULYSSES S. GRANT

✣

POTATOES, MOSES FARMER

✣

BRAISED CELERY, JAMES OTIS

✣

SALAD, EDWIN ABBEY

✣

STRAWBERRIES FLAMBEE, DOLLY MADISON

✣

HORS-D'OEUVRE, JAMES FENNER

Clean 6 smelts. Put them aside for a moment. To 1 pint of water, add 1 chopped onion, ½ chopped green pepper, 2 tablespoons of cream, and the juice of ½ lemon. Slice the other half of the lemon and put it into the water. Add a little chopped parsley, a few chopped tarragon leaves, ½ sliced tomato, 2 whole peeled cloves of garlic, 2 sliced sour pickles, 1 chopped stalk of celery, 2 bay leaves, 1 tablespoon of vinegar, a few sprinkles of pepper and salt. Place the 6 cleaned smelts into the pan and put it in a preheated oven. Let it all come to a boil, which will take about 15 minutes. Let it cool, and then place in the refrigerator. Serve cold.

SOUP, GEORGE ROGERS CLARK

Boil 1 pint of milk, and add a handful of crushed vermicelli. Salt only. Boil for 15 minutes. Put the yolks of 2 eggs into a tureen and stir. Add a generous piece of butter to the tureen, pour the soup over it, and serve. Season.

EGGS, NATHANAEL GREENE

Break 6 eggs into a bowl and stir just enough to break the yolks. Put a handful of fresh green peas, which have been previously cooked in milk, into a separate pan. Add to the peas: 2 tablespoons of cream, 2 thinly sliced mushrooms, 2 tablespoons of white port wine, 1 teaspoon of sugar, a pinch of salt and pepper. Mix and cook for 10 minutes.

Prepare an omelet with the 6 eggs and garnish it with the peas, mushrooms, etc. Season with salt and pepper.

SCRAMBLED EGGS, JAMES OGLETHORPE

Scramble 6 eggs in the usual manner. Broil 4 strips of bacon.
Put a piece of butter into a separate pan with 3 finely chopped scal-

lions. When they begin to cook, add 1 chopped ripe tomato, 2 diced slices of cooked smoked tongue, 1 clove of garlic which has been crushed into a little chopped parsley, 2 tablespoons of red wine, a pinch of pepper and salt. Cook for 10 minutes. Pour over the scrambled eggs and garnish with the bacon.

BROILED SHAD, ROBERT FULTON

Clean a small shad and dry it with a cloth. Place on a baking dish with 1 tablespoon of butter. Salt and pepper. Put in a hot oven, 450° F., for 25 minutes. Drape 5 slices of bacon over the top of the fish and then place it under the broiler for 5 minutes.

Put 2 tablespoons of butter into a separate pan, add 1 finely chopped shallot, the juice of ½ lemon, pepper and salt and cook it until the butter bubbles. Pour over the fish.

GUINEA HEN, ULYSSES S. GRANT

Purchase a 2½ pound guinea hen. Do not wash it. Clean and wipe the inside with a cloth. Salt and pepper the inside of the carcass, and add as well: 2 bay leaves, a few juniper berries, a pinch of thyme, 1 clove of crushed garlic, and 2 strips of bacon. Place the guinea hen into a roasting pan with a generous piece of butter. Salt and pepper, and put into a hot oven, 450 to 500° F. Baste often. To cook a guinea hen of this size, 35 to 40 minutes are required. The hen should be brown, but at the same time juicy. Remove the fowl from the roasting pan. Add to the roasting pan: 1 chopped shallot, 1 tablespoon of butter, 1 pony of brandy. Touch a flame to it and pour over the guinea hen which has been carved and is ready to be served. Salt and pepper.

A slice of broiled ham served as an accompaniment to the guinea hen forms an excellent combination. Toast which has been rubbed with garlic first and then buttered is delicious when served with the guinea hen and gravy.

POTATOES, MOSES FARMER

Use 1 large sweet potato which has previously been boiled. Slice it into a baking dish. Add 1 pared, cored, and sliced apple. Mix together. Put 1 tablespoon of butter into the baking dish. Add the juice of 1 orange, and cover the top with 1 sliced banana. Sprinkle with sugar. Add 1 tablespoon of water and place in an oven of 400° F. for 40 minutes.

BRAISED CELERY, JAMES OTIS

Chop 1 onion and put it into a pot. Add 1 tablespoon of butter and cook for a moment. Cut 1 stalk of celery into the pot, cover, and cook for 3 or 4 minutes. Add 2 cups of consommé, 1 chopped tomato, 1 clove of garlic which has been crushed into a few chopped sprigs of parsley. Salt and pepper. Place in a hot oven for 55 minutes. Five minutes before taking it from the oven, add ½ tablespoon of meat stock. If you think it is necessary, add a little more butter.

SALAD, EDWIN ABBEY

Take 3 black and 3 green olives and remove the pits. Thinly slice: ½ green pepper, 1 celery heart, 1 hard-boiled egg, ½ cucumber. Chop some chives as well as a few anchovies. Cut up 1 white chicory and mix it with the above ingredients. Serve with a very piquant French Dressing.

STRAWBERRIES FLAMBEE, DOLLY MADISON

Wash 1 pint of fresh strawberries and remove the stems. Put them into a chafing dish, add 3 tablespoons of white port wine, and simmer for about 3 minutes. Sprinkle the top of the berries with powdered sugar. Light 2 tablespoons of brandy and pour over the strawberries.

Chapter XIV

THE BANKER OF
THE VILLAGE

To MY YOUNG MIND the title of "banker" was a great mystery; I had never heard of either a bank or a banker. The entire village of Contes was rich in health, and everyone possessed a good digestion. The few *sous* and *écus* that were necessary to daily living caused no one any trouble. My village was like a large family in which each member was well known to the others. In the inexhaustible supply of stories recounted by Giroumetta and other old ladies there had never been one concerning stolen money in Contes. I presume that that was because there had never been any to steal. If money had grown like peaches on a tree there would have been the temptation to fill your pockets with it, as you would fill your pockets with fruit so that your stomach could be filled too.

There came a day when Papa Camous needed three silver dollars, or three *écus* more than he had, in order to pay his taxes in full.

I heard him say to Maman Camous, "I need fifteen francs (three *écus*) to complete the payment of my debt to the Republic of France."

"How much do you have already?"

"I have twenty-five francs and I ought to have forty. My mind is in a turmoil from worry. I've thought and thought and I don't know where I'm going to get them."

A woman is always wisest in the little difficulties which arise, and Maman Camous was no exception. She was not only a wonderful mother, a good wife, and an ideal cook, she was also the lawyer of the family with her good advice.

She said, "Why don't you call on André Cotto, the banker of the village?"

I had been quietly listening, but now I was all attention and my curiosity prompted me to say, "But Maman, Monsieur is the owner of the *auberge,* and he sells tobacco too!"

She replied, "Henri, there are many things that Monsieur Cotto does that no one knows about. He is the second priest in our village. Don Albini takes care of your soul, but André Cotto takes care of any troubles that might cause complications when the time comes for you to leave this world. The French Republic wants things to be settled quickly and without delay, but Don Albini with a few prayers postpones your payment until you reach God. He gives you more time to pray and to pay."

That was how I first learned that André Cotto, the owner of the Café de la Ville, was also the second priest in the village because he helped to straighten out the worries of all those fine people. That, too, was the reason his café was more prosperous than many of the others. He practiced the maxim, "As ye sow so shall ye reap."

That night around eleven o'clock I heard Papa Camous as he walked around downstairs on the creaking floor with his hobnailed shoes. I put my hands over Bacci's nose and mouth and said to him, "You, Bacci, don't move. Stay in bed, and don't follow me."

He wagged his tail and closed one eye to show that he would only be half obedient.

I ran downstairs in my bare feet and followed Papa Camous from a short distance behind. He couldn't see me because there were no street lights in the village and I was careful to remain at a discreet distance. As I became accustomed to the darkness I could see his figure as he stood in the Place de L'Église beneath the window of the Café de la Ville. The whole village was asleep; not a soul was out except Papa Camous and myself. Then I found out that the insubordinate Bacci was following me even as I was following Papa. He was only half obedient, for, although he was quiet, he had not remained in bed. And now I couldn't talk to him without being heard by Papa Camous. So Bacci was the winner; this time it was my turn to shut up. In a few seconds he was at my heels, wagging his tail, which meant, "I won't bark, but let me go along with you." So we both watched Papa Camous from a distance of fifty feet. Because there were no lights on the streets at night, everyone in Contes had the eyes of a cat. Some had the eyes of an old cat; they couldn't see well either.

Bacci and I heard a scratching on the door of the café which must have been a signal between those in trouble and Cotto, the banker. In one moment the window on the first floor was raised, and a soft voice, which I recognized as the voice of André Cotto, whispered, "You are Joseph Camous?"

Bacci and I crouched down, as quiet as mice.

"Yes, Cotto."

"What can I do for you?"

Papa said, "I need 3 *écus* with which to pay my taxes."

André Cotto said, "Just a minute."

The wonderul man who never said "no" in his life when others were to be helped, left the window. Those in the village who could not bring themselves to tell their troubles to others, always brought them to him. He could have put out a gazette if he had only had a printing shop. Then, if it had been permissible, Don Albini might have managed to fill one column with all the stories that were confessed to him. As it was, Cotto could have filled that unborn gazette all by himself.

In a moment he returned to the window and said, "Joseph, hold out your hat."

Papa Camous turned his hat upside down and held it out. I heard Monsieur Cotto count, and his counting surprised me. Instead of saying, "One," he said, "Two," and then I heard the second coin clink against the first which had dropped noiselessly into the hat. I heard him say, "Three," and then another clink. Now Papa Camous had three silver *écus* in his hat, and Cotto said to him, "Only God, you, and I know this."

Tears came to my eyes and Bacci, sensing it, began to lick my face. We ran back home without being seen; Maman Camous never missed us either.

231

That night I learned the meaning of the word banker. In his little way I place André Cotto in the same category as the late J. P. Morgan. Only the humble Cotto helped his fellow citizens without the formality of lawyers or papers and with only God as his witness.

I told that little story, later on, to my American born children, and on one of our numerous trips back and forth from America to Contes it pleased me very much to make a great surprise for that trusting banker of Contes. I took along 100 silver American dollars which I got from the National Bank of Lynbrook, Long Island. At that time Mr. Schanley was the bank's president, and I said to him, "I'm taking this little bag of 100 silver pieces to France to renew an acquaintance and to bring satisfaction to a gentleman who was born a banker without a bank."

My four children: Camille, Josephine, Pierre, and Marcelle accompanied me; and when we arrived in Contes my first desire was to present them to André and be rid of my bag of silver dollars which was difficult to carry. I realized that if all the wealthy people in the world had to carry their fortunes around with them in gold or silver pieces there would be fewer millionaires.

We found Monsieur Cotto sitting down because he was very old and because he was almost as broad as he was tall. But he still had the same smiling face and was still the same fine fellow. He was far from rich, but certainly he was not so poor that he had to go hungry even if he was so fat. The banking system in Contes had never been great enough to supply him with a carriage, since he had always loaned his money without asking for interest. I feel sure that of the few in the village who bought things without paying their debts, Cotto would never demand his money.

After embracing the old man, I presented my children. Pierre, my youngest son, then nine years old, was glad to reach Cotto's with the bag of silver coins which he had been lugging and which had been causing him to perspire. He had insisted on carrying it.

I remembered, then, the expression that had been used by Monsieur Cotto when he had dropped the three silver *écus* into Papa Camous' hat.

I repeated it, using the same words I had heard so many years before, "Only God, you, and I know this." I took his hat from his head and held it upside down. Pierre opened the bag, tipped it up, and poured the clinking silver dollars into it. I put the hat on Cotto's knees and we looked at each other with great emotion. My four Yankee children, André, and I were mute with tear-filled eyes. I thought of Bacci, the irrepressible; he should have been there to lick my wet face another time.

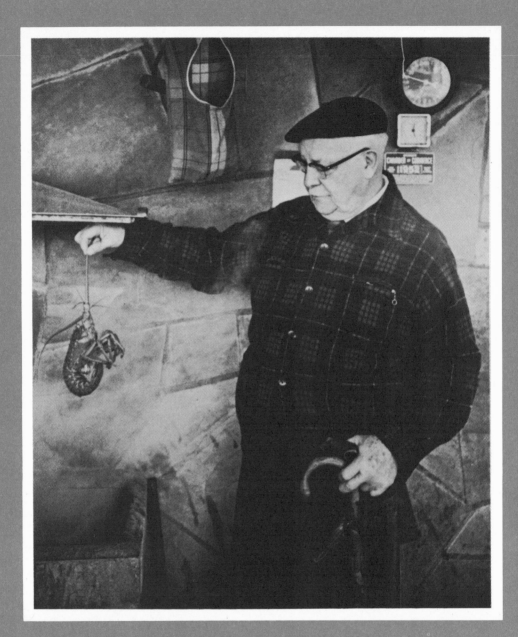

Inspecting lobsters for the night's meal.

RECIPES

✤

HORS-D'OEUVRE, THOMAS STONE

✤

SOUP, GEORGE CLINTON

✤

SHIRRED EGGS, OLIVER WOLCOTT

✤

OMELET, ROGER GRISWOLD

✤

BAKED SEA BASS, WILLIAM H. CRAWFORD

✤

BROILED YOUNG DUCKLING, MARTIN VAN BUREN

✤

POTATOES, JOSEPH HABERSHAM

✤

ASPARAGUS, JACOB CROWNINSHIELD

✤

SALAD, SAMUEL D. INGHAM

✤

VANILLA SOUFFLE, DOROTHEA DIX

✤

235

HORS-D'OEUVRE, THOMAS STONE

Prepare a pancake batter, using 1 egg, 1 tablespoon of flour, 2 tablespoons of milk, and a pinch of salt. Mix well. It should have the consistency of heavy cream. This amount will enable you to make 4 small pancakes, sufficient for your table for 2.

Place 1 teaspoon of butter into an omelet pan, and, I repeat, not one made of aluminum. Let it become very hot. Make 4 very thin pancakes, one at a time, and let each one become brown. Use 1 teaspoon of butter in making each pancake.

Shred 1 cup of boiled salmon, add ½ very finely chopped onion, 1 chopped hard-boiled egg, and 2 tablespoons of French Dressing. Stir well.

Place a pancake on each serving plate and spread with the salmon, etc. Cover with the 2 remaining pancakes. Sprinkle a few chopped chives and a little chopped parsley over the top. They will have the appearance of covered canapés or sandwiches that have been made with pancakes instead of bread.

SOUP, GEORGE CLINTON

Wash and finely chop: 1 carrot, 1 pared turnip, 1 leek, 1 leaf of white cabbage, ½ onion, and ¼ head of lettuce. Put 1 tablespoon of butter into a pot, add vegetables, sprinkle with a pinch of salt and a pinch of sugar. Cover and simmer for 15 minutes. Add 1 quart of clear consommé, or water, cover again and boil slowly for 1 hour. Just before serving, sprinkle with a little chopped parsley or chervil. Season to taste.

SHIRRED EGGS, OLIVER WOLCOTT

Finely chop 1 onion and let it cook in a frying pan by itself until it is brown and soft.

Put 1 tablespoon of butter into a baking platter, melt it, and add 4 eggs. (Eggs should always be tested for freshness by breaking them into a separate dish before adding them to the other ingredients.) Sprinkle the cooked chopped onion over the top and then sprinkle with grated cheese. Bake in a hot oven or on top of the stove for 3 minutes. Season.

OMELET, ROGER GRISWOLD

Chop 2 thin slices of raw bacon. Put them into a pan with 1 finely chopped onion, 1 tablespoon of butter, 2 pinches of paprika, 1 pinch of salt, and 1 pinch of pepper. Cook for 10 minutes. Add 1 tablespoon of cream. Let it come to a boil.

Prepare an omelet, using 6 eggs. Before rolling, place the chopped bacon, etc., in the center. Season.

BAKED SEA BASS, WILLIAM H. CRAWFORD

Take a 1 pound sea bass. Open and clean it. Remove the head. Wash and dry it well. Do not remove the bones. Make a few incisions on both sides with a knife.

Put 2 tablespoons of butter into a baking platter. Add 1 chopped shallot and 2 sliced mushrooms. Lay the fish over this.

Chop 1 peeled tomato. Mix it with 1 clove of garlic which has been crushed into a little chopped parsley, 1 pinch each of thyme, salt and pepper, and 1 crushed bay leaf. Sprinkle this over the bass. Add ½ sherry-glass of white wine. Bake in a preheated oven of 400° F. for 35 minutes. When it begins to bake reduce the heat to 350° F. An accompanying small bottle of white wine will make this fish taste heavenly.

BROILED YOUNG DUCKLING, MARTIN VAN BUREN

Take 1 duckling. After singeing, cut off the head and feet. Split through the backbone from neck to tail. Lay it open and remove the entrails. Do not wash it. Dry it with a clean cloth. Season with a sprinkle of salt and pepper. Place it on the broiling rack bony side up. Put 1 tablespoon of butter on top and arrange 2 thin slices of Virginia ham over the duckling. Place it under a very hot broiler for 5 minutes. Remove the ham and broil the bony side 5 more minutes. Turn the duck, brush it with butter and broil the breast side for 3 or 4 minutes. Then place it (breast side up) on a baking platter and add 2 tablespoons of butter. Finish cooking it by placing it in a preheated hot oven of 400° F. for 15 minutes.

Remove the duck from the baking platter to a hot serving platter. To the baking platter, add 1 more tablespoon of butter and ½ sherry-glass of port wine. When it comes to a boil sprinkle 1 finely chopped shallot into the bubbling sauce. Pour it over the duckling and serve with the broiled slices of Virginia ham. The ham may be separately broiled, if so desired. This is especially delicious when served with applesauce.

POTATOES, JOSEPH HABERSHAM

Peel 4 potatoes and boil in salted water until done. Pour off water and mash. Add 1 tablespoon of butter, 1 tablespoon of grated cheese, 1 tablespoon of cream, and a sprinkle each of pepper and salt. Mix well. Place into a baking dish and distribute 1 more tablespoon of cream over the top. Sprinkle with grated cheese and place under the broiler for 2 or 3 minutes.

ASPARAGUS, JACOB CROWNINSHIELD

Untie, wash, and remove the scales from 1 medium-sized bunch of asparagus. Boil until tender in plenty of water which has been salted. Take them from the water and lay them on a clean cloth for a moment to remove all water. Place on a serving platter and sprinkle with a few pinches of salt and 1 pinch of freshly ground black pepper. Squeeze the juice of ½ lemon over the asparagus and serve with hollandaise.

SALAD, SAMUEL D. INGHAM

Place the leaves of ½ head of lettuce on salad plates. Mix 2 tablespoons of cream with 1 raw egg yolk. Add the juice of ½ lemon, a pinch of pepper, and a pinch of salt. Beat together. Pour it over the lettuce. Sprinkle with chopped chives.

VANILLA SOUFFLE, DOROTHEA DIX

Place a few vanilla beans into a quart jarful of granulated sugar. Let them remain in the jar at least 2 days before using the sugar. This preparation is indispensable in the making of delicate desserts. It is economical and gives a much finer flavor than vanilla extract. If you wish, of course, you may use the extract, 1 teaspoon or more, according to your taste. In that case the ½ vanilla bean in the first step of this recipe may be eliminated. The sugar measurements, however, remain the same.

This recipe calls for the whites of 6 eggs and the yolks of 3. Save the 3 remaining egg yolks for some other recipe.

Have ready the stiffly beaten whites of 6 eggs to be used in a moment.

Put 1¼ cups of milk into a saucepan. Add ⅕ cup of sifted flour and ¾ cup of vanilla sugar.

One-half vanilla bean may be added to the pan during the first stage. Stir constantly over a small fire until it thickens. Remove the vanilla bean, wash it, and put it back into the jarful of sugar for future use. Remove the thickened sugar, flour, and milk from the fire. Pass it through a sieve. Quickly stir in 3 beaten egg yolks. Mix it well and immediately add the 6 stiffly beaten egg whites. Stir it well.

Take a pyrex baking dish that is no more than 2 inches deep. Use your fingers and butter it thoroughly. Sprinkle a little powdered sugar into the empty buttered dish. Pour in the contents of the saucepan. To obtain the best results, the baking dish must be completely filled.

Have the oven preheated and turned to 250° or 300° F. to start. Bake it for 5 or 6 minutes at that temperature and then turn it up to 350° F. Total baking time is approximately 25 minutes. Three minutes before removing it from the oven, sprinkle a little powdered sugar on top of the soufflé to give it a slightly brown and lustrous appearance. Serve immediately.

Chapter XV

THE END OF A BEAUTIFUL LIFE

GIROUMETTA was a bride of forty-seven when she married her sweet-heart, who was fifty-two. They were the parents of Papa Camous. I never knew Grandpapa Camous because he died before I was born.

Giroumetta, that grand old lady, helped to bury a great many of the villagers; those who went to that final resting place had to pass the windows of our house. Looking out at the funeral cortège as it passed, because she could not attend the services, she made the sign of the cross. On each occasion she said, "The next time it will be me."

I reported that to Maman Camous with tears in my eyes; I loved my old Grandmaman, who had taught me to dance. Maman helped me blow my nose and wiped away my tears.

She said, "Henri, your Grandmaman says that just as Don Albini says his mass every day; I've heard it for the last 20 years. Don't cry, Henri, Giroumetta has lost the way to paradise, and she never did like the Devil; consequently, she will be with us many, many more years. She has a lot of fun every day when you drink your three bowls of coffee, but she doesn't tell you that she drinks about fourteen cups a day herself. Every time I ask, 'Mother, do you want a cup of coffee?' she answers, 'Yes, Alesandrina. It will be the first one for me today.' She doesn't remember that I've already served her six. So you run along, Henri, and don't cry."

Giroumetta was a great lover of black coffee, and so was her son, Papa Camous. All the goats and cows could have disappeared from the earth; it would never have bothered Grandmaman, since she never used milk, cream, or butter. But she liked cheese. She always prayed, "Never condemn the animals that produce the last of the four products: milk, cream, butter, and cheese."

Maman asked her quite often, "Why don't you take a little bit of milk in your coffee?"

"Then, Alesandrina, you will certainly kill me before my time, even if I am past 100," was the answer.

"But Mother, you like cheese and that comes from milk."

"No, it doesn't come from milk."

"Then what is it?"

And Giroumetta simply said, "It is cheese."

But Maman was only satisfied after saying, "Cheese is produced by the olive trees."

Then they were both satisfied. Maman Camous could not argue with my old Grandmaman, and I firmly believed that Giroumetta was convinced that cheese actually did come from the olive trees.

That wonderful old lady bore five children after she was forty-seven, three of whom died before she did. There remained only Papa Camous and his sister, who also lived in Contes and who was married to the mayor, Honoré Passeron.

Grandmaman said she never wanted to die, but if she had to it must not be until after Carnival Day.

She always said, "Let people masquerade themselves; let them dance and burn the customary figure which portrays the King of Follies."

Sometimes he was represented by Bacchus, the King of Wine, who for nearly a month every year was crazy with drunkenness and pleasure and made all his people dance and drink until they became the same. Gratitude, which is very seldom born in a human being, condemned Bacchus to be burned to death for no reason at all, and without any crime having been committed.

The great folly of having too much of everything caused the revelers to carry out the burning of the figure, and, when it had been consumed and only ashes remained, they realized too late that they had burned the

King of Pleasure. The ashes were brought to the church where Don Albini became the *chandelier* on Ash Wednesday.

But it was not carnival time, it was December 23, 1887. Giroumetta was like the chanticleer that awakened the household. I think Grandmaman and Maman were the only ladies in the entire village who got up like that fowl, to greet the day with the sun. The roosters of Madame Gasiglia thought they were alone in their crowing, as the hens grumbled to themselves on their roosts, but Giroumetta and Maman Camous were already up ahead of them.

It was the old lady's custom to pass our bed on her way downstairs to the kitchen. And it was Bacci's custom to follow her down. Giroumetta occupied her place by the chimney and Bacci took his on the other side. There they sat like statues while the burning wood in the fireplace crackled and heated the water for the morning coffee. Giroumetta had often said that fire couldn't burn the old ladies anymore, but Bacci still had to worry about it. When one ear got too warm he turned his head so the other side would become toasted.

Maman Camous ran around preparing the coffee for everybody while Grandmaman and Bacci waited. They were entitled to have the first, since they were the first to get up. Like three cooks, they had the right to serve themselves before anyone else.

On that day, December 23, I didn't see or hear Giroumetta pass through our room on her way downstairs. Bacci was still in my bed; he had no watch to tell him it was time to get up, and as long as Grandmaman didn't pass by he was ready to stay there without answering the command of anyone else.

Maman Camous came upstairs to find out what was the matter, and I heard Giroumetta say, "I don't feel very well, I feel tired. Today you had better bring my coffee upstairs."

In less than a minute Celestin, Césarina, Papa Camous, Bacci, and I were in her room. She looked at all of us with a big smile and said, "I don't believe I will be able to see Carnival Day next year. I think Don Albini should come to see me. I want to whisper some little secrets in his ear, secrets of which he alone shall be the guardian. He might give me some information in patois instead of always talking about it in Latin. I never cared to learn what it was before; I thought there would always be plenty of time for it on the day it was needed. That day is here now, and I want him instead of the doctor. He might have a password that I could give to St. Peter, of whom he speaks so often. And in case Don Albini's protection is worthless I certainly will come back and tell him so."

We thought the poor old lady was out of her mind, and Papa Camous gently asked, "Maman, what's the matter with you?" Tears were already forming in his eyes.

She said, "Joseph, bring a nice bottle of old wine, one of those that you're too stingy to offer to anyone. On this twenty-third day of December let us all have a little glass together. I don't think Henri should go to early mass this morning. When Don Albini arrives we'll all make it together by drinking a glass of your wonderful wine. If I have to go I will carry with me to the next world the pleasant memory of this great family with whom I have lived for so many years. You, my good son, Joseph, and you, Alesandrina, who are kinder than my own daughter, may God bless you and the children."

The priest, who had been called by a neighbor, arrived shortly before his early mass. The confession of that kind old lady was never made. She said to the priest, "I didn't call you here, Father Albini, to tell you my sins because I have none on my conscience. But as long as it would have been the first time in twenty years that I would have missed the early mass, and I don't have the strength to go to church, I have asked you to come to me. Now, by seeing you, I am still attending it."

This time Don Albini could not camouflage the tears behind his eyeglasses and say that they were caused by the dust; they rolled down his long nose and dropped onto his robe.

Papa Camous poured wine into the small glasses, which we all clinked together, saying, "Good luck" to please Grandmaman.

So Don Albini, for the first time, missed giving his early mass. The whole village found out that Giroumetta, the most humble of farm women, had become more than a princess by winning, before departing from this world, one mass all for herself. It only took five minutes. With the wine still moist on her lips, she looked at everyone in farewell, and, giving one hand to her son and one to Don Albini, she passed on. That wonderful soul left that ancient house, as had many others who had lived and died there centuries before her. But not one had had the great intelligence to transform that poor bedroom into a cathedral and die sipping, as a last drink, a glass of the best wine that Contes had ever produced.

In my memory, as I write that little story of fifty-seven years ago, I can still see that little fellow Henri as he stood beside the bed of his Grandmaman. At recollecting the very humble but sincere departure of that fine old lady, those many years ago, he can still feel the same original emotion.

Grandmaman was buried the next day, and the entire village crowded the church to the doors. André Cotto sang for Giroumetta in such a beautiful voice and with such feeling that he achieved the title of "the unknown Caruso" without the appearance of his name in the newspapers. I later met and appreciated Enrico Caruso, whose operatic voice was divine. He sang to the people, but Cotto sang to God. One was paid thousands of dollars for singing a few hours, and the other, the unknown, gave thousands of *sous* from his humble earnings to follow the words of God, "Help those in need."

Cotto died many years after Giroumetta. It is my belief that the soul of that grand old lady refused to go further into paradise but waited there, with determination, for Cotto to arrive. She wanted to express her gratitude to him for the lovely voice that had filled the church on December 24, because it had been impossible for her to thank him sooner.

To find you have succeeded in creating a dish which gives pleasure and is satisfying to those for whom you cook, will give you great contentment. —Henri Charpentier

RECIPES

✤

HORS-D'OEUVRE, WILLIAM PACA

✤

SOUP, JAMES PAULDING

✤

EGGS, SAMUEL DEXTER

✤

OMELET, HENRY DEARBORN

✤

BOILED HALIBUT, GEORGE ADE

✤

BROILED PORK CHOPS, ROBERT LIVINGSTON

✤

POTATOES, GIDEON GRANGER

✤

BROCCOLI, PAUL HAMILTON

✤

SALAD, WILLIAM J. DUANE

✤

BRANDY APPLES, AMELIA EARHART

✤

HORS-D'OEUVRE, WILLIAM PACA

Put 1 finely chopped onion into a pan with 1 tablespoon of butter. Cover and let it simmer for 10 minutes until it is cooked soft and becomes a light brown. Put 2 thin slices of boiled ham into the pan and cover them with: ½ head of finely cut red cabbage, 1 cup of consommé, 2 sherry-glasses of red wine, 1 tablespoon of sugar, and 2 tablespoons of vinegar. Season with salt and pepper. Cook for 35 minutes.

Put into a separate pan: 2 tablespoons of French Dressing, 1 teaspoon of English mustard, 1 teaspoon of Worcestershire sauce, 1 tablespoon of chili sauce, 1 teaspoon of sugar and 1 tablespoon of butter. Let it come to a boil.

Place the cabbage, etc., on serving plates. Be sure the cabbage has absorbed all the liquid in which it has been cooked. Pour the sauce, which has come to a boil, over the top.

SOUP, JAMES PAULDING

Wash and finely chop: 1 carrot, 1 pared turnip, 1 leek, ½ onion, and ⅛ head of Savoy cabbage. Put 1 tablespoon of butter into a pot, add vegetables, cover and simmer for 15 minutes. Add 1 quart of consommé and ½ cup of dried beans that have previously been soaked and cooked. Cover and slowly boil for 30 minutes.

Before serving, add 2 tablespoons of cream and 1 tablespoon of butter. Season to taste.

EGGS, SAMUEL DEXTER

Crush 1 clove of garlic into a little chopped parsley and 1 tablespoon of butter. Sprinkle with 1 pinch of salt and 1 pinch of pepper. Mix it all together, making a parsley butter.

Take 2 tomatoes, cut them in halves and place them on a baking platter. Put ½ teaspoon of the parsley butter on top of each half tomato and bake in a preheated moderate oven of 350° to 375° F. for 15 minutes. When the tomatoes become soft gently loosen the center of each with a fork to make room for an egg. Place 1 egg on top of each and garnish with 4 slices of broiled ham. Bake for 3 more minutes.

OMELET, HENRY DEARBORN

Put 1 tablespoon of butter into a pan with ½ finely chopped onion. Add 1 sliced cooked vegetable marrow, 2 thinly sliced mushrooms, 1 crushed clove of garlic, 1 pinch of salt and 1 pinch of pepper. Mix and cook for 10 minutes.

Prepare an omelet, using 6 eggs. Put the onions, etc., in the center before rolling. The omelet must be brown outside and soft inside. Season.

BOILED HALIBUT, GEORGE ADE

Purchase 1 pound of halibut in one piece. Place it into a pot with 2 quarts of water, 1 bay leaf, 2 peppercorns, 1 whole clove, 1 slice of onion,

1 whole clove of peeled garlic, 1 stalk of celery, 1 sprig of parsley, ½ carrot, the juice of ½ lemon, and 1 pinch of salt. When it begins to boil turn the fire low so that the bubbling water will not destroy the fish. Boil for 30 minutes. To determine whether the halibut is done, stick the prongs of a fork into it and touch your cheek with it. If it's hot, it's done.

Put 1 tablespoon of butter into a separate pan with 2 finely chopped shallots. Cook for 3 minutes. Add ½ cup of cream and 3 thinly sliced mushrooms. Let it come to a boil. Remove from the fire and stir in the yolk of 1 egg.

Remove the fish from the boiling water, dry, and serve it with the creamy sauce. Season to taste.

BROILED PORK CHOPS, ROBERT LIVINGSTON

Purchase 2 thick, lean pork chops. Sprinkle both sides with a pinch of salt. Broil each side for 3 minutes. Then brush the first side with melted butter and broil it for 10 more minutes. Do the same to the other side. Place them on a hot serving platter. Sprinkle with 2 finely chopped pickles.

Place 2 tablespoons of butter into a frying pan and when it begins to sizzle throw in 2 finely chopped shallots. Add 1 tablespoon of Worcestershire sauce and stir. Pour the bubbling sauce over the broiled chops.

POTATOES, GIDEON GRANGER

Peel and boil 6 medium-sized whole potatoes in salted water. When they are done, pour off water and place into a baking dish. Melt 1 table-spoon of butter and distribute it over the potatoes. Sprinkle 2 tablespoons of grated cheese and a little chopped parsley over the top. Season. Place in a preheated moderately hot oven of 375° to 400° F. for 10 minutes.

BROCCOLI, PAUL HAMILTON

Take 1 bunch of broccoli. Cut off the large leaves and peel off the woody outer skin of the main stem. Boil whole in plenty of salted water until tender.

Drain off water and let the broccoli remain on the fire for a moment to dry off all remaining water.

Place on a serving platter and squeeze the juice of ½ lemon over the top. Sprinkle with 2 tablespoons of grated cheese.

Separately mix: ½ cup of hollandaise, 1 teaspoon of meat stock, 1 chopped hard-boiled egg, and 1 tablespoon of chili sauce. Pour it over the broccoli. Season with salt and freshly ground pepper. Sprinkle with a few chopped chives.

SALAD, WILLIAM J. DUANE

Take ½ head of lettuce. Remove 2 large leaves, place them on salad plates, and shred the rest, cutting it lengthwise to make it hair-like. Place

251

a portion of shredded lettuce on each leaf.

Fry 4 slices of bacon. Make them crisp. Crush and add to them: 1 tablespoon of finely chopped walnuts, 1 teaspoon of bread crumbs, 1 teaspoon of grated cheese and 1 teaspoon of chopped chives. Mix and place over the shredded lettuce.

Put 1 raw egg yolk into a mixing bowl. Add 2 tablespoons of cream, the juice of ½ lemon, 1 teaspoon of Worcestershire sauce, and a pinch each of salt, pepper and paprika. Mix and pour over each portion.

BRANDY APPLES, AMELIA EARHART

Cut the tops off 2 large apples and scrape out the insides, being careful to leave the shells intact. Stand the shells aside.

Cook 4 tablespoons of the scraped apple until it is sauce. Be sure you haven't used any of the cores. Then add 1 tablespoon of vanilla sugar. Remove from the fire. Beat the whites of 3 eggs until they are stiff, add to the applesauce, and stir thoroughly.

Pour 1 pony of brandy into each apple shell. Turn them so as to wet the entire insides with the brandy. Stuff them with the applesauce, etc., and sprinkle with powdered sugar. Do not replace the tops. Place them on a baking platter and bake for 10 minutes in a preheated very hot oven of 450° to 500° F.

Put 1 tablespoon of butter into a pan with 1 tablespoon of vanilla sugar and 2 tablespoons of cream. Let it come to a boil, remove it from the fire, and let it stand for 2 minutes.

Mix the 3 egg yolks with another heaping tablespoon of vanilla sugar and 1 pony of brandy. After the butter, sugar, and cream have stood for 2 minutes, pour it into the yolks, etc. Do not pour the yolks, etc., into the hot pan. Stir thoroughly, and serve separately accompanying the apples,

Chapter XVI

AN ENGLISH PLUM PUDDING IN CONTES

IT WAS THE INTENTION of Jean Camous to make Christmas in Contes a more happy occasion. It was his generosity and love which prompted him to send us a plum pudding from London, where he was a protégé of the master Escoffier. The name "plum pudding" was entirely new to us; it was a dessert unknown to Contes.

When we received Jean's letter, which preceded the arrival of the pudding, Papa Camous opened it, read it, and passed it on to Celestin who said, "I don't know what plum pudding means, it's not in the story of France."

Césarina said she had never heard of the words.

I stuck my nose into it and shook my head, saying, "It must be something quite new. Why don't we show the letter to Monsieur Draghui?"

Professor Draghui, looking at it, appeared worried and perplexed; in all his vocabulary and past years of study he had never come across that peculiar English name. Poor Jean! He had written it wrong, which made it more difficult for anyone looking up a definition.

After thinking for a long time Monsieur Draghui said, "I'm sorry, but I can't define it. It might be something from India, Africa, or any of the other English possessions scattered around the world. It might be meat from some kind of wild animal, maybe a piece of elephant meat, or some kind of big fish. It might be anything, I don't know. Show this to Don Albini, he might have the answer."

That letter, after having been read by the priest, was passed on to all the wealthy and prominent villagers as if it had been a British gazette. In less than three hours that plum pudding had disturbed the brains of everyone in Contes. One villager said to another, "I wonder what it is that Jean is sending to Papa Camous this Christmas? Nobody can translate his letter."

The whole village buzzed. Some said, "Monsieur Draghui says it might be some part of an elephant, and Don Albini says it might be some part of a crocodile."

Monsieur Faussati, an old gentleman, piped up with, "Maybe it's one of those big smoked fishes that's prepared in the style of the South Sea Islands."

Monsieur Alardi, a very prominent lawyer, said, "It must be something extraordinary. I can't pronounce it myself."

All the varied and indefinite answers of the brainy people in the village worried Papa and Maman Camous.

Papa said to Maman, "Why the devil is Jean sending us such an embarrassing present? It gives us more worry than pleasure."

"Well," Maman replied, "it's too late now. We can't tell him not to send it; it's at the depot in Nice already."

The next morning fifteen year old Celestin hitched Fannie to the wagon and called out, "Henri, come along to the depot with Fannie and me."

It was on a Thursday and there was no school.

Papa Camous said, "There's no use in taking a wagonload of wood or anything else to sell in Nice, because we don't know how big or how heavy the darn thing is that Jean's sending to us. Fannie's too old to pull a heavy load of wood as well as that thing Jean is sending. And if you don't sell any wood heaven knows how much she'd have to pull."

That made it much easier for Celestin and myself and, of course, the old mule; she started off for Nice with great enthusiasm.

Celestin said, "Fannie, try to run and make a little more noise with your feet, because you have nothing to pull. Point your ears up and fool everybody into thinking you're still young. But prepare to sweat on your way home tonight when you'll have to cart that thing Jean sent from England."

Fannie, wearing her funny looking hat, moved her ears as if she were ready for the effort right then. Celestin tried to make a noise with his whip by waving it around and cracking it in imitation of Badou. He never hit the mule and she knew he never would. Even if the whip had touched her her hide was so old and so thick and hard she wouldn't have felt it.

We weren't travelling at any great speed; every horse, mule, and jackass going to Nice passed us up. In that dry locality the roads were very dusty, and in no time at all Celestin, Fannie, and I were covered with a fine, white powder. We looked like bakers full of flour from making bread. Celestin laughed at me, and I laughed at him. Only Fannie, unable to see herself, said nothing; if she had she would have refused to go one step further along the road to Nice. Then she would have known that her dark brown hair had become white because every other mule, horse, and jackass had passed her up.

I made the remark, "I believe Fannie's getting too old."

And Celestin answered quickly, "Don't say that in such a loud voice. She might hear you and refuse to go to the station; then how would we be able to bring that darn stuff home tonight?"

It was my belief that that animal could understand everything she heard, so I shut up.

When the mule was alone on the road the dust rolled in a cloud behind us, Celestin cracked his whip, and Fannie looked young again because she had no competition.

As we entered Nice we left the dusty road behind us. But not the dust. It had settled on us and went with us up the city streets that were paved with blocks of wood.

At last we arrived at the depot. Celestin called to the *chef de gare* and showed him the invoice from London. He laughed when he saw the empty wagon; he laughed as if at some good joke which we didn't understand.

He said, "Fellows, you need a rope to tie the thing up."

Celestin looked at me and exulted, "Didn't I tell you I'd need your help? Wasn't it smart of Papa to throw a rope into the wagon?"

After thanking the *chef de gare,* we went through to the freight office a few blocks distant. On the way Celestin felt the muscles in my arms to see if I had strength enough to help him carry that famous whatever-it-was to the wagon.

The ancient man behind the mesh window said, "All right, young fellows, is everything paid for? If it is, I'll give you the package."

Celestin said, "If you need any help, we're both here to assist you. The *chef de gare* told us we might need a rope to tie up the package."

The old man laughed at that and replied, 'No, it's a plum pudding, not a horse."

The name still meant nothing to us; it was like the Latin Don Albini used in church.

My face became red, and, because of the dust on it, Celestin said, "You look funny, all pink."

I retorted, "I don't know how I look, but I think the *chef de gare* is playing a joke on us. If I were only four inches taller I'd go back and punch his nose and thank him for suggesting that we use a rope."

The good Celestin, who never found harm in anyone, thought the man meant well.

When that shaky old fellow brought us a little box which couldn't have weighed more than ten pounds, carrying it without any exertion, Celestin's face became red. And that flush beneath his dust-covered brown skin made him look like a colored boy. It was my turn to laugh.

"We don't need the rope," I said, "and Fannie'll dance on the way home; she won't have to sweat. We'd better take the best way home, around by the sea, and then wait until nightfall before we enter Contes because the whole curious village will be waiting for us. Everybody's dying to see the stuff in this English package. If those villagers see the ropes we took with us you'll have a new nickname, Celestin, which your great grandchildren will hear even after you're gone."

Celestin, in astonishment, looked three or four times to be sure we had the right package. I told him the first time we looked that the handwriting on it was Jean's, but he couldn't believe anyone would send such a small package from such a great distance. To have caused such a commotion among the people of Contes, it should have been an enormous one.

It was very late when we reached home, and the night was very cold. Thank goodness the villagers were in bed, their curiosity asleep with them. Only Papa, Maman, and Césarina were still up and anxiously waiting for us. They had spent most of the evening peering into the darkness and worrying about us.

Maman kept saying, "I wonder why they're so late?"

Papa said, "Well, maybe the package is too heavy for Fannie to pull. I'm sorry I didn't go along to help them."

The little light on the front of our wagon told our watching family that we were approaching. Papa Camous ran to meet us with, "Maybe it was too big and you couldn't bring it, eh? Then you must return tomorrow."

"No, father," replied Celestin, "it's here in this small box."

Everybody laughed. I shrieked until I was reminded of the time my chums and I had tied walnut shells onto the paws of our cats.

We opened the mysterious package. It contained some kind of a big ball that was sewed up inside of a bag. A short note from Jean was attached to it which read, "Dear Maman, put the whole thing, bag and all, into your big soup kettle, cover it with water and let it boil slowly for three hours. Put it on the fire so that it will be ready to eat after the Christmas midnight mass. Then tear the bag away, place the plum pudding on a large platter, sprinkle some powdered sugar on top, pour some rum over it, and light it with a match. After it has burned for a few minutes, cut it into slices and serve."

When I read what Jean had written, about putting the bag and all into the soup kettle, I thought of Badou and hoped that, whatever was in the bag, it wouldn't be another snake.

All we could hear from the villagers next day was, "What was it that Jean sent from England that has such a funny name?"

Maman Camous said, "We don't know yet, it's in a bag and we have to cook it first. We have to wait four more days until the Christmas midnight mass to find out."

On Christmas eve, the last I was to spend in Contes with my family, we followed Jean's instructions. I went to serve mass with Don Albini, but my mind was on the bag from England that was boiling away in a kettle at home.

When I reached home it was close to 1 A. M. and the house was full of villagers. The leading question was, "What the devil's in that bag?" Everybody, young and old, seemed to be enjoying the anticipation and crowded around the big kettle which made a plopping noise like the lava in Mt. Vesuvius. Papa Camous put more wood on the fire. Badou was there and so were Don Albini and Monsieur Draghui. The house wasn't big enough so Bacci and the cats went outside; they thought someone would step on their tails.

Every guest looked into the kettle at some time or other and wondered if there wasn't some sort of English devil inside waiting to be released.

This gathering gave Papa Camous a chance to serve samples of his wine just so he could hear people say how good it was. He shrugged his shoulders and said, "Oh, well, Christmas only comes once a year. Let's drink to a merry one."

Badou laughed, "Let's eat fewer grapes and drink more wine." He only ate them on his "week of cure," but not because he liked them. He, like Papa Camous, preferred the wine.

At last the big ball was taken from the kettle, but not without difficulty. I looked at it in surprise. The plum pudding had swelled during the boiling and now looked like a monster! Thank goodness the kettle was an ancient one and large enough for a family of twenty. Our largest platter couldn't hold that big thing so Monsieur Cotto said, "Henri, run over to the *auberge* and get a tray." I made a quick trip with Bacci at my heels.

When the bag was finally removed we stood looking at its funny-looking contents, still not certain just what it was. A full quart of rum, generously supplied by Monsieur Cotto, was poured over the top after the pudding had been sprinkled with a pound of powdered sugar. Papa

Camous, with the ceremony of Don Albini, lit it with a match. A big flame shot up and the large ball started to burn, which scared everyone. In a few minutes the sugar, rum, and juice from the pudding combined to form a sauce. Monsieur Cotto sliced it, and everyone had a taste.

The kids didn't like it. I happened to be looking at Badou when I swallowed my first mouthful of strong sauce and pudding. I thought, "There isn't any snake in the bag this time, and I'm not anywhere near the sea, but I'd better get out of here quick; this stuff is making me sick." I didn't like it. When I saw Monsieur Cotto put some more sugar and rum on without making it burn, I took Bacci and went to bed. I thought, "This pudding might make Christmas a merry one in England, but if I ate any more of it it would be a sad one for me."

The rest of our guests, young and old, emptied many bottles of Papa Camous' good wine. The old ones scraped their plates and licked their spoons until the plum pudding disappeared into their French bellies. Messieurs Cotto, Badou, Draghui, Trapenat and the rest began to sing the Christmas eve song, "Minuit Chrétien—" And so the very first English plum pudding to be introduced to and eaten in Contes, after causing a great deal of speculation among the populace, was thoroughly enjoyed by the grown-ups. The villagers regretted the size of that pudding. They would have liked one big enough so that Celestin and I would have had to actually tie it onto the wagon with a rope; one that Fannie, poor old Fannie, would have had to pull home with a maximum of effort, but with a great deal of pride.

Only The Memory
And The Old Hat
Of Fannie Remain

WHEN EVERYTHING LIVING on this earth has completed its destined span of life, whether long or short, death comes and all resistance ends. It is the same with grass, flowers, animals, and humans.

That time came for Fannie, the pet mule of Papa Camous. One day, toward the end of September in the same year that I left Contes and the loving care of my Maman Camous, Fannie left the stable forever, after having lived there for thirty-five years. She was next to Bacci in presiding over that place and had seen many Bismarcks come and go in her lifetime. They would come in as little squealers and leave as big porkers that grunted and screamed because they didn't want to leave their pig-pen. On these occasions both Fannie and Bicou, our donkey, moved their long ears and swished their tails as if to say, "So long, Bismarck, this is your last mile. At the end of your trip you will encounter Baza, the black-smith, who is also the pig killer of our village. We'll see you again when you return as a ham, and then, of all the animals, that fresh Bacci will be the only one to taste you. None of the rest of us would eat you. So long, Bismarck." Even as the big fellow was being led away to the slaughter a tiny newcomer was getting ready to take his place. Whenever Papa Camous or the rest of the family called "Bismarck," the rest of the animals knew it meant the pig and always turned in his direction to look at him. How many calves and kids Fannie must have seen born in that stable!

Papa Camous never went to bed before making the final round of the stable, talking to and petting all of the animals as he passed by. To us, the animals were part of the family.

One evening, when he went to the stable, Papa found Fannie stretched out on the straw. She looked at him in supplication. Her big eyes seemed to say, "You promised that I would never have to die in the stable. You always said I could spend my last moments under the big olive tree where I used to stand while you replenished the earth with the loads of fertilizer that I carried on my back. And, later on, after the grateful land had produced abundantly, I hauled many loads back for you."

Papa Camous hurried into the kitchen. Maman saw his pale face and asked, "What has happened to you? What's the matter?"

He replied, "Well, I guess Fannie's last day is near. Tomorrow we must get up early and help her reach her favorite olive tree near our farm land. But there'll be no load for her to carry this time; she'll hardly be able to make it herself."

About 4 o'clock the following morning, after the coffee had been prepared and he had already had his, Bacci jumped back onto my bed and licked my face, "Get up." I dressed hurriedly and went downstairs. Maman Camous had lined up my three bowls on the kitchen table and filled them with coffee. I drank them in a hurry and ran out to the stable where I found the family there ahead of me. Fannie was standing up, which pleased Papa Camous. But now she didn't want to go, and he asked tremulously, "What's the matter?"

Maman Camous said, "I think she's waiting for her load; she has seldom gone without it."

Papa Camous said, "Oh, you are mistaken."

Celestin shrugged his shoulders. He remembered the plum pudding and the promise he had made to the mule that she would be sweating on the way home. For the first time in Fannie's life she had been fooled.

Césarina only listened, and offered no comments.

I was standing at Fannie's tail and Bacci was near her forelegs when Celestin said, "Suppose we put Henri on Fannie's back so she'll have her load?"

261

Wine and a flower on the table, along with good company and food prepared with care and love, were Henri Charpentier's ingredients for a beautiful dinner.

The moment they put me on her back she started to walk, very slowly, out of the stable.

Maman looked at Papa and asked, "Wasn't I right?"

That made him say, "You are always right."

Bacci was the vanguard of that little caravan which consisted of Maman, Papa, Césarina, Celestin, Fannie, and myself. When I turned my head to look behind me, there was Blanchette in the rear. She had followed us out of the stable, and, since no one had paid any attention to her, kept on following a short distance behind, nipping leaves and ruminating on the way. I didn't say anything because we were too close to home yet; had she known about Blanchette, Maman Camous would have made Césarina take her back to the stable. Bacci, too, must have had an *entente* with Blanchette; he didn't bark either. Our farm was two miles away, and when we had covered half that distance Bacci ran around to the rear; then both devils followed the one on top of the mule. When the Camous family looked back each was surprised, and each asked, wonderingly, "How did Blanchette get here?"

Papa Camous brushed the tears from his eyes. He knew that even an animal could have love for an old friend and that between those pets there was an understanding.

Fannie had said goodbye to all her friends in the stable early that morning, but Blanchette was not satisfied. She wanted to assist and be present at the last few moments of the mule's life.

Finally we arrived under the big olive tree where Fannie had stopped so many times before. I dismounted and caressed her. Bacci jumped to her nose as if to give her a last kiss. Blanchette stopped chewing for a moment in contemplation of that serious moment.

Fannie stretched out on the fresh straw which Papa Camous had carried and spread out for her. He presented her with a pail of water, but she refused to drink. He washed her nose and tried to put some water into her mouth; then he gathered some tender green grass from under the tree—grass that had never been reached by the sun and was as tender as the lettuce in our garden. But Fannie's old teeth refused to accept what a few days before she would have run to claim. Only her eyes expressed gratitude to her great and wonderful master, Papa Camous, who had never used a whip on her. She tried to swish her tail, but she had no energy. Her ears moved slowly and stopped. Only her breathing showed that she was still alive; finally that stopped, too. One eye remained open, indicating that she still wanted to picture the great kindness of the Camous family. All was quiet. Tears rolled down our cheeks. It was Papa who broke the silence with his sobs as he wept for that old pet which he had loved for so many, many years.

RECIPES

✤

HORS-D'OEUVRE, SAMUEL CHASE

✤

SOUP, JOHN MARSHALL

✤

POACHED EGGS, GEORGE W. CAMPBELL

✤

SCRAMBLED EGGS, JOHN ARMSTRONG II

✤

BROILED POMPANO, GEORGE DEWEY

✤

ROAST GUINEA HEN, JOHN C. CALHOUN

✤

POTATOES, WILLIAM T. BARRY

✤

CAULIFLOWER, SMITH THOMPSON

✤

SALAD, RICHARD M. JOHNSON

✤

APRICOTS, MARGARET BRENT

✤

HORS-D'OEUVRE, SAMUEL CHASE

Put 1 tablespoon of chopped chives, 2 tablespoons of cream, the juice of ½ lemon, 1 chopped hard-boiled egg, 1 finely chopped celery heart, and ½ cup of cottage cheese into a mixing bowl. Season with salt and pepper and 2 pinches of paprika. Mix it well.

Cut the tops off 2 large tomatoes and put them (the tops) aside; do not cut off too much. Scoop out the insides carefully, leaving the shells intact. Do not use the insides in this recipe. Stuff the tomato shells with the above mixture and replace the tops.

Shred ½ head of lettuce and arrange it nest-like on 2 serving plates. Place the stuffed tomatoes into the nests.

Cut some celery julienne style as well as some carrots. Mix them together. Arrange them around the bottom of the tomatoes on top of the lettuce. Sprinkle a few chopped chives over the border of celery and carrots.

SOUP, JOHN MARSHALL

Put 1 pint of consommé and 1 pint of milk into a pot with ¼ cup of asparagus tips. Let it come to a boil. Crush a handful of very fine vermicelli and sprinkle it into the pot. Cover and boil slowly for 20 minutes.

Put the yolk of 1 egg into each soup plate as well as 1 tablespoon of cream, a small piece of butter, a sprinkle of pepper, and a sprinkle of salt. Pour the well mixed boiling soup over the egg, etc. Sprinkle with grated cheese.

POACHED EGGS, GEORGE W. CAMPBELL

Place 4 large croutons into a baking dish with 1 tablespoon of butter.

Poach 4 eggs, dry them well, and put them over the croutons.

Pass 1 cup of cooked spinach through a sieve. Place in a bowl and add 3 tablespoons of cream, 1 tablespoon of grated cheese, and 1 tablespoon of melted butter. When it is mixed it should have the consistency of heavy cream. Pour it over the eggs, sprinkle with a little more grated cheese, and bake for 7 or 8 minutes in a preheated hot oven. Season to taste.

SCRAMBLED EGGS, JOHN ARMSTRONG II

Place 3 finely chopped shallots into a pan with 2 tablespoons of butter and cook for 3 minutes. Add 1 dozen oysters and their liquor, 1 cup of cream, 1 pinch each of salt, pepper, and paprika, and a little chopped parsley. After it starts boiling, cook for 5 minutes.

Scramble 6 eggs and garnish with the above mixture. Place it around the eggs, making it look like a nest. Season to taste.

BROILED POMPANO, GEORGE DEWEY

Take a 1 pound pompano. Open and clean it. Do not remove head, tail or bones. Wash and dry thoroughly. Make a few incisions on both sides with a knife. Season each side with a sprinkle of salt. Place it on a baking platter with 1 tablespoon of butter and put it under a preheated moderate broiler for 10 minutes. Then turn it with a spatula and broil the other side for 10 minutes.

While the fish is broiling, peel 1 orange and ½ grapefruit. Remove all the white pulp and break up into sections.

Have 1 finely chopped shallot in readiness.

Place the broiled pompano on a hot serving platter. Sprinkle with 1 pinch of salt, 1 pinch of pepper, a few bread crumbs, and the finely chopped shallot. Put 2 tablespoons of butter into a pan and when they become sizzling hot pour over the top. Quickly arrange the orange and grapefruit sections decoratively over the fish. Pour 2 ponies of flaming brandy over the top and serve immediately.

ROAST GUINEA HEN, JOHN C. CALHOUN

Remove the entrails of 1 guinea hen. Prepare it for roasting. Do not wash it. Wipe the inside dry with a clean cloth and sprinkle a few pinches of salt and pepper inside the carcass. Put 1 whole clove of unpeeled garlic, 1 teaspoon of juniper berries, ¼ raw onion, 1 strip of bacon, 1 sprig of parsley, and 1 bay leaf into the cavity. Tie 4 strips of bacon onto the breast.

Lay the guinea fowl on a baking platter on its side and add 2 large tablespoons of butter. Put it in a preheated hot oven of 400° F. for 40 minutes and turn and baste it every 5 minutes.

Remove the guinea hen, empty the carcass, and place it on a hot serving platter. Keep it hot.

To the platter in which the fowl was roasted, add 2 tablespoons of butter, 1 tablespoon of chopped parsley, 1 finely chopped shallot, and ½ sherry-glass of dry sherry. Stir constantly, and when it comes to a bubbling boil, pour it over the guinea hen. Season.

POTATOES, WILLIAM T. BARRY

Put 1 finely chopped shallot into a frying pan with 1 tablespoon of butter. Peel and slice 3 cold boiled potatoes (that have been cooked with their skins). Add them to the frying pan. At the same time add 1 chopped peeled tomato. Cover and simmer for 10 minutes. Sprinkle with chopped parsley, season, and serve.

CAULIFLOWER, SMITH THOMPSON

Take 1 small, firm head of cauliflower. Cut off the stalk and all leaves. Wash, and boil whole until tender in plenty of water which has been salted. To keep the cauliflower white, add the juice of ½ lemon to the water while it is cooking.

Take it from the water and lay it on a clean cloth for a moment to remove all water. Place on a baking platter.

Mix 1 tablespoon of grated cheese, ½ clove of crushed garlic, and 1 tablespoon of bread crumbs. Sprinkle it over the cauliflower, leaving the center white.

Put 1 tablespoon of butter into a pan and add 2 finely chopped shallots, 2 finely chopped mushrooms, 1 clove of garlic which has been crushed into a little chopped parsley, 1 chopped peeled tomato, 1 sherryglassful of red wine, 1 tablespoon of grated cheese, and 1 teaspoon of Worcestershire sauce. Season with salt and pepper. Stir. Let it come to a boil and then pour it over the cauliflower, again leaving the center white. Over this center sprinkle a little chopped parsley. Place in a preheated hot oven for 10 minutes.

SALAD, RICHARD M. JOHNSON

Dice: 1 celery heart, the heart of 1 cold boiled artichoke, 1 slice of boiled ham, and 2 peeled, cold boiled potatoes (that have been cooked with their skins.) Add 3 tablespoons of French Dressing and mix.

Take 1 head of lettuce. Loosen the leaves, do not break them off, and remove the heart. Shred the lettuce heart. Put the shredded lettuce on a serving platter into the form of a nest and place the loosened head on top. Put the diced vegetables in the middle.

Cut 1 hard-boiled egg into quarters lengthwise and arrange it on top.

Sprinkle with a little chopped parsley. Slice 1 tomato and arrange it into a border around the edge of the shredded lettuce.

APRICOTS, MARGARET BRENT

Take 8, or more, canned or fresh apricots. If fresh they must be very ripe and must be sliced. Do not peel them. Put them into a pan and sprinkle with 1 tablespoon of vanilla sugar. Gently mix with 2 table-spoons of melted butter.

Prepare 3 slices of buttered toast. Cut each slice into 3 pieces. Butter a baking dish, place 3 strips of the toast on the bottom, and cover with half of the partially cooked apricots. Lay 3 more strips of toast over the apricots so that they are criss-cross with the ones on the bottom. Make another layer with the rest of the apricots. Place the last 3 strips of toast over the top so that they are parallel with the bottom strips. Sprinkle a little vanilla sugar on top and distribute 1 tablespoon of melted butter over it.

Bake in a preheated hot oven of 400° F. for 15 minutes.

This apricot dessert may be accompanied by any one of the 3 follow-ing sublime additions: first, by 2 ponies of any flaming cordial, brandy, rum or whiskey. It should be lit first and then poured over the top. Second, by a sauce which consists of 1 tablespoon of melted butter and 2 ponies of any kind of cordial. Mix and pour it over the dessert with-out making it flame. Third, by a sauce made of 1 tablespoon of melted butter, 1 tablespoon of cream, 1 tablespoon of vanilla sugar, and 2 ponies of any kind of cordial, etc. Mix and pour it over the dessert without mak-ing it flame.

Chapter XVII

A GREAT SURPRISE FOR MONSIEUR DRAGHUI

THE CERTIFICATE which is presented at the completion of the primary school is very seldom given to a pupil before he has reached the age of thirteen or fourteen. But, to spur the boys on, the tricolor belt was given to the best student of the week, and he was permitted to wear it only on Sundays and for special occasions. Every Saturday Monsieur Draghui gave us an oral examination. My rapid development permitted me to give a quick answer so that the other kids didn't have a chance. It pleased me and gave me more pep and power which facilitated my mind and prompted me to give still speedier answers.

But one week I was sick and had to spend several days in bed. Many of the kids asked Maman Camous when I would be able to return to class.

She said, "Well, Henri is very sick. He might have to stay in bed for a long time yet."

On Friday morning I was mad at myself. I thought I would have to surrender my tricolor belt to someone else that Saturday night or Sunday morning. It was a very long day to me, and from Friday night to Saturday morning I felt like a sentry. I was guarding that belt and was not ready to surrender it.

When I asked Maman Camous for my three bowls of coffee on Saturday morning, she said, "Henri, I think you are getting better."

"Yes, Mom."

She said, "I'm going to the farm now; you'll find everything your need here. Césarina will take care of you. Don't get up, and I think on Monday morning you'll be able to return to school."

After she had been gone a short time Césarina said, "I think I'll go to school now, Henri. If you want anything you'll probably find it on the table. I'll be back at noon."

Some of the kids came over to see me during the noon hour; one of them pointed to the tricolor belt and announced, "This belt might be mine today."

A second boy said, "I'll punch your nose. It's going to be mine."

A third said, "I'll kick you both out."

And still a fourth kid, whose name was Georges, stroked it and with a mocking look on his face said, "This belt will fit me wonderfully well tomorrow morning."

That last crack was too much for me. I said, "Oh, yes? I'll be ready to go to school with you this afternoon."

My four chums, in one moment, had almost become four enemies. Before they knew what was happening, I grabbed my tricolor belt and was out of the room. Bacci understood exactly what I meant to do, and he was ready. This time, instead of licking the faces of my chums, he would have bitten the leg of any one of them had they tried any funny business. They knew they couldn't catch me once I started to run.

Bacci barked with joy. He loved excitement because it gave him a chance to be noisy. He ran ahead of me in the street, barking and proclaiming that I was well again. He forgot that school was not for dogs· and jumped onto my desk, impatient with me for taking so long. When I arrived out of breath a few seconds later, he started some sort of dog talk as if he were saying, "Well, we beat them." I think I understood him to say also, "I'll be back at 4 o'clock with Blanchette, and then we'll run up the street together and make everyone get out of our way. Everybody except Maman Camous. But when we get here see that the tricolor belt is still yours." He kept on muttering to himself. I thought he was preparing to answer Monsieur Draghui's questions himself so we would be sure of getting the belt again.

In a moment he went out, and the class came to order. Monsieur

Draghui complimented me on having the will power and determination to overcome my sickness. My pale face, which made my freckles more pronounced, flushed with happiness at that encouragement from my grand professor.

We began answering the questions he asked us. In a flash my hand went up, and I called out the answer on the heels of his question. Every query was followed by such a quick answer that the whole class, instead of trying to compete, sat back and admired me. What surprised the teacher was the fact that on Friday morning the kids had all signed a paper which stated that if I were not present there would be no test. When I won, it pleased Monsieur Draghui; but when one of the older boys came forward with the list of signatures he was still more pleased, and his face showed great emotion. He placed the paper on his desk and ordered all of us to stand. Then, in a hushed voice, he said, "I am proud of all of you."

He shook hands with me and said, "Henri, you give us an example of determination which entitles you to the friendship of all the school. And the entire classroom, because it was already prepared not to take the tricolor belt from your sick-room in case you could not participate in the examination, gives us an example of loyalty. I am very proud of you."

It was too much for my freckled face, and I cried like the little kid that I was.

I managed to keep that tricolor belt for sixty weeks; it gave me the opportunity to obtain my diploma before the usual age.

Every year, a few days before Bastille Day, a professor from the Academy and a few of his assistants arrived to give an examination to those pupils who were ready to graduate. The mayor and the village dignitaries, including the four musicians: Straforello, flute; Ganzi, violin; Zaveri, cornet; and François Baza, bass viol, awaited their arrival at the entrance of our village. François Baza was the brother of the official pig killer of Contes. At the arrival of the professor and his colleagues, the musicians began to play the "Marseillaise." It was my privilege to be present among the celebrities of Contes since I was the proud possessor of the tricolor belt. After the mayor had finished shaking hands with the visitors each of the village dignitaries did the same. I was last in line, and when I shook the professor's hand he asked, "Is this the second mayor?"

"Yes, Monsieur le *professeur*," I said, " and I feel that I am a man already. I would like to have my diploma presented to me."

Monsieur Draghui, astonished but pleased nevertheless, said, "A very intelligent little fellow, very stubborn and well-deserving, but too young. He's not quite ten."

"Well, Monsieur Draghui," the visiting professor said, "we'll break the rule, and if the boy passes the examination, then he shall have his diploma. But if such a thing happens it will be the first time in all my career."

I was so pleased I stood on tiptoe like a ballet dancer, which made everyone laugh, even Monsieur Draghui, and caused the professor from the Academy to say, "My heavens! He has grown a few inches already and in only a few seconds."

I think I would have remained in that position indefinitely if he hadn't said, "It's all right, I've seen you."

That trick of standing on tiptoe was going to help me a few months later when I sought employment for the first time from Monsieur Charles Ulrick, manager of the Riviera's finest hotel, the Cap Martin.

Our four village musicians started to play a patriotic French march and produced enough noise to make the occasion a complete success. I was filled with emotion, but my face remained serious as my short legs tried to march in step with the man next to me who was twice my size. I was supposed to open the door of the schoolhouse for our guests and take the professor's brief case and place it on the table. We were almost there when I got out of line and ran to take my place at the door.

What a surprise it was for my chums, who were a few years older, to see me approach the benches that had been placed in front of the class for those who were to be questioned.

Every one of the big boys said, "Oh, oh, not here, Henri."

But I insisted, "Yes," pushing them aside.

In front of me I saw that the eyes of Monsieur Draghui and those of the visiting professor were upon me, and that elsewhere in the classroom there were hundreds of other eyes looking in my direction. They belonged to the rest of the kids and the villagers who were always present at the final examination. Only the fathers were allowed to attend the one given for the boys. Papa Camous was there in the rear. When the girls, who were taught by Madame Draghui, were given their examination by the visiting professor, mothers and fathers and everyone else attended.

In no time questions were ready to be fired at the prospective graduates. Each boy was to be questioned on the different subjects and later each was to answer, at great length, a question pertaining to the history of France.

I was seated at the last bench, and to everyone's amazement it was decided that I should be first. The questions demanded of me were answered with machine-gun rapidity, which pleased Monsieur Draghui immensely. The visiting professor turned and complimented him. To me he said, "Sit down."

Then I knew everything was all right; if you didn't pass the examination you were asked to sit at another bench.

After a few of my older chums had been questioned, the professor called on me again.

My face became pale and I thought he was going to change his mind and tell me to get out.

But on the contrary, he said, "Little fellow, tell us what you know about the French Revolution."

I felt as if all those beautiful souls who had died for the liberty of France were there in my heart and that I must speak for them. I felt the courage of Danton, the eloquence of Mirabeau, the terrible determination of Robespierre. I saw Chaumette, Lafayette, and Marat; the kindness of the beheaded King Louis XVI, and his beautiful and inimitable Queen, Marie Antoinette. I saw their orphaned children, the Dauphin, Louis XVII, who died in prison without attaining his crown, and his sister, the Princess, who was freed after much suffering and later became the Duchess D'Angoulême. Many other wonderful souls came at that moment to inspire me. A pupil was generally permitted five minutes in which to answer a question such as I had been given, and then a bell was rung by the professor, and the boy sat down. I became so enthusiastic I forgot where I was and kept talking on and on about the French Revolution, which I had learned to love so much at such an early age. I don't remember how long I talked, but no bell ever rang. I stopped only when I became aware of the classroom again. I saw moisture in the eyes of the visiting professor, and many others used handkerchiefs to blow their noses and to surreptitiously wipe their eyes. The professor himself applauded with the rest who made so much noise that if Badou's whip had been cracked in the classroom no one would have heard it.

The professor asked, "Who is the father of this boy?"

Papa Camous stood up. In one hand was his hat, one of those which I had won at the races. In the other he held a red handkerchief and, with it, reached up to wipe away the tears that were rolling down his cheeks.

I was surprised to hear the professor say, "Monsieur Charpentier, I compliment you on your son."

I'm sure it was the first time Papa Camous had ever been addressed by a name that was not his own. He had taken the place of my real father, a deceased lawyer whose name I bear and whom I never knew. Papa Camous had always loved me as his own.

The professor signed my diploma and handed it to Papa, whom he still addressed as "Monsieur Charpentier."

He said, "I have signed this diploma and now give it to you. Please give it, in turn, to Monsieur Draghui who will present it to the boy. My felicitations to all three of you."

There was no sign of jealousy on the part of my chums. I was very proud because I not only left the classroom wearing my tricolor belt, but I was the only kid with a diploma in his hand. The rest of the graduates had to wait until the next morning at eleven when they would receive theirs at the graduating exercises.

My Departure From Contes
My Arrival At The Cap Martin

A FEW WEEKS before my last evening in Contes, Jean Camous, the great and immortal chef, paid a visit to his home. That was after he discovered I had received my diploma. I informed him that now I was a grown man.

I wore the long pants which I had begged Maman Camous to let me have, and strutted in front of him. I stood on tiptoe and said, "Jean, look how tall I am. I want to work with you."

He looked at me, observing my tallness without looking at my feet, and said, "You're a big fellow, all right."

Jean knew there was no money in the Camous family with which to further my education. And I was just as pleased. I wanted to go to work so that I might start gratefully repaying all the kindness which had been bestowed on me by my foster-family.

"All right," he said, "I'll take you back with me tomorrow to see Monsieur Ulrick, and if he says it's all right, it'll be all right with me, too."

The next morning I accompanied my foster-brother to the office that Monsieur Ulrick maintained in Nice. After Jean shook hands with him he presented me and said, "This big man, my little brother Henri, wants to work. He has his diploma."

As Jean spoke I stood on tiptoe. My healthy looks, freckles included, seemed to help very much. I was not bashful and answered all the questions that were asked.

Monsieur Ulrick turned to Jean and said, "All right, Monsieur Camous, take that big man, your little brother, to the tailor and see that he is measured for three uniforms."

That meant I was engaged. Jean, who was only 23 and the head chef at the Cap Martin with 150 men under him, pulled his goatee and laughed because I twirled on the toes of my clumsy farmer shoes. How could I know that Nijinsky, the greatest dancer of them all, had been born that very same year?

After I had been measured for my uniforms, two for daily use and one for special occasions, such as the arrival of royalty, the tailor said to us, "Come back again in a week and we'll try them on. Then, if they fit, we'll send them directly to the Cap Martin."

We returned to Contes; and when the week was up, went back to the tailor. After everything had been arranged my foster-brother placed me in the care of Badou who took me safely home on top of his diligence. Jean went back to his work at the Cap Martin.

The same night I explained to all my school chums that I had three uniforms.

I said, "One is full of gold braid and gold buttons and has lace all over it. I look like Henri IV of Navarre."

One of them asked, "What does he look like?"

And I said, "Why! He looks like me!"

"But you look just like you did yesterday."

"Yes, but you didn't see me when I had my uniform on this morning. I looked beautiful."

Now they were envious.

One said, "Oh, you'll come back to Contes after you've been there a few days. How can you stay away from Bacci and Blanchette? And what will Don Albini do without you? There won't be any early mass without you."

I believe they were sincere. I liked them and they liked me; however, destiny will have its way and no tears will ever impede it. Those days were very short in one way and interminably long in another.

The last evening arrived. My chums came over to say goodbye; each mentioned some escapade or other and told me not to forget.

"Remember the cats, Henri?"

"Remember the licking you got for stealing the birds? You'd better save the pants so you'll remember it."

"Remember the frogs in the holy water?"

"And the time you let the donkey of Jacques into the church? We won't forget you, Henri."

And now, after fifty-four years, I know I haven't forgotten them.

After much laughing, because we were ashamed to cry, my friends went home.

Maman Camous said, "It is best that we go over to see Madame and Monsieur Draghui and Don Albini so you can say goodbye in person, Henri."

After a very sincere farewell on their part, we started out for home. On our way we had to pass the Place de Trinco and its fountain that was permitted to bubble continuously; sparkling water flowed into a receptacle at its base for the animals. I will always remember its tinkling music; its memory has journeyed with me throughout the five continents and is with me yet.

It was ten o'clock when Maman and I reached it. The October night was splendid. We stood there alone under a sky that was brilliantly studded with stars. The moon, in its third quarter, lit the mountainside and gave the effervescent water in the fountain a silvery gleam. It lit the face of my lovely Maman Camous.

After a few moments of silence, I said, "Maman, tomorrow I must leave you. I don't know how far the future will take me, and I don't know whether I'll always have the three *sous* or the five *sous* with which to buy stamps to write to you. But I do know that every day of your life you have risen before the sun. I promise you that every morning there will be a kiss for you in the sun from me. It'll be more regular than the postman."

She embraced me, and together we mixed a few tears. She wanted to say something, but couldn't find her voice. Later, before reaching our doorstep, she said, "Henri, you don't have to go. You are one of us and have always been in our hearts."

Papa Camous, Césarina, Celestin and Bacci were still up when we arrived home, and had very little to say; they were too filled with emotion. Bacci couldn't comprehend. He knew the stable was in order, with the exception of Fannie. She was gone and no other mule had, as yet, taken her place. Now then, here was some new tragedy of which he knew nothing.

The night was long and Bacci and I couldn't sleep. He licked my face for so long that I think he removed some of my freckles.

In the morning my last three bowls of coffee were waiting for me, but I could only get one down. Like a good soldier I didn't want anyone to come down to the diligence with me. My trunk was already at the station in Nice, where Badou had taken it the day before. It was a beautiful piece of English luggage and had previously belonged to Jean. Into that trunk, which was large enough to hold me, I had put four pairs of stockings that Maman Camous had knitted and two old pairs which Giroumetta, bless her, had made for me a few weeks previous to her death three years before. I kept them in memory of her. There were six handkerchiefs, the kind that were almost as large as tablecloths, and two old pairs of pants. That was the extent of my wardrobe, and there was plenty of room to spare. I was sorry Maman had sent the trunk away the day before; I fully intended to put Bacci into it, too.

I went out to say goodbye to the animals. I patted and embraced Bacci and told him to stay there in the stable. This time he obeyed. He licked my face once more and came to understand what it was that he could not comprehend the night before. The three devils had finally come to a parting of the way. Blanchette moved her whiskers in mastication and was surprised that I had no pail to use for her milk. Bicou, the donkey, moved his ears and swished his tail. The cow looked at me significantly with her soft eyes, and even Bismarck grunted, "Au revoir." He squealed, "In case you come back before Christmas, I'll see you again." Every pig Papa ever had could be sure of two things. First, that he would be called "Bismarck"; and second, that he would be butchered the week after Christmas. It was Papa's belief that to start the New Year right he must have blood sausage made from the freshly killed pig. Maman could make them with great artistry.

As I left that stable I felt I was leaving behind me dear friends that I had never thought of as animals. I knew that that evening one of them, Bacci, would be hopefully waiting for me, and that the rest of them would be waiting for him to tell them what it was all about. Alas! The days go by and time slowly takes care of everything.

I went back into the house, said goodbye to everyone again, and went alone down to the entrance of the village where Badou was stationed with his diligence.

From Contes he took me to the station in Nice, where I was to take the first train to Menton. That soft-hearted old fellow embraced me and said goodbye. He knew I had never told anyone the story of his famous soup.

I got into the third-class coach and felt like a grown man because I was travelling alone. In 45 minutes the train would reach Menton. It was quite different from my first trip to Monte Carlo with Maman Camous three years before, when I had met the great Escoffier. When we reached Monte Carlo I saw the elevator which Maman Camous had paid one *sou* to ride on, and my eyes became blurred. I was glad when the train started again. I pulled out my big handkerchief, wiped my eyes, and then remembered the way in which Jean Camous had presented me to Monsieur Ulrick. "This big man, my little brother," he had said. I thought, "A man doesn't cry." From that moment on, whenever I felt like crying, I swallowed my tears instead, and, like Madame Gasiglia, went on without showing them.

When we arrived in Menton I recognized the Hotel Cap Martin coachman by his uniform. He met all the trains and brought the guests to the hotel. This time, however, there were none; instead, there was the new page boy, Henri. The coachman placed my beautiful trunk on top of the stagecoach. No one would have believed that it could possibly belong to a little fellow from Contes. No. It was a trunk that should have belonged to a lord from England. We drove two miles to the Cap

Martin. The *concierge,* seeing the approaching stage-coach, couldn't tell how many people were inside. He pushed a button that rang bells on all four floors of the hotel. There were two valets on each floor who not only cleaned the shoes, suits, etc., of the guests, but also the parquet floors, which were always spick-and-span. Monsieur Ulrick, the eight valets, and the two main floor chambermaids were all assembled in the lobby ready to greet and accommodate the newly arrived guests. How surprised they were when the door of the stage-coach opened and only the new page boy stepped out!

But Monsieur Ulrick played his part. He said to the group, " A grand reception for the big man, the little brother of the chef Monsieur Camous."

One of the valets remarked, "Such a big trunk for such a little fellow."

When it was pulled down someone else said, "I think the trunk's empty. Maybe he thinks we have no room and he must sleep in it."

I smiled brightly at them and bowed to Monsieur Ulrick, who shook hands with me. Then I shook hands with the rest of them, and with that royal welcome I started the first day of my career.

That evening when the sun was setting I went out onto one of the porches of the hotel and addressed Old Sol, "Please give a kiss to my Maman Camous tomorrow morning and every morning. She'll be there in Contes preparing the coffee and waiting for you to arrive with the caress which I give to you to convey to her."

How wonderful is the heart of a woman. In the year 1935 Maman Camous reached the age of 100. On the twenty-eighth of December in that year she was destined to leave this life and enter another, the eternal, the immortal. On that morning she called her daughter-in-law Virginie, the widow of Celestin, and said, "Virginie, will you push my bed over to the window, please?"

"Yes, maman, but what for?"

"I want to see the sun rise; he'll have a kiss for me from Henri."

Those words were almost her last; she died an hour later.

I was in New York when, two weeks later, I received a letter that told me of her passing. "On that day," Virginie said, "the sun shone very, very brightly." My memory took me back to the little village of Contes and to that little fellow of ten. It took me back to that last evening, to the bubbling music of the fountain, to those eloquent moments of silence, and to the moonlight which illuminated the surrounding mountains and fell softly on the face of my lovely Maman Camous.

RECIPES

✦

HORS-D'OEUVRE, CHARLES CARROLL

✦

SOUP, EDWARD LIVINGSTON

✦

POACHED EGGS, HENRY KNOX

✦

SCRAMBLED EGGS, PETER B. PORTER

✦

BAKED OYSTERS, WILLIAM PINKNEY

✦

BEEF STEW, JOHN STEVENS

✦

POTATOES, JOHN NILES

✦

BRAISED LETTUCE, FRANCIS GRANGER

✦

SALAD, GEORGE M. DALLAS

✦

PUDDING, ANNA SHAW

✦

HORS-D'OEUVRE, CHARLES CARROLL

To 1 cup of cold cooked rice add: 1 chopped slice of boiled ham, 1 chopped hard-boiled egg (the egg must be cold), 2 finely chopped scallions, 1 chopped peeled tomato, 1 clove of garlic which has been crushed into a little chopped parsley, 2 tablespoons of bread crumbs, and 1 tablespoon of grated cheese. Season with salt and pepper. Mix well.

Cut the tops off 2 large green peppers, remove the insides, stuff with the above mixture, and pour a tablespoon of French Dressing over each.

SOUP, EDWARD LIVINGSTON

Put 1 tablespoon of butter into a pot and add 1 finely chopped leek, 1 finely chopped celery heart, 1/2 finely chopped onion, and 2 sliced mushrooms. Cover and simmer for 15 minutes. Then add 1 quart of consommé, cover, and boil for 40 minutes.

Place 1 tablespoon of cream and a small piece of butter into each soup plate. Season with salt and pepper. Pour the boiling soup over the cream and butter and sprinkle with a few chopped chives. Add croutons if you wish.

POACHED EGGS, HENRY KNOX

Boil 4 potatoes with their skins. Peel and slice them into a pan. Add 1 tablespoon of butter and cook until slightly browned. Place them into a baking dish.

Poach 4 eggs, dry them well and put them over the potatoes.

Put 1 tablespoon of butter into a separate pan. Add 1 finely chopped shallot, 2 thinly sliced mushrooms, 1 pinch of salt, 1 pinch of pepper, 2 pinches of paprika, 6 cooked shrimps which have been cut into small pieces, 1 tablespoon of grated cheese, 1/2 cup of cream, and 1 teaspoon of meat stock. Stir, and when it comes to a boil add it to the eggs and potatoes, and bake in a preheated oven for 8 minutes.

SCRAMBLED EGGS, PETER B. PORTER

Place 1 tablespoon of butter into a pan with 2 finely chopped shallots. Cook for 3 minutes. Add 5 thinly sliced mushrooms and place in a hot oven until they become crisp. Then take them from the oven.

Separately mix 1 finely chopped shallot which has been crushed into a little chopped parsley and 1 tablespoon of bread crumbs. Sprinkle it over the mushrooms. Add 1 pinch of salt, 1 pinch of pepper and 1 more tablespoon of butter. Stir.

Beat 6 eggs, add the above mixture and scramble. Season to taste.

BAKED OYSTERS, WILLIAM PINKNEY

Dry 1 dozen large oysters. Dip them into bread crumbs and place them into a baking dish.

Crush 2 cloves of garlic into 2 tablespoons of chopped parsley and mix it with 3 tablespoons of melted butter, 1 pinch of salt, and 1 pinch of pepper. With a spoon, distribute the parsley and garlic butter over the oysters. Arrange 6 partly broiled strips of bacon over the top and place in a preheated hot oven of 400° F. for 10 minutes.

BEEF STEW, JOHN STEVENS

Cut 1 pound of lean beef into small pieces, place into a frying pan and, without seasoning, butter, or anything else, fry the pieces until they become brown (about 10 minutes).

Then add 2 tablespoons of butter, 1 finely chopped onion, 2 finely chopped carrots, 1 pinch of salt, and 1 pinch of pepper. Stir and cook 5 more minutes.

After that add 2 cups of consommé, 3 peeled and sliced raw potatoes, 1/4 cup of diced green beans, 1/4 cup of fresh green peas, and 2 chopped peeled tomatoes. Place in a preheated hot oven of 400° F. for 1 hour, and look from time to time to see if there is enough juice on the stew so it won't burn. If necessary add water or consommé, 1 tablespoon from time to time.

Put 1 tablespoon of butter into a pan with 2 finely chopped shallots. Add 1 clove of garlic which has been crushed into 1 teaspoon of chopped parsley, 2 sherry-glasses of red wine and 1 teaspoon of mustard. Let it come to a boil and pour it over the stew after it has been in the oven 1 hour. Put it back in the oven for 5 more minutes. Season to taste.

POTATOES, JOHN NILES

Bake 2 large Idaho potatoes. Cut their tops off lengthwise (do not throw the tops away). Remove the insides.

Put 1 tablespoon of butter into a pan with 1 finely chopped shallot, 2 finely chopped mushrooms, ½ cup of cream, and a pinch each of salt and pepper. Cook over a small fire for 10 minutes. Then add the potato pulp. When it becomes thick add 1 egg yolk. Stir. Stuff the above mixture into the potato shells and replace the tops. Bake in a preheated hot oven of 400° F. for 10 minutes.

BRAISED LETTUCE, FRANCIS GRANGER

Wash 1 large head of lettuce and cut into quarters. Place into a baking dish with 1 cup of consommé. Put into a preheated hot oven for 40 minutes. Baste every 10 minutes and, if necessary, add a little more consommé.

Put 1 tablespoon of butter into a separate pan and add 2 finely chopped shallots, ½ cup of cream, 1 tablespoon of sweet sherry, 1 tablespoon of grated cheese, and 2 pinches of paprika. Season with pepper and salt. When it comes to a boil pour it over the braised lettuce.

Mix 1 tablespoon of bread crumbs, 1 tablespoon of grated cheese, and a little chopped parsley. Sprinkle it over the braised lettuce and place it back in the hot oven for 10 minutes.

SALAD, GEORGE M. DALLAS

Place the white leaves of 1 crisp chicory salad into a bowl. The green part may be saved and cooked later as a vegetable. Add 1 chopped peeled tomato. Sprinkle with a few large croutons that have been rubbed with garlic and cut into small pieces. Mix. Add 3 tablespoons of French Dressing and mix again.

PUDDING, ANNA SHAW

Beat the whites of 4 eggs until they are stiff, and stand them aside for a moment.

Put ¾ cup of vanilla sugar into a pan. (Or, ¾ cup of sugar and 1 or more teaspoons of vanilla extract, according to your taste.) Add the yolks of 4 eggs, ½ cup of melted butter, and ⅕ cup of cornstarch (which has been dissolved in a little cold milk). Place over a very low fire and stir constantly with a wooden spoon to mix it well. Do not let it boil. Remove the pan from the fire when the ingredients are nicely mixed. Then add the stiffly beaten whites. Mix thoroughly.

Butter a mold and sprinkle it with a few pinches of flour. Pour the contents of the pan into it and place it in a pan of boiling water. Put in a preheated hot oven of 400° F. for 30 minutes.

Put 1 more tablespoon of vanilla sugar (or just 1 tablespoon of plain sugar if you have used the vanilla extract) into a pan with 2 more egg yolks and 2 sherry-glasses of sweet white port wine. Place it on the fire and beat constantly until it becomes thick.

Remove the pudding from the mold and place it on a serving platter. Accompany it with the above thickened sauce, but serve separately.

Chapter XVIII

MY FIRST NIGHT IN THE CASTLE OF KINGS

I COULD TELL that my entrance to the Hotel Cap Martin had been a disappointment to the valets and chambermaids. They had expected a king or a queen, or at least some royalty, and the only arrival had been a freckle-faced kid from Contes. One of the porters, Michel, a native of Menton, took possession of the big trunk which contained my meager wardrobe. He was surprised at its light weight and said, "Some kings come to the Cap Martin with twenty trunks and depart with only three, but this fellow brings an empty one and expects to take it home full."

He winked an eye, and I understood. I didn't expect to buy shoes, hats or suits; at that time I believed a fellow should have only one suit at a time. In Contes, Maman and Papa Camous always believed as well as practiced the same thing. Papa had two suits, one that he wore every day, and another that he called a new suit but which was really fifteen years old. In my mind my trunk was going to hold everything that Contes had never seen before. I thought of brightly colored empty cigar and cigarette boxes. As long as Contes had never seen a colored cigar box, it would be an innovation there. I knew that Don Albini would like one in which to put some of his relics so that people would exclaim every time he showed them. It was my opinion that the *gendarmes* would have arrested anyone who threw away one of those beautiful boxes, and placed him in jail as a vandal.

I was shown to my room and saw that it was furnished with three beds. One was already occupied by Jean Devisse; the second was to be occupied later by a Swiss boy named Antoine; the third was to be occupied that very night by the ten year old ex-champion runner of Contes. The room was very beautiful compared to the humble ones in the farmer homes of my village. Such a room did not exist in Contes. There was a large mirror on the wall; it was the first time I had ever seen my complete self from head to toe. Maman Camous had a looking-glass whose back was so worn that I could only see one eye at a time. In those days the ladies of Contes did not rouge or powder and, therefore, had no need for mirrors. When I saw all my freckles I realized that no matter where I went I could never be lost. I thought, "Now I know why Bacci licked my face so much. He thought the freckles were something to eat. But he fooled himself, because the more he licked the shinier they got, and still he couldn't remove them. One thing about him, though, he was never discouraged; he tried the same thing over the next day."

Jean Devisse, who was thirteen, came into our room and asked, "Who shot you in the face?"

"What do you mean?"

"Where did you get all those freckles?"

I answered him with, "Don Albini, the priest of my village, says there's a lot of mystery in this life. Why don't you write and ask him?"

At our first meeting Devisse found out that the fellow who had been "shot in the face" was far from bashful; we stood there together looking into the mirror. He extended his arm, shoulder high, and I stood under it. He wanted to show me how tall he was and how small I was. By a look he tried to impress on me that he was the boss. I leaped across the bed without touching it, doing it so fast that Jean was astonished.

He said, "If you do that in front of the guests you'll make money without having to clean the floors. But don't run away. Here, take this broom, cloth, brush, sponge, pail, and soap, and come with me. I'll give you your first lesson."

I was entranced. No matter where I looked or stepped, everything was shining. On our way, because he saw that I walked between the rugs, he said, "Do you think that's the road to take to reach the lobby?"

We stopped and looked at each other. The boy from Contes had never seen rugs like those before. The clean stone floors of Maman Camous and every lady in the village had never been covered with carpets or rugs. Even Madame Gasiglia had none.

I asked, "Do you mean that you walk on such beautiful things with your dirty shoes?"

To Jean Devisse, I realized, it was only a rug, but to me it was a picture that should have been been hung on the wall. Those large and beautiful Oriental rugs in the lobby, I thought, had never been walked on before by such funny shoes as mine. I stepped on one, and then thought that Jean might be playing a trick on me and trying to get me into trouble, so I walked between and around them for the rest of the day and evening. The marble walls and mosaic floors were also something new to me.

I was given instructions to proceed with the cleaning. I didn't have much time to look at the walls in the lobby; I was occupied with watching where I put my feet. I was intrigued by those rugs. When I finally did raise my eyes to look around, my surprise surpassed any that I had felt since my arrival that morning. I saw Jean Devisse and myself reflected in so many mirrors I was scared. I needed him to lead me around, because if I had been left alone I would have bumped my nose on too many of them before finding an exit. When I saw all of the Henris reflected there, I thought of Bacci and Blanchette and what they would have done had they been there. Bacci would have barked at all the other Baccis, and Blanchette would have rushed into the mirrors in pursuit of those other one-horned Blanchettes. What destruction! Blanchette might even have lost her other horn! It would certainly have been even more confusing to them than it had been to me.

Devisse took me into the kitchen where I saw my foster-brother Jean. He embraced me and asked for news from Contes. He asked me if I was hungry. But the excitement of everything I had seen and felt took away my desire for food. I couldn't eat.

In order to get to work at 4:30 in the morning, we had to go to bed early in the evening. We had to wash the marble walls, wax the mosaic floors, and clean the rugs; and that had to be done early. We had to clean the lamp chimneys, because electricity and gas had not yet been installed in the hotel. The Cap Martin was kept like the palaces of the old kings. Perfumed candles were burned at the same time as the kerosene lamps to take away the disagreeable odor of the oil. We had to polish the chandeliers that held the perfumed candles.

When I found myself in bed that first night I missed the sweet voice of Maman, the kind face of Papa, and my bed companions, Celestin and Bacci. I thought of Césarina, too, and the whole village rolled in a panorama before my closed eyes. My young heart realized for the first time the meaning of the words "Home, Sweet Home." I had lost my sweet home in Contes and was on the way to new adventures and a new life, one that was to be my very own. I forgot my newly acquired manhood, and tears wet my pillow. Thank goodness Jean Devisse was asleep so I could cry my heart out without disturbing him. Now my face was being washed by my own tears and not by Bacci's tongue.

I didn't sleep all night. I got up, washed my face, dressed, and then noticed by Jean's alarm clock that it was 4 A.M. As long as I couldn't sleep myself, I was anxious to wake him up even if it was a half hour too early. I shook him, and he looked at me out of sleepy eyes and asked, "What time is it?"

"Five o'clock."

He jumped out of bed without looking at the clock. He was confused and mad because he thought he was late.

He said, "Hurry up! Hurry up!"

"I don't need to hurry, I'm ready."

Still he didn't look at the time, and when we arrived in the lobby, ready for work, the quarter hour chimed. He looked at the clock, opened his eyes wide for the first time that day, and exclaimed, "What? It's only 4:15?"

He looked at me as if he were the big boss and said angrily, "You told me it was 5 o'clock."

I asked, "Why make so much noise? We're only 15 minutes early."

Then he said: "When I say 4:30 I don't mean 4:15."

I found out that my new teacher, the little Devisse, was worse than Don Albini and Monsieur Draghui put together. Fifteen minutes to him meant more than it did to the other two.

When he saw that I was biting my lips and that my fists were ready for anything that might happen, he realized that he, too, was just another page boy and not the boss. From then on we became good friends; and the freckle-faced fellow from Contes became the freckle-faced fellow of the Cap Martin. The good teachings of Monsieur Draghui and Don Albini were to remain with me, the guiding influences that attended every decision I ever made. Today, half a century later, those bright and shining fundamental truths are still in my possession, and have never become rusty from disuse.

Jean Devisse and I cleaned and polished until it was 8 o'clock. It was the first time 8 o'clock had come and I had not had my breakfast. No three bowls of coffee, I thought, and no Bacci to lick them after I had finished.

Jean took me to the kitchen, where I sat down at the table while he poured out two bowls of coffee. There was a new kind of fancy French bread that I had never tasted before but which I liked very much. It took only a moment to break it into the bowl and eat it. I sat and waited to see what that fellow Devisse, who was a slow eater, would do. When he saw that my bowl was empty he said, "You can take as much coffee as you like here." With that good news, and almost before he finished the sentence, my bowl was filled again. More French bread, and the second bowl was finished before Jean had his first. I filled it for the third time without waiting for any new orders, and he looked at me and asked, "How long are you going to keep that up?"

I had the best of him when I said, "Three is the limit."

My third bowl of coffee had disappeared before Devisse, the slowpoke, had finished his second.

On the way back to the lobby to finish our cleaning, he placed his hand over my belly and asked, "How can a little guy like you hold so much coffee?"

Later on, when we became better acquainted, he learned the story

of the three bowls of coffee that I had had every morning in Contes.
Years later, in 1925, when Devisse was 48 and *concierge* at the Riviera
Palais in Nice, I arrived at his home to pay him a visit. His wife placed
five bowls of coffee on the table. One for Jean, one for herself, and three
for me.

Jean asked, "Do you remember your first morning at the Cap
Martin?"

We smiled affectionately at each other in remembrance, and to
please them both, as well as myself, I finished all three before they finished theirs.

Jean turned to his wife and said, "Didn't I tell you he would?"

But to return to my first morning at the Cap Martin and the two
boys of ten and thirteen. We finished our cleaning at 10:30 and then
went to change into our page boy uniforms. At 11 o'clock we went to
have lunch. It was then that I received another big surprise. I went
up to Tony, one of the cooks in charge of feeding the staff, held out
my plate and said, "Monsieur Tony, if you please."

His big fork and knife reached down and brought up an enormous
piece of roast veal which he placed on a board and cut. He put a
very large piece onto my plate, and I asked, "How many is this for?"

He said, "All for you, my little fellow, you need to grow."

I thanked him, thoroughly hypnotized by the size of that meat. I
thought of the Camous family and how happy I would have been to
offer them my piece of veal. I remembered the roast that Madame
Christini had offered to Maman Camous, and also the potato meat that
Maman had made which contained no meat at all. I remembered her
meat and potatoes which contained one pound of meat and fourteen
pounds of potatoes. I finally reached the table where each one seated
had a pint of claret and was enjoying his lunch. I kept looking at the
big piece of meat which weighed over a pound. The aroma was exciting, but the thought of Contes was more powerful, and I cried as only
a boy my age could cry when his whole heart longed for home. Once
more my stomach lost its desire for food; my heart and mind were filled
with emotion, and I couldn't eat.

Today, fifty-four years later, when I think of the poverty of Contes and the richness with which I was in contact, I can cry afresh from the original emotion.

My Initiation

THE FIRST FEW DAYS at the Cap Martin were spent in just looking around. I was impressed by the grandeur, and after a short time decided that, having seen it all, I was, indeed, a man of the world.

Monsieur Ulrick called me to him and said, "Henri, I think you have shrunk since the last time I saw you."

I stood on tiptoe and then said, "Monsieur, I present myself."

He said, "Wait a minute, *petit,*" and then called to his wife in English, "darling, come here."

Never having heard the word "darling" before, I thought it was her name. A tall and slender blue-eyed blonde, the perfect type of English beauty, entered the room. She didn't speak very good French and whatever she said had an English accent. I bowed deeply and graciously, even at that early age, and she made a remark to Monsieur Ulrick that I didn't understand.

He said, "Do that again. Stand on your toes."

Madame "Darling" Ulrick looked at me and, because I raised myself so quickly, they both laughed. She asked, "Can you walk that way?"

I didn't wait for permission from Monsieur Ulrick but twirled around the room on my toes. They both laughed so hard they had to sit down.

Madame came over to me and said, "You must be very polite and nice to the guests. Before long her Majesty Queen Victoria, my own queen, will arrive, and since you're the smallest page boy and your actions are so quick, I've chosen you to attend her personally. It will be your duty, when her Majesty arrives, to present your arm so that she may use it as a balustrade in descending from her carriage. You'll then assist her to the elevator where you'll give her into the care of her ladies in waiting."

I said, "Yes, Madame 'Darling' Ulrick."

Madame and Monsieur screamed. They said something in English and laughed still more. I was stupefied and, not knowing at what they were laughing, joined in the merriment. Why should I cry when everyone else was laughing? Neither of them explained, and for a long time whenever I spoke to, or about, Madame I always addressed her as Madame "Darling" Ulrick. I believe she was pleased to have everyone know she was the darling of that fine man, Charles Ulrick. I learned later from Jean Camous, who spoke perfect English, that "darling" meant *"cherie"* in French and is a word which is very intimate, gentle and sweet. I realized I had intruded on the privacy of Madame and Monsieur Ulrick.

Later that day when I had a package to deliver to Madame "Darling," I went to their apartment and found that Monsieur was there too.

In a very polite and humble way I said in French, "Madame Ulrick, please excuse me for calling you Madame 'Darling' Ulrick. I thought it was your name, and only discovered the significance of the word 'darling' this morning. I hope you will forgive me."

She said, "There is nothing to forgive because the word is so lovely and so sweet coming from you. When you call me that in front of other people they'll know that Monsieur and I are very happy together. All your life I hope you'll remember that the first time you met Madame Ulrick you gave her the name of 'darling' in your mind."

I had never heard Papa Camous call Maman anything but Alesandrina, and everyone else had always been called by his first name.

Monsieur Ulrick said, "Call Madame Ulrick 'darling,' but don't call her *'cherie.'* "

I became as red as a ripe tomato, and they both patted my face; she the left cheek and he the right.

Madame Ulrick said in English, which I tried to remember, "This little fellow is all right."

Instead of going directly to the lobby I ran down to the kitchen where Jean Camous was ordering his men about, and demanded, "Quick, Jean, quick, I have something I want to ask you before I forget!"

He laughed and asked, "What is it?"

I told him about Madame and Monsieur Ulrick and asked him what she meant by "this little fellow is all right."

"That means you have taken a step forward, now don't change."

Then I knew that at the Cap Martin I had two good friends in Madame and Monsieur Ulrick.

My days of apprenticeship, which were served in learning the ways of life in a hotel, were full of problems for me. From the humble village of Contes to the great Cap Martin was a tremendous jump for the incorrigible freckle face.

One day, while I was serving as inside doorman, a very tall English gentleman approached calling, "Boy" in English. At first I didn't answer because in the dialect of Contes there was a word similarly pronounced that meant "rascal." I wondered how he knew about my actions in Contes. I knew that none of my school chums would have squealed on me, since Monsieur Draghui was the deadly enemy of a squealer.

When I didn't answer, he said in French, *"Petit."* By his speech I could tell he was not a Frenchman. He spoke with an accent that was similar to that of Madame "Darling" Ulrick.

He repeated, *"Petit"* and then added, "water closet."

I was embarrassed again. I had never heard the last two words before. If Bacci had been there I believe he would have bitten me in the leg to urge me on with some sort of a reply, and at the same time he would have asked himself, "Why doesn't he speak patois or French?"

The Englishman himself came to my rescue when he said, *"Urinoir."*

Then I understood. I stood on tiptoe once more because the English gentleman was so tall and I was, by comparison, so small. He looked at me in surprise to see how much I had suddenly grown.

I said, *"Par ici,* monsieur," and led the way.

I didn't know at the time that there was such a thing as a lavatory for the employees as well as one for the guests. I thought a man was a man and a lavatory was a lavatory. We reached the narrow service stairs, which were comfortable for me but not for the tall Englishman. They were dark so I said, "Thirty-two steps down, monsieur." I couldn't offer him my shoulder to lean on because he was too tall. We reached our destination, and I stood outside the door and waited for him to come out so I could lead him back. When we returned to the lobby, he gave me a silver *écu,* one silver dollar.

He said, *"Au revoir,* boy."

I liked the *"Au revoir"* part but not the "boy." However, the silver dollar paid for the last word, which I thought meant "rascal." I was still trying to guess who could have squealed on me.

There was a big surprise in store for me. A few days later Monsieur Ulrick received a letter from the English gentleman telling him what had happened. The manager hurried to the lobby and demanded to know who had taken a gentleman downstairs to the lavatory. I proudly came to the front and said, "I did." Monsieur Ulrick turned in anger to the concierge, "I blame you for this. Why don't you instruct the boy?"

When Monsieur disappeared into his office, the concierge, his face red from the undeserved rebuke, called Jean Devisse and said, "Take this farmer to the lavatory for the guests and submerge his head in the toilet. Maybe the next time he'll know better."

Jean took me to a wonderful salon of porcelain, the white fixtures of which were magnificent. I couldn't believe my eyes. Even as Devisse carried out his instructions, it occurred to me that Maman Camous and everyone else in Contes, had they been there, would have said, "Such a place should be made into the kitchen."

The German concierge hated me for the humiliation my error had brought him. Every time a guest was ready to depart he would send me up to the tower telegraph station with a dispatch. That intriguing place would have delighted any boy's heart. The semaphore signals,

298

as they flashed across the sapphire sea, were very mysterious to me. But when I discovered that the concierge had sent me up there so I would miss my final opportunity to receive pay for many errands that I had, in the past, profitlessly performed for the departing guest, those semaphore signals lost their charm. I returned to the lobby three different times, and each time the derisive concierge hailed me as stupid while the other boys bragged of their tips. I decided that I was smarter, and the next time I was sent off with a dispatch I took it obediently. However, when I was beyond his sight I ran back, climbed through a first floor window, and as the departing guest came down the circular stairs I saluted, bowed and made flattering remarks, all out of sight of the concierge, who was hidden from view by the heavy draperies. To me the guest who departed was, in rank, no less than a baron; several I made counts, and occasionally in a burst of enthusiasm I said, "Farewell, *mon prince*." Some of them were flattered; others, I think, found my smallness wistful and pathetic. I received ten francs where other boys would have received three. I had a ten franc gold piece in my pocket at the very moment that day when the concierge said once more, "Stupid, you don't run fast enough. Another guest has departed." I grinned behind my hand.

That morning while Monsieur Ulrick had been reprimanding the concierge I noticed that he had one eye on my shoes, the shoes of Contes and the same ones that caused someone to remark that first time I had been to Nice with Maman Camous, "With those freckles and those shoes, you'll never lose him." They had been handmade by the shoemaker of Contes and had cost Maman eighty cents (four francs); in those days that was a great expense to her. They were made to fit either foot; the left one could be worn on the right, and vice versa. I could always tell by the knots I left in the strings which foot I had worn the shoe on the day before, and so I reversed them each day. All the boys in the village of Contes wore the same kind.

I sensed what was coming when, later in the day, Monsieur Ulrick called me to his office and said, "Henri, those shoes you have on can't be worn here. Change them."

I said, "Yes, monsieur," and compared for the first time my clumsy, rough farmer shoes with his that were as soft as a lady's gloves and were so highly polished that they mirrored the blue pattern of the huge porcelain vase beside which he was standing. I found Michel, the porter, and begged him to tell me where Monsieur Ulrick had purchased his shoes. He said, "They are made by Monsieur Verrane, the shoemaker in Menton."

I went to Menton and spoke to Monsieur Verrane, who laughed at me and thought he was ending the matter when he declared, "Why, shoes such as Monsieur Ulrick's cost twenty francs!"

I said, "Twenty-two francs if I have them by tomorrow night."

To show that I could pay for them I drew more than that sum out of my pocket.

When I returned for them the next evening the shoemaker threatened his big son with the back of his hand, saying, "You'd better take an example from this boy. He has only worked a few days and now he's able to step from these old farmer shoes into the ones I've made, and for which I'm charging him eighteen francs. I only wish I were rich enough to make them for nothing."

I gazed in admiration at Monsieur Ulrick's shoes in miniature.

Jean Devisse and Antoine slept like tops, but I woke twice that night to reach down and touch those shoes.

I put them on in the morning and before 7 o'clock brought myself under the gaze of Monsieur Ulrick.

I said *"Bonjour,* Monsieur Ulrick" three times before at last he exclaimed over them. Then, when he realized what I had done, he handed me twenty francs.

He said, "I want to pay for them, Henri."

"But," I exclaimed, "Monsieur Verrane, the shoemaker, only charged me eighteen francs!"

"Then keep the two extra ones anyway for being so honest."

RECIPES

✤

HORS-D'OEUVRE, PHILIP LIVINGSTON

✤

SOUP, ROBERT SMITH

✤

POACHED EGGS, ALEXANDER J. DALLAS

✤

SCRAMBLED EGGS, LEWIS CASS

✤

BAKED TROUT, SAMUEL OSGOOD

✤

VEAL SAUTE, JAMES RUMSEY

✤

POTATOES, AMOS KENDALL

✤

CELERY, SAMUEL SOUTHARD

✤

SALAD, DANIEL D. TOMPKINS

✤

SOUFFLE, ANNE HUTCHINSON

✤

HORS-D'OEUVRE, PHILIP LIVINGSTON

Prepare a pancake batter, using 1 egg, 1 tablespoon of flour, 2 tablespoons of milk, and a pinch of salt. Mix well. It should have the consistency of heavy cream. This amount will make 4 small pancakes, enough for 2.

Put 1 teaspoon of butter into an omelet pan and let it become very hot. Make 4 very thin pancakes, one at a time, and let each one become brown. Use 1 teaspoon of butter in making each pancake.

Finely chop: 1 stalk of celery, 2 cold boiled potatoes that have been cooked with their skins, 1 peeled tomato, 1 hard-boiled egg, 5 anchovy fillets, and 2 shallots. Add 2 tablespoons of French Dressing and mix well.

Place a pancake on each serving plate and spread the above finely chopped well mixed ingredients over them. Cover with the 2 remaining pancakes.

SOUP, ROBERT SMITH

Fry 2 small, very thin pancakes in butter. Roll and cut them very fine, like shoestrings. To 1 quart of consommé, add ½ cup of cooked shelled green peas. When it comes to a boil add 2 beaten eggs and stir it well. Add the finely cut pancakes and remove from the fire immediately. Season. Sprinkle with grated cheese.

POACHED EGGS, ALEXANDER J. DALLAS

Boil 1 handful of noodles and strain them well. Add 1 tablespoon of butter and place them into a baking dish in the shape of a nest.

Poach 4 eggs, dry them well, and place them on the nest of noodles.

Into a separate pan thinly slice 1 mushroom. Add 1 tablespoon of butter, 1 finely chopped shallot, and 2 chopped peeled tomatoes. When it comes to a boil add ½ cup of cream. Let it come to a boil again, season, and pour it over the eggs and noodles. Bake for 8 minutes in a preheated hot oven.

SCRAMBLED EGGS, LEWIS CASS

Dice ½ pound of fresh codfish. Put 1 tablespoon of butter into a pan with 2 finely chopped shallots. Cook for 3 minutes. Add the diced raw codfish. Brown it. Then add 2 chopped peeled tomatoes, ½ sherry-glass of sherry, another tablespoon of butter, 1 pinch of salt, 1 pinch of pepper, 1 clove of garlic which has been crushed into a little chopped parsley, and 1 leaf of basil. Cook for 35 minutes.

Scramble 6 eggs and garnish them with the codfish, etc. Season to taste.

BAKED TROUT, SAMUEL OSGOOD

Take a 1 pound trout. Open and clean it. Leave on head and tail. Do not remove bones. Wash and dry thoroughly.

Put 2 finely chopped shallots into a baking platter with 1 tablespoon of melted butter, 2 finely chopped mushrooms, 1 pinch of pepper, and 1 pinch of salt. Lay the trout on the platter. Finely chop 2 more shallots and 2 more mushrooms. Mix them with 2 finely chopped English walnuts and a little chopped parsley. Sprinkle it over the fish. Distribute 2 tablespoons of melted butter over the top and place in a preheated hot oven of 400° F. for 25 or 30 minutes. Season to taste. An accompanying small bottle of white wine will give this trout a delicious taste.

VEAL SAUTE, JAMES RUMSEY

Purchase 1½ pounds of shoulder veal. Cut it into small pieces.

Put 1 finely chopped onion into a frying pan with 2 tablespoons of butter. Add the veal and sauté for 15 minutes until it becomes brown Place it in a casserole and add 3 diced boiled carrots, ½ cup of cooked fresh green peas, 1 cup of consommé, and 1 sherry-glassful of white wine. Season with a sprinkle of salt and pepper. Stir and put in a preheated hot oven of 400° F. for 45 minutes.

After that time place 1 tablespoon of butter into a separate pan with 1 finely chopped shallot. Cook for a moment and then add ½ cup of cream. Let it come to a boil.

Chop 2 hard-boiled eggs, mix them with a little chopped parsley and sprinkle over the sauté. Then pour the cream sauce over the eggs. Put it back in the hot oven for 5 minutes. Serve with either boiled noodles, spaghetti or rice. Season to taste.

POTATOES, AMOS KENDALL

Bake 2 large Idaho potatoes. Cut their tops off lengthwise (do not throw the tops away). Remove the insides.

To the insides, add 1 cup of cooked chopped cauliflower, 1 tablespoon of cooked rice, 1 tablespoon of grated cheese, 1 tablespoon of chili sauce and 1 tablespoon of butter. Season with salt and pepper. Mix well. Stuff the mixture into the potato shells. Sprinkle a little grated cheese over each and replace the tops. Put in a preheated hot oven of 400° F. for 10 minutes.

CELERY, SAMUEL SOUTHARD

Take 2 bunches of celery. Cut off the roots and leaves. Clean thoroughly. Leave whole. Boil until tender in plenty of water which has been salted.

Take them from the water and lay them on a clean cloth for a moment to remove all water.

Broil 2 thin slices of raw ham and lay one at each end of a baking platter. Arrange the celery so that the ham can be seen at the ends of the platter.

Stir 2 tablespoons of grated cheese into ½ cup of cream. Add 1 pinch of paprika and 1 tablespoon of melted butter. Mix well and pour it over the celery.

Mix 1 tablespoon of finely chopped walnuts, 1 tablespoon of bread crumbs, and 1 tablespoon of chopped, crisply broiled bacon. Sprinkle it over the top. Place in a preheated hot oven for 10 minutes. Season

SALAD, DANIEL D. TOMPKINS

Wash a few handfuls of tender young dandelions. Clean them well and let them remain in cold water for a while to become crisp. After the leaves have been removed from any green salad, they should be put under cold running water for a few minutes. Unlike the cooked vegetable, the fresh salad must be crisp and its dressing must not be put on until the moment of serving.

Shake off water without bruising the greens. Cut the dandelions. Add 2 peeled and sliced cold boiled beets, 1 chopped hard-boiled egg, and a few large croutons that have been rubbed with garlic. Mix and place in a salad bowl. Pour 3 tablespoons of French Dressing over it.

SOUFFLE, ANNE HUTCHINSON

Beat the whites of 6 eggs until they are stiff, and stand them aside for a moment. The yolks of 3 eggs only are used in this recipe.

Put 1¼ cups of milk into a saucepan. Add ⅕ cup of sifted flour and ¾ cup of vanilla sugar. (Or, ¾ cup of sugar and 1 teaspoon or more, as you like, of vanilla extract.) If, however, you do use the already prepared vanilla sugar, add ½ vanilla bean during this first stage. Stir constantly over a small fire until it thickens. Remove the vanilla bean, wash it, and put it back into your jarful of vanilla sugar for future use. Remove the thickened sugar, flour, and milk from the fire. Pass it through a sieve. Quickly stir in 3 beaten egg yolks. Mix it well and immediately add the 6 stiffly beaten egg whites. Stir it well.

Take a pyrex baking dish that is no more than 2 inches deep. Butter it thoroughly, using your fingers, and sprinkle a little powdered sugar into the bottom.

Have ready 2 crushed macaroons. Mix them with 1 tablespoon of curaçao. Stir into the saucepan and then pour the contents into the dish. To obtain the best results, the baking dish must be completely filled.

Have the oven preheated and turned to 250° or 300° F. to start. Bake it 5 or 6 minutes at that temperature and then turn it up to 350° F. Total baking time is approximately 25 minutes. Three minutes before removing it from the oven sprinkle a little powdered sugar on top of the soufflé to give it a slightly brown and lustrous appearance. Serve immediately.

Chapter XIX

HOW I MET QUEEN VICTORIA

I WAS READY and anxiously waiting to carry out the instructions Madame "Darling" Ulrick had given me concerning Queen Victoria.

Alas! When Her Majesty arrived at the hotel I was absent. I had been sent to Monte Carlo on a very urgent errand by the Duchess of Rutland. Consequently Jean Devisse was the mobile balustrade for Her Majesty Queen Victoria.

When I returned from Monte Carlo he laughed, "Ha, ha, ha!" He made me think of Gris, the donkey of Jacques. I was far from pleased, and, to tell the truth, I was mad enough to kick like Gris, too.

However, I was recompensed for having missed Queen Victoria by that grand old lady, the duchess, whom it was a privilege to serve. She gave me a twenty franc gold piece for my errand. That was four dollars.

She said, "Take this and buy some bonbons for yourself, or send some to your maman."

I replied, "If you'll permit me, *Madame la duchesse,* I'll save this money and later help Maman and Papa Camous whom I would like to repay for all the kindness and love they have given me."

The duchess asked for more of my family history. She discovered that my name was Henri and that I was an orphan, and then she gave me a bill of 100 francs extra to send to Maman Camous. She asked me for Maman's address, which I gave to her.

She said, "I'll take care of the bonbons myself, Henri."

And from that day until she died, which was fourteen years later in

1904, the Duchess of Rutland sent Maman Camous a ten pound box of the best chocolates every month. The whole village tasted them, even Don Albini. Contes named the boxes of candy "Duchess Chocolates."

I first met that grand old lady in the lobby of the Cap Martin. It was almost time for dinner, and she was seated there reading a newspaper. Her hair was white and there were blue pencilings on the back of her hands. Each of her finger-nails had been cared for as if it were a jewel. I stood close to her chair and followed the direction of her gaze, and, although I couldn't read English at that time, I marked her place as she rose to answer the gong that signaled everyone to dinner.

I went to the kitchen, and word came back that *Madame la duchesse* desired to eat Chicken Beaulieu, which I later learned to make under the supervision of Jean Camous and still make today.

When she emerged from the dining room two hours later I could have told her better than a clairvoyant why she smiled; I had actually seen her smile compounded. She returned to her chair in the lobby where I knelt to bring her footstool into position and then handed her the newspaper. With my finger, I indicated the place where she had stopped reading.

She asked with amazement, "But, how do you know the very line?"

"I followed Madame's eye. I hope I was not impertinent."

She patted my face and my nostrils were filled with the delicate odor of her violet perfume. With big eyes, I watched her take a little purse of gold fabric from the pocket of her skirt. She opened it and selected a gold coin, twenty francs, and placed it in my hand.

If a day passed in which she didn't see me she would pretend to be worried and ask, "Let me look at you, *petit,* have you grown up?" Every Sunday she gave me a gold piece, and very often she would commend me to Monsieur Ulrick.

She said, "Ulrick, I like this little fellow. He's polite and nice."

She patted my cheek and I inhaled the violet perfume again. The first time she spoke those words to Monsieur Ulrick I knew that the German concierge had lost his last remnant of power over me.

To return to Jean Devisse. His "ha, ha, ha" didn't mean that I had lost the battle. The next day I took the letters addressed to Queen Victoria to Her Majesty's suite. I was told explicitly to deliver them to one of the ladies in waiting. I was very curious to see a queen. So I forgot the lady in waiting and acted in my own way. I knocked directly on Her Majesty's drawing room door. I heard a melodious yet commanding voice say in English, "Come in." Once again I was in a quandary. I knew that someone was in the drawing room, but couldn't tell if the command meant "come in" or "stay out." After a few seconds of silence the same voice said in French, "Entrez." I turned the knob and slowly opened the door. I bowed deeply and reverently and then said, "I beg your Majesty to excuse my impertinence for entering, and also for directly bringing your Majesty's letters."

I think she was surprised at my size. With my cap under my arm and with the silver letter-filled tray held in the palm of my hand, I was still six feet from Her Majesty. I awaited a second command to advance. The schooling of Monsieur Draghui has never failed me yet.

Her Majesty said in French, "Come here, my little fellow."

I was amazed; in my imagination a queen was different from other women. I thought she always wore her crown and never took it off, like the lion who perpetually wore his in the picture that adorned the wall of Monsieur Draghui's classroom. I was confused by another temptation. Her Majesty was seated at a table on which there stood a large basketful of luscious chocolates. There was one green-centered piece on top which proved to be pistachio; something I had not yet tasted and something which I had never seen before. The candy was more tempting to me and overshadowed my interest and curiosity in Her Majesty, who, I had discovered, didn't wear her crown. One eye was on Her Majesty and the other on the chocolates, especially the green-centered one. I believe she saw that, too, because she asked for my name.

I replied, "Henri, your Majesty."

"Do you like bonbons, Henri?"

My face flushed with happiness; I was approaching my goal.

"Yes, your Majesty."

"Help yourself then," she said.

I extended my hand in the direction of the basket which I could only see out of the corner of my eye because I was still looking at Her Majesty. I hoped that my thumb and index finger would have eyes of their own so that they could see the green-centered chocolate and then have the intelligence to choose it. I succeeded, and when I had the much desired bonbon in my fingers I held it poised in the air because I had received no order that would permit me to eat it. I stood like a statue. That pleased Her Majesty, and she said, "Eat it." I put the whole thing into my mouth, and she asked, 'Only one?" She selected a chocolate herself and fed it to me. I bowed my thanks to her, and before I had time to swallow the second one, a third and a fourth were placed in my mouth, which completely filled it and made a happy prisoner of my tongue. My eyes alone expressed my thanks. When Her Majesty bent down to feed me a fifth bonbon, the saliva from my mouth wet her fingers, causing them to become brown with chocolate. She touched them to her lips, saying, "Yes, they're very sweet."

In later years I told the story of how a freckle-faced fellow had kissed Her Majesty Queen Victoria without the usual contact of lips. When Mr. David Sarnoff, who knew me, heard the story he gave me a world-wide broadcast of one-half hour, saying, "It's possible that you might reach her Majesty in the other world, Henri, where radio may be heard, too, and she'll be pleased that she acted toward you as any mother would to her little boy."

That's why, on that broadcast, I mentioned Queen Victoria as being not only the greatest queen of all time but the greatest grandmother as well.

But to return again to the Cap Martin. Madame "Darling" Ulrick was more than pleased when Her Majesty, in person, told about the little interview with the boy Henri and the pleasure she had received in feeding him bonbons. From that day I was Her Majesty's good friend, thanks to the Duchess of Rutland who had sent me on an errand, thereby causing me to miss the arrival of England's beloved Queen Victoria.

A Fairyland
In The Eyes Of Little Henri

SOMETHING NEW and something grand happened every day at the Cap Martin; things which my little head could not imagine became realities. The hotel was a rendezvous for kings, queens, emperors, empresses, princes, princesses, dukes, duchesses, in fact all the nobility; the greatest artists, merchants, bankers, and people of wealth. All of them passed before my eyes like a cavalcade, and all this happened long before the discovery of motion pictures. When I saw my first movie I was overjoyed to see that some means had been discovered by which the kaleidoscope of life could be captured. I have always felt like Thomas, the doubter, and, like him, have always discovered the actuality of a thing for myself.

At that tender age it surprised me greatly to see ladies wearing the skins of fur bearing animals. A fur coat was something I had never heard about. And my doubt that it could be fur from a real animal made me venture closer so that I might, with one small movement, caress it; but without impertinence, because I always had something on a tray, water or mint candies, to offer the ladies. I held the tray with one hand and gently stroked the fur with the other, and, because I was so small, no one thought I was being impolite.

I was reminded of a story that I had heard in Monsieur Draghui's classroom which concerned a French nobleman in England. A *soirée* was being given by King Edward III. The ballroom of the palace was crowded with noble knights and ladies and visiting royalty of other

311

lands. A waltz was being played and couples gaily twirled in their exuberance. The rustle of silken costumes, the perfume of the ladies mingled with that of the candles, and the captivating music all served, without the aid of wine, to intoxicate everyone. The language spoken those days in the highest circles was French, which everyone at the *soirée* knew and spoke perfectly.

The queen was dancing when tragedy struck! By accident, one of Her Majesty's garters had become detached. When one of the visiting German noblemen saw what had happened he ignored it and refused to comment. An Italian said, "Too bad." A Russian dignitary exclaimed in Russian, and they whispered together so seriously that it looked as if they were discussing an approaching war.

A young French nobleman glanced at the group of whispering royalty, who were resplendent in their costumes and decorations. When he heard, "Si, ja," etc., he knew that something momentous had happened. His intelligent eyes quickly darted around the room and immediately came to rest on the diamond-studded garter of the queen, as it dragged on the floor. With a gracious politeness he joined the dancers and deftly waltzed unnoticed by the others until he reached Her Majesty. He fell to his knees, which caused everyone to think that an accident had occurred, and the music stopped. The nobleman, on his knees, spoke the words which were later to become famous, "Honi soit qui mal y pense," which means, "Shamed be he who thinks evil of it." Edward III, from that expression, founded the highest and most distinguished "Order of the Garter," which is still known in France as "Honi soit qui mal y pense."

In my sincere heart I, too, felt like that French nobleman who meant nothing wrong. I meant nothing wrong in my caressing of those furs, which I didn't know by name.

When I returned from serving the ladies, the manager and the rest of the page boys sniffed me, and I'll never forget the words of Monsieur Ulrick when he said, "Henri, where did you buy that perfume? I'd like to offer a bottle of it to Madame 'Darling'; I'm sure she would love it."

I said, "Monsieur, I don't know what perfume is. What is it?"

He explained, "Well, Henri, when you go close to the beautiful ladies I think each of their different scents wants to grab you. You smell like a bouquet of all kinds of flowers. You would present confusion to the best perfumer who has never been able, as yet, to obtain such an aroma."

I was very young, but, because of my parentage, the seeds of knowledge and curiosity had already been deeply implanted in me. And now the seeds were sprouting; their thirst drove me on to acquire new knowledge and new experiences at that magic fairyland, the Hotel Cap Martin.

Of the several hundred postcards Henri Charpentier received from "Diamond Jim" Brady, these were the last two sent by the famous financier before his death in 1917. They were addressed to "Henri, The Best Eating Place in the World" and "Henri, The Best of Them All, Lynbrook, Long Island, New York."

RECIPES

✠

HORS-D'OEUVRE, BENJAMIN HARRISON

✠

CREAM OF TOMATO SOUP, THOMAS McKEAN

✠

OMELET, JAMES McHENRY

✠

EGGS, JOHN H. EATON

✠

FRIED FROGS' LEGS, JOHN M. BERRIEN

✠

HAM TIMBALE, JOHN McLEAN

✠

POTATOES, BENJAMIN STODDERT

✠

VEGETABLES, RICHARD RUSH

✠

SALAD, LEVI WOODBURY

✠

CHESTNUT PUDDING, ANN CUNNINGHAM

✠

315

HORS-D'OEUVRE, BENJAMIN HARRISON

Take 4 leeks. Leave them in one piece but slit them lengthwise in order to clean thoroughly.

Place them on a baking platter. Slice one large onion over them and add: 1 chopped peeled tomato, 2 peeled whole cloves of garlic, 1 bay leaf, 1 whole clove, 1 pinch of basil, 2 sprigs of parsley, 1 pint of consommé, 1 tablespoon of butter and 1 tablespoon of olive oil. Season with pepper and salt. Put into a hot oven for 1 hour. Be sure the leeks, etc., have absorbed all of the consommé; then remove from the oven. Slice 1 peeled tomato over them.

Finely chop 2 shallots and mix them with a little chopped parsley and 2 tablespoons of bread crumbs. Sprinkle it over the tomatoes. Pour 4 tablespoons of French Dressing over the top.

CREAM OF TOMATO SOUP, THOMAS McKEAN

Put 1 tablespoon of butter into a pan. Add 1 finely chopped onion, 1 finely chopped stalk of celery, and a little chopped parsley into which ¼ clove of garlic has been crushed. Cover and simmer for 5 minutes. Add 5 chopped peeled tomatoes, cover again and simmer for 5 more minutes. Pass the whole thing through a sieve and place it, and any water there may be from the tomatoes, into a double boiler. Add 1 teaspoon of sugar, 1 cup of cream, 1 pint of milk, 1 tablespoon of butter, and a sprinkle each of pepper and salt. When it comes to a boil add 1 teaspoon of cornstarch that has been dissolved in a few tablespoons of milk.

Before ladling the soup, place 1 tablespoon of cream into each soup plate or cup. Season to taste. Serve with very small croutons.

OMELET, JAMES McHENRY

Place 1 large tablespoon of butter into a pan and add 1 finely chopped shallot, 3 thinly sliced mushrooms, 1 pinch of pepper, and 1 pinch of salt. Let it become brown.

Slightly beat 6 eggs and add the above mixture as well as 2 pinches of chopped chives, another pinch of pepper, and another pinch of salt.

Put 1 tablespoon of butter into an omelet pan and when it becomes hot pour in the eggs, etc., and roll the omelet.

EGGS, JOHN H. EATON

Put ½ chopped onion into a pan with 1 tablespoon of butter. Cut 1 head of lettuce into quarters and add it to the chopped onion. Add also ½ cup of consommé and simmer for 20 minutes.

Place it into a baking dish, juice and all. Cover with 4 sliced hard-boiled eggs. Then add 2 chopped peeled tomatoes.

Crush ½ clove of garlic into a little chopped parsley. Mix it with 2 tablespoons of chili sauce, 1 pinch each of basil, salt, and pepper. Stir it into 1 tablespoon of olive oil and with a spoon distribute it over the top. Bake in a preheated hot oven for 20 minutes. Season to taste.

FRIED FROGS' LEGS, JOHN M. BERRIEN

Take 1 pound of frogs' legs. Dip them into flour and shake off the excess. Mix 1 clove of garlic (which has been crushed into 1 teaspoon of chopped parsley), 1 pinch of pepper and 1 pinch of salt, and stand it aside for a few moments.

Place 2 tablespoons of butter into a frying pan with 4 finely chopped shallots. When the butter becomes hot put the frogs' legs into the pan. When they become brown place them on a hot serving platter. Sprinkle the sizzling frogs' legs with the garlic parsley. Add 2 tablespoons of butter to the same frying pan and when it begins to bubble squeeze the juice of ½ lemon into it. Pour over the top.

HAM TIMBALE, JOHN McLEAN

Use ½ pound of lean, raw or cooked ham in this recipe. Put it through a meat grinder, or have the butcher do it. It must be ground fine. Mix 1 finely chopped shallot with the ham, put it into a pan, add 2 sherry-glasses of sweet sherry, and let it come to a boil. Remove it from the fire and stir in the white of 1 egg. Put the whole thing through a fine sieve.

Beat the whites of 2 more eggs until they become stiff, and stand them aside for a moment.

Stir ½ cup of cream into the yolks of the 3 eggs. When it is well mixed, add the stiffly beaten egg whites. Then add the ham. Mix well and pour into a buttered mold. Place the mold into a *bain-marie* (a pan of boiling water) and put it in a preheated moderate oven of 350° F. for 35 minutes.

Put 1 tablespoon of butter into a pan. Add 1 sherry-glassful of sweet sherry, 2 tablespoons of cream, and 2 pinches of paprika. When it comes to a boil thicken it with 1 teaspoon of cornstarch which has been dissolved in 1 tablespoon of sweet sherry and 1 teaspoon of meat stock.

Remove the ham from the mold and place it on a hot serving platter. Pour the boiling sauce over it. Crush and sprinkle 4 crisply broiled strips of bacon over the sauce. Season to taste and serve with fried apples.

POTATOES, BENJAMIN STODDERT

Potatoes prepared in 3 different ways are used in this recipe.

Boil together ½ head of cabbage, 1 turnip, and 4 peeled potatoes. When cooked, strain, chop fine, and season with pepper and salt. Add 1 tablespoon of butter and stir well.

Put 1 tablespoon of butter into a baking dish. Add a layer of peeled and sliced cold boiled potatoes (that have been cooked with their skins). Now add the chopped cabbage, etc. Over this place 1½ cups of creamy mashed potatoes.

Mix 1 tablespoon of grated cheese with 1 tablespoon of bread crumbs and sprinkle over the potatoes. Bake in a preheated hot oven of 400° F. for 10 minutes. Season.

VEGETABLES, RICHARD RUSH

Take 1 cup of diced carrots, 1 cup of shelled green peas, and 1 cup of diced green beans. Cook in salted water until tender. Pour off the water. Add 1 tablespoon of chopped parsley, 2 tablespoons of cream, 1 tablespoon of butter, a sprinkle of salt, and a sprinkle of pepper. Let it come to a boil and pour into a serving dish.

SALAD, LEVI WOODBURY

Place 1 handful of water-cress on each salad plate. This recipe serves two.

Dice: 1 peeled cold boiled beet, 2 peeled cold boiled potatoes (that have been cooked with their skins), and 2 cold boiled oyster plants. Mix with 1 chopped peeled tomato.

Separately mix 3 tablespoons of French Dressing, 1 tablespoon of chili sauce, 1 teaspoon of Worcestershire sauce, and 2 pinches of paprika. Pour it over the diced beets, etc., and mix well. Place it around the edge of the water-cress as a border.

Chop 1 hard-boiled egg and sprinkle it over the water-cress in the middle.

CHESTNUT PUDDING, ANN CUNNINGHAM

Beat the whites of 4 eggs until they are stiff, and stand them aside for a moment.

Very finely chop ½ cup of roasted chestnuts.

Put 1½ cups of milk into a pan. Add 2 tablespoons of vanilla sugar (or 2 tablespoons of sugar and 1 teaspoon, or more if you like, of vanilla extract), and 1 tablespoon of butter. When it comes to a boil add the cup of finely chopped roasted chestnuts. Stir well and when it begins to boil again remove it from the fire. Quickly stir in 4 beaten egg yolks. Then immediately add the stiffly beaten whites. Mix throughly.

Butter a mold and sprinkle it with a few pinches of flour. Then pour in the above ingredients. Place the mold in a pan of boiling water and put in a preheated hot oven of 400° F. for 30 minutes.

Place 1 tablespoon of vanilla sugar (or just 1 tablespoon of plain sugar if you have used the vanilla extract) into a pan with 2 tablespoons of cream. When it comes to a boil remove from the fire and stir 2 beaten egg yolks into it until it thickens. Then add 1 pony of rum and 1 tablespoon of cranberry jelly. Stir it well and pour it over the pudding which has been removed from the mold and placed on a serving platter.

Chapter XX

THE PAGE BOY BANKER WITHOUT A BANK

I WAS A LITTLE GREENHORN when it came to hotel life and business, but not for long. I had learned in Contes that "God helps those who help themselves." In the short days of apprenticeship served under Jean Devisse, I learned to clean and wax floors, sweep rugs, dust furniture, etc., until I became very proficient. Everything had to be spick-and-span, and no place escaped the concierge's long fingers as he explored secret cubby-holes for dust. I found that Jean had taught me too much in the cleaning business and not enough in the ways of making money. Day after day I hid myself and listened to him conversing with the ladies and gentlemen. When I heard Jean say, "Oui, monsieur" and "no, madame," I asked Monsieur Ulrick's secretary who "monsieur" and "madame" were.

She answered, "Madame is the Duchess so and so, and Monsieur is Prince so and so."

It wasn't long after that I met them again, face to face, and, instead of addressing them as "madame" and "monsieur" the way Jean had done, I added a little, making it, "Madame *la duchesse*" and "*Monsieur le prince.*" Those who had no titles, no matter what their nationality, I would greet with at least, "*Monsieur le baron.*" I thought only titled people were permitted at the Cap Martin so I gave them titles myself without further questioning the secretary. Those I gave depended on the size of the tip I received. That polite little game succeeded in making a banker out of the freckle-faced page boy! Many times the various

321

guests said to me, "The last time I was here you addressed me as *'monsieur le baron.'* Then, why do you receive me today as *'monsieur le prince'*?"

"Because, *Monsieur le prince,* on that occasion I didn't know you, and after helping you into your carriage I was surprised to find, on opening my hand, that you had recompensed me as though you were a prince. I can only, by listening to my heart, call you what God inspires me to call you. You may be merely 'monsieur' to the rest of the world, but to me, the page boy at the Cap Martin, you'll always be *'mon prince.'*"

That guest, who was not of the nobility, told others to look for the smallest page boy in the Cap Martin; the one with the freckles. "And be generous with him, because if you've never been called a prince in your life he'll call you one. But don't make the mistake of not tipping him handsomely, or then he'll very politely leave you with only the title of 'monsieur,' and everybody knows that even a pauper is called that in France. So, if you receive a 'monsieur' from him, then you'll indeed be a nobody."

It seemed that, as my gold pieces increased, my freckles disappeared. I became known because of my freckles, but my name was not widely used until they had disappeared. Then I became Henri. The German concierge, who had at first disliked me, gradually came to favor me because I never said "no" or "it's impossible" to him. I always did anything he asked; consequently, in time he recognized that I was obedient and polite, and so he put aside his grudge.

The next thing I knew Jean Devisse had suddenly become jealous. He wore a long face and refused to speak to me for several days. One morning, instead of waking him gently, I took a glass of water and threw it in his face. He woke up screaming and swearing and ready to fight.

I said, "Thank goodness, I thought you had become a deaf mute."

He was mad but saw by my remark that I liked him, and we became fast friends, which we still are to this day.

My diplomacy didn't stop with the guests of the Cap Martin. In 1890 automobiles were not, as yet, used extensively, and carriages were still the most popular means of transportation. After assisting people who had driven many miles to the hotel for dinner, I turned to their coach-man and said, "Come with me and I'll show you where to leave your horses and carriage so you can get some food and drink, too." I never called him "coachman," but "monsieur coachman." That made him, as well as the horses, happy. The latter were proud to hear that the one who took care of them was a gentleman, and not just a servant. With that little politeness I paved the way for the question, "What are the names of your customers?" When he told me I marked them down in a little note-book and kept asking questions until I found out the towns they came from, and if they lived in hotels, which ones. I placed all that information under the respective names, and, to make it easier, I added their descriptions: the color of their hair, their size, the color of their eyes, etc. I put down the coachman's name and even the color of the horses.

I began carrying a silver cigar case which held two or three cigars that cost me three *sous each*. It was always in my pocket, and a smoke was ready to be offered to "monsieur coachman" with the words, "The compliments of the Cap Martin management."

The information I had gleaned, concerning the visiting dinner guests, gave me the opportunity, when the time came, to announce the readiness of their carriages with more enthusiasm. I went to the table and stated, "Madame and Monsieur So and So, your carriage awaits, and I am at your service." The surprise and delight they felt at hearing their names was great. They couldn't imagine how they had become known to the little page boy when not even the manager or anyone else could have had the occasion to find out in that short time. Why, they had only come for dinner!

Monsieur Ulrick was astounded to hear so many outsiders say, "Hello, Henri, don't forget to order my carriage for two o'clock, and call my 'monsieur coachman,' Jacques. The hotel management is very kind to offer him such a good cigar." The manager's face changed color, and I thought that it was goodbye for me at the Cap Martin. I tried to escape into the lobby but heard approaching footsteps behind me as they fell on the uncovered floor between the rugs. I recognized them as belonging to someone who wore the same kind of shoes as my own. It was the manager.

He called, *"Petit,* I want to see you in my apartment, and bring an English newspaper for Madame 'Darling' Ulrick. Then I knew he wasn't angry and decided that if he asked me I'd tell him everything. I hurried to get the paper, selecting the *Manchester Gazette* because that was the town in which Madame had been born. I knocked on the apartment door, and it was opened by Monsieur Ulrick himself. He glanced at the headlines, said, "Just a minute," and went back into the apartment. I waited outside the door and presently he returned, holding Madame "Darling" by the hand. She was all smiles when the door was again opened for me.

Monsieur said, "Hello, new manager."

I smiled and said, "But you're still the boss," and added, "Madame 'Darling' Ulrick, here's your newspaper."

She asked, "Why do you bring me the *Manchester Gazette?"*

"Because I've seen you reading it many times, and one day I over-heard you telling a guest that you were born in Manchester; your home town is always in your heart just as Contes is in mine. Only Contes doesn't have a newspaper."

They were both very pleased. Madame "Darling" offered me a full box of candy while Monsieur said, "Sit down, Henri." I sat down between them.

The manager said, "Now, tell me all about the cigar business, and how you, who've been here the shortest length of time and are the smallest in size, can have so many people call you by name."

My face became red. I said, "I've kept it secret, Monsieur, but you're my boss, and, because you're almost a new Don Albini, I'll confess to you."

I pulled out the small note-book and also the silver cigar case, which had been filled and emptied three times that day already, and handed them to the manager. He opened the note-book and read off the names, addresses, and descriptions to Madame "Darling." He saw the diagrams I had drawn of the surrounding localities. Madame turned and embraced me.

The manager said, "We'll keep your secret and it'll remain just between the three of us. Keep on using the same tactics. I've learned something today that so far has escaped me: that the coachman and horses are entitled to the politeness which you give them."

He gave me a bill of 100 francs and said, "That's to reimburse you for the silver cigar case, and when the season's over I'll pay you for the cigars you've given away. Don't tell anyone, not even Jean Devisse, because other people might steal your system and use it even though it doesn't belong to them. And, between the three of us, you're the second manager."

It was my small note-book that made me realize for the first time that hotel life is the greatest life of all. The continuous flow of people permits the forming of new contacts, and it is that constant renewal which frustrates stagnation.

Another Midas Who Changed Silver To Gold

THE WONDERFUL CLIENTELE of the Cap Martin became the wonderful clientele of Henri. I, too, in a short time, was favorably regarded by all the guests, royal and otherwise. Among the list, which was headed by Queen Victoria, were: Empress Eugénie, wife of the dethroned Napoleon III; Empress Elizabeth, of Austria; Queen Margherita, of Italy; the Prince of Wales and his gracious Princess Alexandra; the Grand Duke Alexis, of Russia; the Romanoff family; the Spanish Bourbons; a prince of China; and most of the nobility of the world. The hotel became a fairyland in which those fine people temporarily dwelled. Destiny made me their servant for a short time, a rôle that I have filled many times since. Empress Eugénie demanded that I leave and join her staff of servants at the new villa that she was having built. She subsequently spent many winters at Villa Cyrnos and returned every summer to her castle in Farnborough Hill, England. Jean Devisse accepted the position that had been offered to me and remained with Her Majesty for more than ten years.

I received many silver five franc pieces as tips which I later changed into gold ten franc pieces; these, in turn, I changed into gold twenty franc coins. I didn't believe in the security of paper money. I thought, "You can burn paper money but you can't burn gold."

I discovered later in life that my real mother and her brothers and sisters had played in childhood with Prince Eugéne, the son of Napoleon III. The Prince became an officer in the British army and was later killed in Africa. My grandfather, the Marquis Ribaud de Guibaud, had been an intimate of Napoleon III. How ironic it was that Empress Eugénie had wanted me as her servant when my mother had often dined at her table. But I only found it out at the age of twenty when it was told to me by my grandfather whom I met for the first time.

Empress Elizabeth of Austria was a most humble and kind person, and very democratic. Monsieur Ulrick ordered me to always assist Her Majesty when she stepped from her carriage. On those occasions I wore a band over the forearm of my coat sleeve; on it the Austrian coat of arms had been stitched. When she stepped from her carriage she was to rest her hand on the band. I was very excited the day Empress Elizabeth was to arrive, and, after having rehearsed two or three times in front of Monsieur Ulrick, I was told, "If you do that you'll be all right."

Finally Her Majesty's carriage arrived, and the French soldiers, who had been ordered to the Cap Martin, presented arms in the name of the French government. That salute seemed to say, "May her Majesty have many pleasant days filled with tranquillity in the country she has chosen for her sojourn." The sound of the bugle, the beating of the drums, and the clicking of the guns as the soldiers presented arms, touched my young heart and tears filled my eyes. As I extended my arm Her Majesty, instead of placing her hand on the band, put her hand on top of mine. She had noticed the tears in my eyes.

To Monsieur Ulrick, who was a born Austrian, it was a great surprise. After Empress Elizabeth reached her apartment he called me to him and said, "If you were an Austrian boy you would become a nobleman now because her Majesty touched your hand."

The next day Don Rosso came from Cabbé Roquebrune, a village two miles distant, where Jean Devisse had been born. Madame "Darling" Ulrick chose me to be the altar boy, which was nothing new to me. Don Rosso was only Don Albini by another name. A chapel had been specially built for Empress Elizabeth and her ladies in waiting; and every morning we held a mass for them. Every morning Her Majesty, like the priest at the altar, made her communion. She was the only one of those attending who did. I ventured to ask Don Rosso a few days later, *"Monsieur le curé,* can you tell me why such a kind woman makes her communion every day?"

He said, "Her Majesty wants to become a priest, but because she is a woman she cannot be one."

I found out, too, that he, as well as Don Albini, had his mystery. But he didn't have three pairs of eyeglasses, which proved that Don Albini was one mystery ahead of young Don Rosso.

I continued assisting at the special mass, holding my gold tray under Her Majesty's chin as she swallowed the wafer. I can still remember the picture she made as she knelt there before the priest, her mouth slightly open and her eyes half closed. Don Rosso and I knelt in prayer as long as she remained in the chapel; and when she rose to her feet the priest made the sign of the cross. I said, "Amen," and then Her Majesty, Don Rosso, and I made the sign of the cross together. That little mass began the day in a beautiful way.

I received numerous tips from the lovely people at the Cap Martin, and, large or small, they were converted that same day, starting with the little silver ten *sou* piece. When I had enough of them I changed them into a five franc silver *écu;* then into gold ten franc pieces; then into gold twenty franc pieces; and sometimes I kept on until I had a large gold coin evaluated at 100 francs.

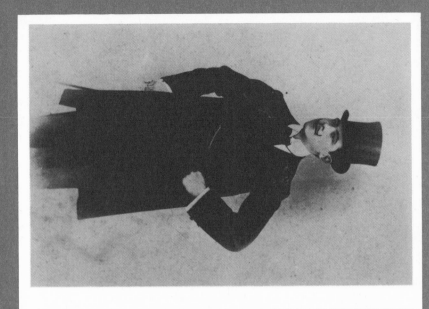

Charpentier, age 18, at the Four Seasons Hotel in Munich, Germany.

Every time I changed my silver into gold I ran up to my room, locked the door, and opened an iron box that I had in my trunk. There were two boxes that fitted into the tray of that trunk, one of iron and one of wood. I kept about twenty-five cigars in the wooden one and had to replenish them quite often. I kept my money in the iron box, and when I opened it noticed that it hadn't been disturbed. I wrapped each gold coin, as I accumulated it, into a little piece of paper as if it were a flat bonbon. I marked the amount of each one in a little note-book and locked both money and note-book in the strong box. In that way I knew every day what I had made, and also the total. When I reached my first 1,000 francs I thought, "I'm no longer a page boy, I'm a rich fellow." But when I passed two, three, four, five, six, and reached 7,000 francs, about $1,400 in those days, I thought, "Now I have a fortune." Men like Papa Camous could work a lifetime and not make half as much; farmers then worked for thirty cents a day. I became another Midas; but instead of asking God to turn everything into gold I asked Him to turn gentleness into gold. This He did, and also gave me more gentleness, which has been the foundation of my success. He knew and understood that that boxful of gold was designed to be my first gift to Maman Camous. Now I could begin to reward her for her kindness in caring for me. I have always compared that wonderful woman and myself with the hen and the duckling that were our neighbors in Contes. I was the duckling that had found a home under her protective wing.

A place where one may dine slowly and gently, where the service is impeccable and the food sublime, is the type of restaurant in which I have always worked or supervised, and in which I have accepted, as well as given, orders.

— Henri Charpentier

RECIPES

✤

HORS-D'OEUVRE, ROBERT MORRIS

✤

SOUP, CYRUS H. McCORMICK

✤

SHIRRED EGGS, ETHELBERT NEVIN

✤

OMELET, ORVILLE WRIGHT

✤

BAKED HERRING, JOSEPH HOOKER

✤

CHICKEN TIMBALE, LORADO TAFT

✤

POTATOES, HERMAN MELVILLE

✤

BROCCOLI, HENRY SHAW

✤

SALAD, GEORGE WESTINGHOUSE

✤

PANCAKES, ABRAHAM LINCOLN

✤

331

HORS-D'OEUVRE, ROBERT MORRIS

Prepare a pancake batter, using 1 egg, 1 tablespoon of flour, 2 tablespoons of milk, and a pinch of salt. Mix well. It should have the consistency of heavy cream. The above ingredients will make 4 small pancakes, enough for 2.

Put 1 teaspoon of butter into an omelet pan and let it become very hot. Make 4 very thin pancakes, one at a time, and let each one become brown. Use 1 teaspoon of butter in making each pancake.

Place ½ cup of cottage cheese in a mixing bowl and add 1 large tablespoon of chopped chives, 2 finely chopped shallots, 1 tablespoon of sweet cream, and the yolk of 1 raw egg. Season with salt and pepper. Mix thoroughly and add ½ sherry-glass of sherry, and 1 pinch of cayenne pepper. Mix well.

Place a pancake on each serving plate and spread with the cottage cheese, etc. Cover with the 2 remaining pancakes. Beat 2 large tablespoons of sour cream and spread over the top. Sprinkle with chopped chives.

SOUP, CYRUS H. McCORMICK

Place 1 tablespoon of butter into a pot and add 1 finely chopped onion, 2 finely chopped stalks of celery, 1 chopped peeled tomato, a little parsley into which 1 clove of garlic has been crushed, a sprinkle of pepper, and a sprinkle of salt. Cover and let it simmer for 15 minutes. Add 1 quart of consommé and ½ cup of rice, cover and boil slowly for 30 minutes. Remove from the fire and stir in 1 tablespoon of olive oil just before serving.

SHIRRED EGGS, ETHELBERT NEVIN

Broil a few slices of bacon. Place 1 tablespoon of butter on a baking platter, melt it, and add 4 eggs. Season with 1 pinch of pepper and 1 pinch of salt. Arrange the bacon over the eggs and sprinkle with grated Swiss cheese. Place a few tablespoons of cream around the eggs and put in a hot broiler for 3 or 4 minutes.

OMELET, ORVILLE WRIGHT

Put ½ cup of cooked fresh green peas into a bowl. Add 2 diced slices of American cheese, 2 tablespoons of small croutons (which have been fried in butter), 1 pinch of salt, and 1 pinch of pepper. Mix.

Place 1 tablespoon of butter into an omelet pan. Gently beat 6 eggs; to them, add the above ingredients. When the butter becomes hot pour in the eggs, etc., and make a flat omelet by baking it in a preheated hot oven for 5 or 6 minutes. Watch it so it doesn't become too hard. Season to taste.

BAKED HERRING, JOSEPH HOOKER

Take 2 large herrings. Open and clean. Remove the heads and tails. Do not remove the roe, or the bones. Wash and dry thoroughly.

Place them on a baking platter with 2 tablespoons of butter. Mix ½ minced onion with a little finely chopped parsley, 1 finely chopped stalk of celery, and 2 thinly sliced mushrooms. Sprinkle it over the fish. Season with 1 pinch of salt and 1 pinch of pepper. Put into a preheated hot oven of 400° F. for 25 minutes. Then remove from the oven and sprinkle with the juice of ½ lemon.

Put 1 tablespoon of butter into a separate pan and add 1 crushed clove of garlic, 1 teaspoon of Worcestershire sauce, 1 teaspoon of mustard, and 1 sherry-glassful of red wine. Let it come to a boil and pour it over the fish. Serve immediately.

CHICKEN TIMBALE, LORADO TAFT

Use the entire breast of 1 uncooked chicken in this recipe. Put it through a fine meat grinder. Mix 1 finely chopped shallot and 1 tablespoon of butter with the ground chicken, put it into a pan, add 1 pinch of salt, 1 pinch of pepper, 2 sherry-glasses of sweet sherry, and let it come to a boil. Remove it from the fire and stir in the white of 1 egg. Put the whole thing through a fine sieve.

Beat the whites of 2 more eggs until they become stiff, and stand them aside for a moment.

Stir ½ cup of cream into the yolks of the 3 eggs. When it is well mixed, add the stiffly beaten egg whites. Then add the chicken. Mix well and pour into a buttered mold. Place the mold into a *bain-marie* (a pan of boiling water) and put it in a preheated moderate oven of 350° F. for 35 minutes.

Put 1 tablespoon of butter into a pan. Add 1 sherry-glassful of sweet sherry, 2 tablespoons of cream, 2 pinches of paprika, and 2 tablespoons of chopped *pâté de foie gras*. When it comes to a boil thicken it with 1 teaspoon of cornstarch which has been dissolved in 1 tablespoon of sweet sherry and 1 teaspoon of meat stock.

Remove the chicken from the mold and place it on a serving platter. Pour the boiling sauce over the top. Crush and sprinkle 4 crisply broiled strips of bacon over the sauce. Season to taste.

POTATOES, HERMAN MELVILLE

Peel and chop 4 cold boiled potatoes (that have been cooked with their skins). To them, add 1 raw egg and 1 large tablespoon of flour.

Place 1 tablespoon of butter into a frying pan with 2 finely chopped shallots. Add 1 finely chopped canned red pepper. Mix. When they begin to bubble add the chopped potatoes, etc.

Put 3 tablespoons of oil into a frying pan. When it comes to a boil add the potatoes, etc., and then roll as you would an omelet. Let it become very brown, but don't burn it. Remove from the oil and season.

BROCCOLI, HENRY SHAW

Take 1 bunch of broccoli. Cut off the large leaves and peel off the woody outer skin of the main stem. Boil whole in plenty of salted water until tender.

Drain off water and let the broccoli remain on the fire for a moment to dry off all remaining water.

Place on a serving platter and squeeze the juice of ½ lemon over it. Season with salt and pepper. Serve with hollandaise.

SALAD, GEORGE WESTINGHOUSE

Take ½ head of lettuce. Remove 2 large leaves, place them on salad plates, and shred the rest, cutting it lengthwise to make it hair-like. Mince ½ green pepper and mix it with the shredded lettuce. Place a portion on each leaf. Sprinkle with 1 chopped hard-boiled egg. Mince 1 canned pimiento and sprinkle it over the top. Pour 1 or more tablespoons of French Dressing over each portion.

PANCAKES, ABRAHAM LINCOLN

Place 2 tablespoons of butter into a frying pan. Add 6 ripe apricots that have been cut into very small pieces. Add, also, the skin of ½ tangerine cut julienne style and 1 tablespoon of vanilla sugar. Simmer until the apricots are done. Then add the strained juice of 1 tangerine.

Take 2 more tangerines. Peel and remove all pulp. Separate the sections and remove seeds. Mix sections with 2 ponies of brandy, and sprinkle with 1 tablespoon of vanilla sugar. Let it stand for 10 minutes and then add it to the cooked apricots. Remove it from the fire and mix well. Do not cook the tangerines.

Prepare a pancake batter, using 1 egg, 1 tablespoon of flour, 2 tablespoons of milk and a pinch of salt. Mix thoroughly. The batter should have the consistency of heavy cream. Place 1 teaspoon of butter into an omelet pan (one which is not aluminum), and let it become very hot. Make 4 very thin pancakes, one at a time, and let each one become brown. Use 1 teaspoon of butter in making each pancake.

Place a pancake on each serving plate and cover with the cooked apricots, etc. Arrange the two remaining pancakes over the fruit and sprinkle with powdered sugar.

Mr. Lincoln was right when he said, "You can't fool all of the people all of the time." This recipe won't fool anyone; it's delicious.

Chapter XXI

ONE ROYAL EVENING

On one evening a week the dining room at the Cap Martin was reserved exclusively for the guests of the hotel. A few days before, the management announced that on such and such an evening a certain queen would be dining at the hotel and that on that evening guests only could attend. They were informed by the ladies in waiting as to the color of the queen's attire, her perfume, and her flowers so that they would dress harmoniously. Queen Victoria almost always wore black, and I remember one Saturday evening that she chose to grace the dining room. The guests were informed as to the color in which she preferred to see everyone attired.

The morning and afternoon of that anticipated day were spent in elaborately preparing for the dinner party. Flowers and ferns filled the whole lobby and every corner of the dining room. The gardens of the Cap Martin outdid themselves for the occasion. Luncheon and tea that day were served in the *Salon de Midi* to give us ample time to put the dining room in readiness. I helped, too, and as I stood there among the quantities and quantities of beautiful flowers, I felt that it was really a privilege to spend my apprenticeship in such a place.

Cassut, the Swiss maître d' and an artist in his line, saw to it that shortly before receiving the guests all the windows in the dining room were opened for a while and then closed. Under his direction Jean Devisse and I walked around the empty dining room with pots of fragrantly burning herbs such as: rosemary, thyme, bay leaves, clove, and cinnamon. Whether they were mixed or not depended on Monsieur Cassut and Jean Camous, the chef; but it really was the *pièce de résistance* that decided the matter. We called those smoking pots "the pipes of Cassut," because he wouldn't permit anyone to smoke in the dining room no matter who he was. Not even kings were permitted to desecrate his sacred temple. It seemed sacred to me, too; those burning herbs reminded me of Don Albini and his censer. Monsieur Cassut didn't have to show me how to distribute the incense; I was an expert. That time I reversed things and became Jean Devisse's teacher.

On such evenings dinner consisted of seventeen courses and lasted three or four hours. No cocktails were served, only the finest of sherry and eight or nine other kinds of wine, which had been poured into decanters. The bottles, themselves, were not placed on the table, since they were too old and were often found to have sediments. Champagne was served last. Coffee, and black coffee only; liqueurs, cigars, and cigarettes were served later in the enormous lobby of the Cap Martin, a combination vestibule and lounge that was used for various hotel functions. In those days ladies didn't smoke in public; on such occasions men smoked cigars and cigarettes with the serving of coffee and liqueurs, but never a pipe.

The final preparation had been made, and Monsieur Cassut was ready to receive the guests. The dining room, a veritable fairyland, soon became filled. The ladies represented a vast bouquet of flowers with their lovely dresses, corsages, and jewelry. The uniforms and dresses of the titled guests of various nationalities made the place look like a room in the palace of some king who had invited other nobility and ambassadors. On that festive night every guest was seated before the entrance of Her Majesty, and when Queen Victoria entered the room everyone rose to his feet and remained standing until she was seated.

The food presented was arranged in such an artistic manner that Queen Victoria said, "It's almost a crime to destroy such a beautiful piece of art." Jean Camous, with tear-filled eyes, bowed his thanks to Her Majesty. She noticed his emotion, and the next day sent word to

Monsieur Ulrick that he was to be complimented on having a chef with such deepness of feeling.

One of the cooks remarked, "I think Jean rubbed some raw onion on his goatee so he could produce those tears."

Years later, whenever I saw Jean Camous caress his beard I thought of that exciting night when I was ten.

No guest would have dared to enter the dining room once Her Majesty had seated herself, and no guest would have dared to leave his seat before she left. Only when the sherbet was served was there an *entr'acte* of twenty or twenty-five minutes. It was served fifteen minutes after the roast course had been finished and before the game and cold dishes, *pâte de foies gras,* terrines, etc., etc. One could either eat the sherbet or leave the dining room during that period. The gentlemen usually went into the lobby to smoke. When Monsieur Cassut received orders that Her Majesty would be ready in a few moments, he sent Jean Devisse, the other page boys and myself to announce, *"Mesdames et messieurs, à table, s'il vous plaît. Le dîner continu."* There was never any need to repeat ourselves, for *noblesse oblige* existed and politeness was in the blood of those people.

The dinner progressed, and the cooks tried to outdo each other in creating dishes with promptness. The waiters noiselessly vied with each other in serving those superb dishes with finesse. The light from the crystal chandeliers shone on the crystal glasses; filled with various colored wines, they made a picture of scintillating beauty. The perfumed candles that burned in the chandeliers were made of orange blossom beeswax.

The manners and politeness of the young and old servants of the hotel, who loved their business, made Monsieur Ulrick very proud. He went to the kitchen and said to Camous and Cassut, "Gentlemen, you are at the head of the finest group of highly efficient cooks and waiters who, themselves, are all gentlemen. And, because of all of you, I've received a great compliment from her Majesty Queen Victoria; the highest one that has ever been paid to me. I thank you both. I know you will share with those under you the great appreciation I feel.

Here is an envelope that her Majesty herself gave me to distribute among all of you. Please see that it is done." Every one of the employees, except Camous and Cassut, received one English pound. Those two received merely her Majesty's thanks, because they considered themselves above tipping and felt that they were, more or less, representatives of the Cap Martin. Jean Camous for his wonderful culinary art, and Cassut for his magnificent service and impeccable dining room.

After dinner when Queen Victoria rose to depart the guests stood respectfully, and the double doors of the dining room were opened wide. Jean Devisse and I had unrolled a special carpet from the door of the dining room to the grand staircase just a moment before, and now we stood at attention on either side of the large doorway attired in our gala uniforms. The many mirrors in the lobby had not been numerous enough in which to view ourselves. But now we were at attention. It was my duty to stand at the door to the left of Her Majesty. As she approached I bowed deeply, saying nothing. I presented my arm so that she might use it as a support for the few steps she had to take to the staircase and up the ten steps to the elevator. Queen Victoria always had a pleasant word or two to say, but no matter what she said we were only permitted to answer, "Thank you, your Majesty." When we arrived at the elevator I exceeded myself by saying, as I bowed deeply, *"Bonne nuit, Votre Majesté."* She smiled and thanked me, saying goodnight also. As long as Her Majesty liked those expressions no one had the right to deny them, not even Monsieur Ulrick. I thought many times that if Maman and Papa Camous and Don Albini had been there they would have gone down on their knees and would have been afraid to sit down at the table. It was no wonder that I couldn't sleep after such an evening. The next morning I was up before the clock rang and shaking Jean Devisse who, as usual, was sound asleep.

RECIPES

❧

HORS-D'OEUVRE, FRANCIS HOPKINSON

❧

SOUP, CHARLES WICKLIFFE

❧

POACHED EGGS, MAHLON DICKERSON

❧

EGGS, BENJAMIN F. BUTLER

❧

BAKED SMELTS, LEVI LINCOLN

❧

MINUTE LAMB STEAK, WILLIAM B. BANKHEAD

❧

POTATOES, JOEL R. POINSETT

❧

BRUSSELS SPROUTS, WALTER FORWARD

❧

SALAD, WILLIAM WIRT

❧

PUDDING, HELEN KELLER

❧

341

HORS-D'OEUVRE, FRANCIS HOPKINSON

Boil a small chicken and remove the breast. Put the rest aside for another time. Chop the breast very fine.

Into a separate pan put 1 tablespoon of butter, 2 finely chopped shallots, and 2 finely chopped mushrooms. Cook for 3 or 4 minutes. Add the finely chopped breast of chicken, ½ cup of cream, and 2 tablespoons of grated cheese. Let it come to a boil and remove it from the fire. Then mix in the yolks of 2 raw eggs, 2 pinches of paprika, 1 pinch of red pepper, ½ teaspoon of sugar, and 1 tablespoon of butter. Stir it well.

Make 2 slices of toast. Place them on a baking platter, pour the finely chopped chicken, etc., over the toast, and sprinkle each with 1 teaspoon of grated cheese. In the middle of each, place a small thin slice of tomato. Put the whole thing under the broiler for 2 minutes, just long enough for the cheese to melt. Watch it so it doesn't burn.

SOUP, CHARLES WICKLIFFE

Boil 1 pound of spinach until it is tender. Pass it through a sieve and place the purée into a double boiler. Add 1 pint of milk and when it begins to boil add 1 cup of cream and 2 tablespoons of butter. When this begins to boil remove it from the fire, add 2 egg yolks and stir quickly. Season to taste. Serve with croutons.

POACHED EGGS, MAHLON DICKERSON

Pour 1 pint of milk into a pan. Add 1 tablespoon of butter and 1 pinch of salt. When it comes to a boil, add enough cornmeal to make it thick after 10 minutes of cooking. Don't let it burn. Stir it constantly with a wooden spoon. When it has thickened, put 1 tablespoon of butter into a baking platter, melt it, and pour in the cornmeal.

Have ready 4 poached eggs. Dry them well and place them on top of the cornmeal.

Put 1 tablespoon of butter into a separate pan and add 1 finely chopped shallot. After cooking for 1 minute, add 1 cup of cream and 1 thinly sliced mushroom. When it comes to a boil pour it over the eggs. If you like, sprinkle a little grated cheese over the top. Bake in a preheated moderate oven of 350° to 375° F. for a few minutes. Season to taste. This recipe may also be prepared with a tomato sauce.

EGGS, BENJAMIN F. BUTLER

Mince 2 onions. Boil them in a little water, 1 pinch of pepper, and 1 tablespoon of butter. Use very little water so that it will be absorbed by the time the onions are cooked.

After the onions are cooked, add 4 chopped hard-boiled eggs, 1 cup of cream, 3 tablespoons of bread crumbs, 2 minced shallots, 1 pinch of salt, and 1 pinch of pepper.

Have ready 1½ cups of carrot purée and stir it into the onions, etc.

Place 1 tablespoon of butter into a baking dish, melt it, and pour in the above ingredients. Arrange 4 slices of bacon on top. Put in a preheated moderate oven of 375° F. for 10 minutes. Season to taste.

BAKED SMELTS, LEVI LINCOLN

Clean, wash and dry thoroughly 1 pound of smelts. Do not remove heads, tails or bones.

Place 1 tablespoon of butter on a baking platter, melt it, and sprinkle the bottom with 3 finely chopped shallots. Lay the smelts on top of the shallots, making only one layer. Season with a sprinkle of salt and pepper. After 7 minutes in a preheated hot oven of 400° F., sprinkle with grated cheese and bake for 5 more minutes.

MINUTE LAMB STEAK, WILLIAM B. BANKHEAD

Have 2 frying pans in use at one time. Take ½ pound of lamb steak from the leg or chops. Cut it very thin and hammer it as flat as possible. Make one of the frying pans very hot and lay the steak into it without butter or seasoning. Fry for 2 minutes on each side.

While the steak is frying, separately crush 1 clove of garlic into 1 teaspoon of chopped parsley. Mix with 1 pinch of salt and pepper. Place the steak on a very hot serving platter and sprinkle with the garlic parsley.

In the other frying pan have ready 2 tablespoons of sizzling hot butter. This must be poured over the steak immediately after the garlic parsley. Season.

POTATOES, JOEL R. POINSETT

Put 1 finely chopped shallot into a frying pan with 1 tablespoon of butter. Cook for 3 minutes. Add 4 sliced cold boiled potatoes (that have been cooked with their skins), and 2 finely chopped mushrooms. Sauté for 5 minutes.

Place it all into a baking dish and add 1 chopped peeled tomato, 1 cup of cream, and 1 tablespoon of butter. Season with pepper and salt. Bake in a preheated moderately hot oven of 375° to 400° F. for 20 minutes.

BRUSSELS SPROUTS, WALTER FORWARD

Clean and wash 1 quart of first quality Brussels sprouts. Pick them over carefully, place in a colander, remove all wilted leaves and let cold water run over them until they are thoroughly washed. Boil for 30 minutes in plenty of salted water. Drain, and let them remain on the fire for a moment to dry off all remaining water.

Broil 2 thin slices of raw ham and dice them. Put the Brussels sprouts on a baking platter and sprinkle the diced ham over them.

Stir 2 tablespoons of grated cheese into ½ cup of cream. Add 1 pinch of paprika and 1 tablespoon of melted butter. Mix well and pour it over the Brussels sprouts and ham.

Mix 1 tablespoon of finely chopped walnuts with 1 tablespoon of bread crumbs and 1 tablespoon of chopped, crisply broiled bacon. Sprinkle it over the sauce. Place in a preheated moderately hot oven of 375° to 400° F. for 10 minutes. Season.

SALAD, WILLIAM WIRT

Wash 2 handfuls of tender young dandelions. Clean them well and let them remain in cold water for a while to become crisp. Shake off water without bruising the greens. Cut them. Cut 1 carrot julienne style and add it to the dandelions. Mix, and place in a salad bowl.

Make 1 slice of toast and dice it into a separate bowl. Crush 1 clove of garlic into 1 tablespoon of chopped parsley and add it to the diced toast. Broil 6 slices of bacon very crisp, crush, and add also. Mix and sprinkle over the dandelions and carrots. Pour 3 tablespoons of French Dressing over and mix.

PUDDING, HELEN KELLER

Beat the whites of 4 eggs until they are stiff, and stand them aside for a moment.

Put 1½ cups of milk into a pan. Add 2 tablespoons of vanilla sugar (or 2 tablespoons of sugar and 1 teaspoon of vanilla extract), and 1 tablespoon of butter. When it comes to a boil add ½ cup of boiled rice. Stir well, and when it begins to boil again remove it from the fire. Quickly stir in 4 beaten egg yolks. Then immediately add the stiffly beaten whites. Mix thoroughly.

Butter a mold and sprinkle it with a few pinches of flour. Then pour in the above ingredients. Place the mold in a pan of boiling water and put in a preheated hot oven of 400° F. for 30 minutes.

Place 1 tablespoon of vanilla sugar (or just 1 tablespoon of plain sugar if you have used the vanilla extract) into a pan with 2 tablespoons of cream. When it comes to a boil remove from the fire and stir 2 more beaten egg yolks into it until it thickens. Then add 2 ponies of rum. Stir it well and pour it over the pudding which has been removed from the mold and placed on a serving platter.

Chapter XXII

MONEY MAKES MONEY

THE SIX GOLD 100 FRANC PIECES that I had received from Mr. Bennett didn't remain six pieces very long. A few days later destiny ordained that I, a boy of not quite eleven, was to make another large sum of money. Later on, in Chicago, my hope was renewed by the memories of those early days and gave me the courage to work fourteen hours a day for much less money. It's true that my associates in Chicago were not like the magnanimous Mr. Bennett.

Three days after the "Battle of the Flowers" at Menton I had that rendezvous with destiny. I had resumed my duties as page boy at the Cap Martin, and my turn came, on the third evening, to do extra duty and serve on the last watch. I waited, by myself, for the last guest to come in before locking up. If one decided he wouldn't return that evening he always called the concierge on the telephone and said, "There's no use waiting for me, I won't be in tonight." In those days a hotel was more like a large home in which each guest was a member of the family. The manager, concierge, or any other employee took care of him with a full sense of duty, and with manners and affection. Those employees learned that it was the tradition of the hotel to live and die in the business. Each was like a branch on a tree and fulfilled his duty without counting the hours he worked. The guest was there to be pleased, and the employees were happy to accommodate him. Princes, kings, etc., were not too proud to shake hands and talk to them, because they knew those faithful people were part of their lives.

That night when I was on late duty the hours seemed to drag. There was no noise except the snoring of the German concierge and the pendulum of the clock in the lobby, as it ticked away the minutes. Every quarter of an hour the little carillon struck musical notes that went up and then down the scale. It was up to me not to fall asleep, and at my tender age that's just what I wanted to do. But it was my duty to act like the man I felt I was. I was the policeman at the front door, the only sentry who guarded the sleeping royalty. It's nice to say that nothing out of the way ever happened at the Cap Martin in the three seasons I worked there, nor in the subsequent years. The tranquillity of that charming hotel was never disturbed. I still believe that the perfume of the flowers was enough to change any bad instincts into good ones, since that place was literally the gateway to another paradise. I think Bailet would have stopped at the entrance, afraid to go in because his stable odor would have spoiled the atmosphere. And he, in his kind heart, would have been the first to recognize it.

I looked through the glass door and strolled over to the clock whenever the quarter hour struck. I kept walking around the lobby, afraid that the title of "man" would disappear if I fell asleep. All the guests had been accounted for except one, and I wondered if he was ever going to come in.

At 2:30 A.M. a Victoria pulled by two horses stopped at the entrance. I opened the door to receive that last guest, an English lord. Pipou, the coachman, who was well known to me, had often driven to the Cap Martin. I always addressed him as "Monsieur Pipou." One of those who had kindly given me the names of numerous passengers for the furtherance of my career, I had offered him many cigars in the time I had known him, and he felt kindly disposed toward me. The English lord was intoxicated and needed assistance. Pipou helped me, and, together, we got him into the lobby. Milord may have had too little strength in his legs, and too much liquor may have gone to his brain, but, and to my wonderment, he still had strength in his hands. He gripped a leather bag in his right hand as if it were riveted to him.

Pipou took the English lord by the shoulders, and I took his feet; we carried him to his apartment, which was on the main floor facing the sea. The leather bag, which he still tightly clutched, bumped along the floor. After we stretched him across the bed, Pipou left; he had been paid in advance. It was a good thing, too, that the coachman had been Pipou and not one that was unknown, because of the contents of the leather bag.

The English lord tried to rise from the bed, but instead rolled off onto the floor, dragging the bag with him. As it landed, the catch opened, causing gold pieces and bank notes to spill out over the rug. It was raining gold! The Englishman had won more than $50,000 at the roulette wheel in the casino at Monte Carlo.

Two thoughts flashed through my mind: I must lock the door from the inside and watch milord and his treasure; and, nothing must happen to that money, or I'd be blamed for it.

The little white light burning in the lobby showed that the page boy was still on duty. It was customary for him, on finishing work, to extinguish it and light a small red one. But I couldn't leave milord and his money to do that; some one might come and trick us both.

I opened the Englishman's collar, vest, and trousers. He was too heavy for me to lift back on the bed so I took two pillows and placed them under his head, and covered him with a blanket. I thought, "Now I've really matured into a man. I have a grown man's duty to perform. Very few people have ever seen this much money, or have ever had the chance to acquire it."

I closed and locked the windows. I locked the door to the adjoining room in his suite and placed furniture in front of it. I sat down in an armchair and looked at the Englishman, my prisoner. It was an easy victory for Morpheus who, ten minutes later, made us both his captives.

Time passed. Jean Devisse came on duty at 4:30 A.M. and saw the little white light still burning. And no Henri. He was afraid to tell anyone and thought he'd wait a few hours to see what would happen. Time passed, and still no Henri. Monsieur Ulrick made an appearance, and Jean, hesitating at first, told him that he couldn't find me anywhere.

The manager asked, "Isn't he downstairs?"

"No, sir."

It was up to the boy who closed for the night to be in the lobby ready for work at ten the next morning. It was only nine, but Monsieur Ulrick asked, "Who was the last guest to come in last night?" He looked in the book and saw the name I had written, that of the English lord in apartment six. He and several employees, who had gathered, went into the foyer of that apartment and listened. They heard the snoring duet of the prisoners, and when Monsieur Ulrick said, "Yes, he's in there," it woke me up.

I asked, "Is that you, Monsieur Ulrick?"

I opened the door just a little, enough to admit his head and shoulders. When he saw the English gentleman on the floor, covered up like a baby, and all the money scattered around the room, he pushed the others out of the foyer, saying, "Go back to your duties in the lobby."

I told him my story, of how I had been afraid to leave the room long enough to extinguish the light in the lobby for fear that someone might come, in my absence, and take the money.

He complimented me on the way I had acted, saying, "It's no wonder that Madame 'Darling' likes you so much."

He patted my cheek, and my eyes became misty. "You don't like me, Monsieur?"

He said, "Certainly, I like you very much. What you have done proves once more that, even though you've only been in the hotel business a few months, you've converted yourself into a hotel man in the same way that a priest gives himself into the service of God."

Our talking awoke the English lord, who yawned and stretched himself on the floor. In my boy's mind I thought of Bacci. That dog always went through those same maneuvers every morning before he got up and trotted downstairs for his coffee.

Milord got up and began conversing with the manager in English. What they said was a mystery to me. Monsieur Ulrick asked me what had happened. I told the Englishman that Pipou and I had carried him into the room and stretched him across the bed. I explained how he had dropped his bag on the floor, and that when I saw all the money

I had decided it was my duty to remain and watch both milord and the treasure.

He told me to recover the gold and place it in the bag again. When it had all been restored, he dipped into the bag and brought out a large handful of coins and said, "That's for you, young fellow." I cupped my hands and held them out; there were too many for one hand. I put them into my pockets and thanked him very much.

I went to my room, as I usually did when I received a large remuneration, and locked the door. I emptied my pockets. There were thirteen 100 franc gold pieces, or about $260. Since that day I have always considered thirteen as my number. All the good and bad luck that I have had has always occurred on the thirteenth.

In less than four days I had earned nineteen 100 franc gold pieces; six from Mr. Bennett and thirteen from the English lord. Those coins amounted to 1900 francs, or about $400. Money certainly makes money.

A Jack Among Four Queens

IT WAS MID-SEASON at the Cap Martin. Flowers, in their huge vases, and plants, in their variously colored pots, adorned the entire hotel and gave it the appearance of being dressed in a new gown for another festive occasion. The sun helped to create this illusion. By its warmth, and with the assistance of a little breeze, the aromas of the jasmine, rose, carnation, violet, and geranium flowers in the garden were gently wafted through the windows and permeated the hotel. The landscaped beds of flowers that made a paradise of the Cap Martin could not be cut; to do that would have destroyed their scenic beauty. But they, too, wanted to join the blossoms within the hotel in presenting their message to the royal guests. So the sun and the breeze, in their understanding, assisted them in achieving their desire. The orange trees that were in blossom sent their perfume and, along with the fragrant rosemary and thyme, completed the ensemble. Those flowers may not have been in evidence, but their fragrances were idealistically present throughout the hotel.

And festive occasion it was, too, I found out later. That certain morning, in addition to my various duties, I had to change the ink at the tables in the writing room. I took the inkwells to the bottom of the service stairs to clean them. Brooms, wax, candles, etc., which were used by the page boys, were kept underneath the stairs. Jean Devisse opened the door and yelled down, "Henri, Monsieur Ulrick wants to see you at once."

In my hurry to be prompt I forgot there was a full quart bottle of ink standing on the stairs.

The manager said, as I entered his office, "Henri, her Majesty Empress Elizabeth of Austria is having a tea this afternoon at 3 o'clock. It will be served under the direction of Monsieur Cassut. At that time I want you to have on your gala uniform and be ready and waiting in the suite which has been set aside for her Majesty. Monsieur Cassut, however, wants to see you in the suite at one-thirty so he can give you your instructions."

I returned to the inkwells at the bottom of the stairs and found the quart bottle broken and ink spattered on the steps, floor, and walls. Who had done it was to remain a mystery; no one seemed to know anything about it. So I took the blame for it. I scrubbed the ink stains with a brush and some soap, but couldn't remove them.

Thirty years later, when I returned to the Cap Martin for a visit I surprised another little page boy by handing him a generous tip and saying, "Well, little fellow, I used to be a page boy in this same hotel."

The boy began to laugh and said he didn't believe it.

I asked, "Is the big ink spot underneath the service stairs still there?"

His face paled and his eyes opened wide. "*Oui* monsieur," he said.

I said, almost proudly, "I'm the fellow who was guilty of spilling the ink, or at least I was blamed for it."

But to return to the newly made ink stains. After scrubbing for a while I became tired with the futility of it all and quit. I was glad the guests of the hotel didn't have to use those stairs, especially that tall English gentleman who might write another letter to Monsieur Ulrick and be the cause of more useless scrubbing by myself.

At 1:30 P.M. I went to the suite where the tea was to be given.

Monsieur Cassut greeted me with, "Are you here too, little mouse?"

It was to be my duty to place the four footstools at the feet of the royal guests when they sat down.

The maître d' asked, "How would you do it?"

He watched me rehearse with the four empty armchairs and footstools. I placed a footstool, in readiness, at the left side of each chair, which must have been all right because he asked, "What are you going to do now? Her Majesty Queen Victoria will be seated in this chair; her Majesty Empress Eugénie will occupy the one on her right; her Majesty Queen Margherita of Italy will be next; and her Majesty Empress Elizabeth of Austria will be seated in the fourth chair. What now?"

I said, going through the motions at the same time, "First, I'll take the footstool from the left of the chair, bow to her Majesty Queen Victoria, rest on one knee, place it at her feet, bow again, and retire. I'll do the same with each of the footstools, approaching from the left and returning the same way so that I won't have to pass in front of their Majesties at any time."

Monsieur Cassut said, "All right, if you do it exactly that way, it'll be fine."

Monsieur Ulrick had said tea would be served, and I thought, "What a disturbance for a cup of tea." I was very surprised, when I looked at the long buffet table, to see such a great assortment of *galantines* and *pâté de foies gras* on ice. There was a sculptured eagle that had been shaped from a large block of ice, with a huge box of fresh caviar resting in its base. On either side of the eagle there were different colored baskets made of candy and filled with *pâtisseries* and *petits fours*. Next to each basket were horns of plenty, also made of candy. They gave the appearance of being filled with fruit which overflowed into two large baskets.

I understood, then, why there was so much ado, but I couldn't figure out why the insignificant cup of tea should receive such acclaim. Why should that elaborate feast be called a tea? Tea to Maman Camous was an entirely different thing. She and the people of Contes only drank it when they didn't feel well. Later, when I told her the story I never mentioned the beverage because she never would have understood. If I had said that a mere cup of tea went with that royal feast, it would have spoiled the story for her.

It was an hour yet before the arrival of our royal guests, and so, after the rehearsal with Monsieur Cassut, I went to the lobby for a moment where I saw Monsieur Ulrick standing with his high hat in his hand. That meant the reception committee was all ready.

He saw me and asked, "What are you doing here?"

I couldn't answer. My curiosity had prompted me to see what preparations were being made outside the hotel, and what the French soldiers and the committee of French politicians and diplomats looked like. I was saved from my embarrassing situation by old Mr. Marriott, a wonderful, deaf, English gentleman, who permitted me to make four or five francs regularly every day, besides an additional five on Sunday. Every time his cane dropped I picked it up, and he gave me one franc for my courtesy. The manager saw me retrieve it many times a day; he also saw that when the old gentleman rested his hand on something else his cane always received a little assistance in falling. I looked at Mr. Marriott and, with my foot, tapped it a little to make it drop onto the floor. Then I picked it up, gave it to him, and received another franc. If he kept on talking to me the same thing happened again, and again I became one franc richer. One day I made three francs in less than ten minutes and then discovered that Monsieur Ulrick had been watching me. I could have made a few more if the manager hadn't called me.

I said, "At your service, monsieur."

He let his newspaper drop onto the floor, and when I picked it up he said, "This time there'll be no franc. I'm not Mr. Marriott. You must use, but not abuse."

He didn't give me a franc, but he did give me a bit of logic in the words "use, but do not abuse," as well as the idea that I must look around before I pushed Mr. Marriott's cane again. During my first season at the Cap Martin I made close to a thousand francs because of that cane. No wonder Mr. Marriott laughed when I kissed it every time I picked it up! I think he was onto my little trick and the money I was making because of it. But he was tremendously wealthy and very old and expected to die at any moment, while I was very young and filled with the desire to live. So his cane helped both of us, and every time I kissed it I was reminded of Don Albini who kissed the cross during mass.

That afternoon, when Monsieur Ulrick demanded to know what I was doing in the lobby, Mr. Marriott saved me by sending me to his apartment to get his cigarette case, which he had forgotten. That gave me a chance to return to the lobby once more to satisfy my curiosity and to please Mr. Marriott without disobeying the manager.

Everyone was ready and at his post when Queen Victoria, the first of the royal guests, arrived. Each came separately, but on time, and in great splendor. Empress Elizabeth, who had a suite on the main floor, came to the lobby and engaged in conversation with Queen Victoria. Then Empress Eugénie arrived, and a moment later Queen Margherita. After chatting for a few moments they were escorted to the party room where they seated themselves. Little Henri performed exactly as he had at the rehearsal. A long line of noble ladies and gentlemen passed in front of the royal guests, bowed and went on. That continued for half an hour, during which time I acted as doorman. The invited guests gathered in the antechamber, and when Monsieur Cassut pushed the large sliding doors open, the serving of the famous tea began. I was there, in attendance until the finale, a jack among four queens.

HIGH  HAT

s a Cuisine of Ours

ER 20 yrs. at Lynbrook, which
in Long Island, Mr. Henri
iculous cuisinier in America, is picking up his pos-
tter. Here in a modern French setting, Mons. Charpentier, probably the most skilful
s in New York. There he will hang his shingle—
ving them over to a new stand at Radio City.
Henri Charpentier—right smack on the walls of the new
Francaise and make room for 350 diners. The ter-
ving on the sunken court (which sports a statue of
liers Going Whoops) will allow for 200 outdoor feed-
s and when it rains, or seals—there is room for 150
In other words, the whole menage will echo the
e and atmosphere of the Café de Paris itself, which
ris (which is in France).
ever, one should not mention feeding & the new
s the same breath. It is sacrilege gastronomic. One
at Charpentier's—one dines. For, as there is
nce of astronomy, so is there the art of gastronomy.
Charpie has never been one to stint himself of Na-
best when it comes to preparing a meal. He is indeed
antavara—the idealist—of the kitchen range.
He will import his own wines, serving Champagne

tues. M. Henri is privy to
—champignons Cepes Mor
—will be imported in sea
are cultivated mushrooms, it
are gathered at certain phases of the moon fro
cial beds which nestle between olive trees and
in the Provence District, which is in France.
these are mushrooms which hardly have had
background of the ordinary mushroom, they a
vated and aristocratic, they practically speak
an Oxford accent. It is familiar French legen
are set up with at nights when ill.

(Page

HENRI
OF LYNBROO
AND RADIO C

La Maison Française in Ra
has acquired for its chef the
ing Frenchman, Monsieur
Lynbrook, whose famous cre
ette and other delicacies are
with the subtleties of his ow
Says Henri to Redbook: "It
great pleasure to give to
original recipe for my own
the crepes Suzette which I se
the first time to the Prince
(later Edward VII of Englan
early days of my career." H
it is: Make a very thin pa
the usual way—i. e., eggs, fl
and water, pinch of salt.
cake into this mixture: The
an orange and part of the
lemon, sliced very thinly, fre
vanilla sugar, Maraschino,
Kirschwasser, and Curaçao
all melted together in a cho
Now add and set, fire to
quantity of cordials you care
before, moving the chafing
and forth over the burner s
flaming solution reaches al
the pancake. Then remove
cake to plate, and pour o
cordial sauce in which it w

HENRI
CHARPENTIER

AFE Henri Charpentier, the rendezvous of gourmets,
New York's finest restaurant in the continental man
ner. Here in a modern French setting, Mons. Charpentier, disciple of the great Auguste Escoffier and host
Royalty, concocts those amazing dishes for which he is so
mous: Tortue Verte au Vieux Madère; Rognon de Veau
s au Vin Blanc; Champignons Cepes Morilles; and Fraise
u Bois—those tiny wild strawberries imported all the way
m France and served with double cream in little earthen
are pots.

AFE Henri Charpentier

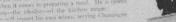

Mingling with Kings Gave
M. Charpentier His Finesse

So Now Lynbrook Restaurateur, Planning to Open in Radio
City, Will Employ Only Gentlemen—Found Empress
Eugenie Sweet, but Hates Gum Chewers

Henri Charpentier, the sage restaurateur of Lynbro
who will open a big restaurant in Rockefeller Cente
Maison Française this month, talked today of the times w
he mingled with kings and of the qualities of a true ge
man and of the soul.

Mingling with kings, half a lifetime ago, got him
the restaurant business, he said.
He was a boy of 16 at the Cap Mar
tin on the Riviera, and though he
was impressed then, this is what he
has learned since:
"Nobility is not carried on by
title but by the soul. I know many
Americans and they are very so
much nobler. They need no title."
Yet there was one who, long ago,
made an indelible mark upon him.
She was Empress Eugenie

in the jacket of the maître
But in case monsieur sees me
out either of them, I am th
gentleman.
His theory of the square
elucidated thus:
"When you give somethi
is wrong, you do wrong to
you want the beautiful e
of the men you serve."

HENRI CHARPENTIER, host to royalty
and gourmets of two continents, trans-
forms the beautiful HOUSE OF MORGAN
into a paradise for epicures.

And Now
Liqueur
Suzette

That grand old man himself,
Henri Charpentier, internationally famous chef and originator
of Crepes Suzette, has now been
done in china—chef's cap, white
uniform, mixing spoon and all
—to hold Liqueur Suzette, that
special blend of choice liqueurs
prepared by the master himself
to enable everyone to make
Crepes Suzette in the authentic
way—to give an air of authen-
ity to home kitchen or bar.
With Liqueur Suzette, even
nat a "fairly good cook can be
re of achieving perfect
wa the

THE
STAGE

Helen's
BACK
AT THE
House of Morgan

Luncheon - 12 to 3 P.M. One twenty-five per person

Cocktail Hour - Every afternoon 4 to 7

On Saturdays
CHAMPAGNE SUZETTE DANSANT
(The smartest innovation in town)

One-fifty { Canapé Nicois
            Crepes Suzette
            Coupe Champagne

Dinner
From 6:00 P.M . . . Prix Fixe Two-fifty per person

Henri Charpentier will also dispense his world renowned
a la carte service at your pleasure

(George Jean Nathan calls him the greatest Chef in Christendom)

owners of restaura
ke usually write v
tudy script. Since the
good food invariabl
teristic of a good coo
fe to look for heav
ure. A thin cook is a
owever, that does no
ll heavy scripts deno
'cooking'!
M. Charpentier doe
pressions. It is inky a
phasis in on the curve
—another indication o
in material things. H
angular and it is in the
ter formations that w
telligence and shrewd
made him top one
fession. He is quick a
efficient and exacting.
like i-dots are evidenc
critical mind. One ca
heavy, closely written
he is a good judge of
demands it, yet is not

HOUSE OF MORGAN » 49 East 54th at Madison » NEW YORK

N. Y. Times
"All Hail The House of (Henri) Morgan"

Henri Charpentier, who best made crepes
Suzette, making crepes Suzette at his own han

RECIPES

✤

HORS-D'OEUVRE, WILLIAM WHIPPLE

✤

SOUP, JAMES M. CRAFTS

✤

SCRAMBLED EGGS, LYMAN R. BLAKE

✤

EGGS, WILLIAM S. BURROUGHS

✤

BAKED CRABMEAT, BOOKER T. WASHINGTON

✤

CHICKEN, ALEXANDER GRAHAM BELL

✤

POTATOES, CHARLES ALBERT SPENCER

✤

CAULIFLOWER, THOMAS EWING

✤

SALAD, HENRY WADSWORTH LONGFELLOW

✤

SOUFFLE, GRACE ABBOTT

✤

HORS-D'OEUVRE, WILLIAM WHIPPLE

Prepare a pancake batter, using 1 egg, 1 tablespoon of flour, 2 tablespoons of milk, and a pinch of salt. Mix well. It should have the consistency of heavy cream. Mix well and stir in 1 large tablespoon of chopped chives. This preparation will make 4 small pancakes, enough for 2.

Place 1 teaspoon of butter into an omelet pan and let it become very hot. Make 4 very thin pancakes, one at a time, and let each one become brown. Use 1 teaspoon of butter in making each pancake.

To 1 finely chopped shallot, add 2 large tablespoons of caviar. Stir together very gently.

Place a pancake on each serving plate and spread with the caviar, etc. Cover with the two remaining pancakes.

Beat 3 large tablespoons of sour cream and spread over the top. Sprinkle with 1 chopped hard-boiled egg and 1 teaspoon of chopped chives.

SOUP, JAMES M. CRAFTS

Boil separately until tender: ½ cup of shelled green peas, ¼ cup of asparagus tips, and ½ cup of diced green beans. Pour off water and put vegetables together.

Put 1 quart of consommé into a pot and when it begins to boil add the vegetables. Cover and boil for 2 minutes. Season with salt and pepper.

Put the yolk of 1 egg into each soup plate as well as 2 tablespoons of cream and a small piece of butter, before ladling the boiling soup.

SCRAMBLED EGGS, LYMAN R. BLAKE

Put 1 tablespoon of butter into a pan with 1 finely chopped shallot and cook for 3 minutes. Add 1 finely chopped leek, 1 finely chopped celery heart, 2 thinly sliced mushrooms, 2 chopped peeled tomatoes, ½ finely chopped green pepper, ½ clove of garlic which has been crushed into a little chopped parsley, a few leaves of basil, ½ sherry-glass of red wine, and 1 teaspoon of meat stock. Cook for 20 minutes. Sprinkle with 1 pinch of pepper and 1 pinch of salt. Stir.

Scramble 6 eggs and pour the garniture over the top. Season to taste. Large croutons that have been rubbed with garlic should be served with these eggs.

EGGS, WILLIAM S. BURROUGHS

Chop 1 onion and place it into a pan with 1 tablespoon of butter. Brown it.

Take the green part of 1 chicory salad (keep the white part for a salad). Chop it fine and add it to the onion. Cover and simmer for 15 minutes. Then add 4 chopped hard-boiled eggs, 1 clove of garlic that has been crushed into a little chopped parsley, 2 chopped peeled tomatoes, 1 more tablespoon of butter, 1 teaspoon of meat stock, 1 pinch of pepper, 1 pinch of salt, and 1 sherry-glassful of claret. Cook for 5 minutes.

Boil 2 handfuls of noodles for 15 minutes. Strain. Be sure they are free of all water. Place them on the bottom of a baking dish. Cover with the chicory, etc., and bake in a preheated moderate oven of 350° F. for 15 minutes. Season to taste.

BAKED CRABMEAT, BOOKER T. WASHINGTON

Use 1 pound of crabmeat for this recipe.

Place 2 tablespoons of butter into a pan with 2 finely chopped shallots and cook for 3 minutes. Add 4 thinly sliced mushrooms, 1 cup of cream, 2 sherry-glasses of sherry, 2 ponies of brandy, 2 chopped hard-boiled eggs, and 1 pinch each of salt, pepper and paprika. Then add the crabmeat. Stir, and when it come to a boil place it into a baking dish. Sprinkle with small croutons that have been fried in butter. Sprinkle also with a little grated cheese and bake in a preheated hot oven of 400° F. for 10 minutes. An accompanying small glass of sherry would be appreciated with this dish. Season to taste.

CHICKEN, ALEXANDER GRAHAM BELL

Clean, wash, and boil a 2 pound chicken for 40 minutes. Let it remain in the hot consommé for the moment.

Boil 1 cup of rice in some of the chicken consommé.

Put 2 tablespoons of butter into a pan and add 2 finely chopped shallots, 1 cup of cream, 1 pinch of salt, 1 pinch of pepper, 1 teaspoon of curry powder, 2 pinches of paprika, and 2 sherry-glasses of dry sherry. When it comes to a boil thicken it with the beaten yolks of 3 eggs.

Place the whole boiled chicken on a nest made of the boiled rice. Pour the boiling sauce over the chicken and sprinkle with chopped chives. Season to taste.

POTATOES, CHARLES ALBERT SPENCER

Bake 2 large Idaho potatoes. Cut their tops off lengthwise (do not throw the tops away). Remove the insides.

Boil 1 whole green vegetable marrow for 15 minutes. Pour off the water and squeeze it to remove all the water it may contain. Put it into a frying-pan and add: 1 tablespoon of butter, 1 finely chopped shallot, 1 tablespoon of bread crumbs, 1 tablespoon of cream, and 1 tablespoon of chili sauce. When it comes to a bubbling boil add the potato pulp, 1 more tablespoon of butter, and 1 more tablespoon of cream. Stir well, season, and stuff into the potato shells. Sprinkle with a little grated cheese. Replace the tops and bake in a preheated hot oven of 400° F. for 10 minutes.

CAULIFLOWER, THOMAS EWING

Take 1 small firm head of cauliflower. Cut off the stalk and all leaves. Wash and boil whole until tender in plenty of water which has been salted. To keep the cauliflower white, add the juice of ½ lemon to the water while it is cooking.

Take it from the water and lay it on a clean cloth for a moment to remove all water. Place on a serving platter and sprinkle with a few pinches of salt and 1 pinch of freshly ground black pepper. Squeeze the juice of ½ lemon over the cauliflower and serve with hollandaise.

SALAD, HENRY WADSWORTH LONGFELLOW

Take the white leaves of 1 small chicory salad, 1 handful of water-cress, and 1 handful of field salad.

Put a large lettuce leaf on each salad plate and arrange the chicory salad, water-cress, and field salad on top in separate piles. In the middle place 1 peeled and diced boiled beet. Sprinkle with 1 chopped hard-boiled egg.

Mix 1 tablespoon of chili sauce with 3 tablespoons of French Dressing and 1 teaspoon of Worcestershire sauce. Pour over each salad.

SOUFFLE, GRACE ABBOTT

Beat the whites of 6 eggs until they are stiff, and stand them aside for a moment. The yolks of 3 eggs only are used in this recipe.

Put 1¼ cups of milk into a saucepan. Add ⅓ cup of sifted flour and ¾ cup of vanilla sugar. (Or, ¾ cup of sugar and 1 teaspoon or more, as you like, of vanilla extract.) If, however, you do use the already prepared vanilla sugar, add ½ vanilla bean during this first stage. Stir constantly over a small fire until it thickens. Remove the vanilla bean, wash it, and put it back into your jarful of vanilla sugar for future use. Remove the thickened sugar, flour, and milk from the fire. Pass it through a sieve. Quickly stir in 3 beaten egg yolks. Mix it well and immediately add the stiffly beaten egg whites. Stir it well.

Take a pyrex baking dish that is no more than 2 inches deep. Butter it thoroughly, using your fingers, and sprinkle a little powdered sugar into the bottom.

Have ready 1 large tablespoon of ground roasted hazelnuts. Stir into the saucepan. Then pour the contents into the baking dish. To obtain the best results, the baking dish must be completely filled.

Have the oven preheated and turned to 250° or 300° F. to start. Bake it for 5 or 6 minutes at that temperature and then turn it up to 350° F. Total baking time is approximately 25 minutes. Three minutes before removing it from the oven sprinkle a little powdered sugar on top of the soufflé to give it a slightly brown and lustrous appearance. Serve immediately.

Chapter XXIII

THE END OF
THE SEASON

THE END OF THE SEASON at the Cap Martin was marked by the blossoming orange trees. The noble clientele began to make reservations for their journeys home: some to Russia, some to England, Holland, Austria, etc., etc. During that first season of mine the "Iron Chancellor," Bismarck, the mortal enemy of Papa Camous, was a guest of the Cap Martin. He was one of the last to leave. When I assisted him to his carriage for his return home to Germany, he gave me a gold piece of twenty German marks. I didn't thank him because I pictured that coin as one of the many billions that France had given in payment for the Prussian war of 1870. Mention of that payment always made Papa Camous fighting mad. I think the "Iron Chancellor" noticed, because he turned to the man who was with him and muttered something about, "Another Frenchman, you can't buy 'em."

He asked, "Are you a French boy?"

I replied, "Yes, monsieur," ignoring the fact that he had the title of a prince, "in 1870 my Papa Camous fought in the war."

I was ready to tell him about our pigs, but the Cap Martin had already inculcated in me the proper attitude one should have toward a guest.

The gentleman who terminated that short interview and speeded the departure of the "Iron Chancellor" was Mr. J. P. Morgan, Sr.

The first time I ever saw Mr. Morgan I thought, "What a funny nose." That was several months before, when he had stopped me and asked, "What's your name, little fellow?"

"Henri, monsieur."

Then he said something I'll never forget, "When you meet me in the morning you must look at my nose and then say, 'Bonjour, Monsieur Morgan.' "

With that, bit of psychology he did away with any comments that might have been made concerning his nose. My deepest respects to that grand American gentleman who knew how to make a path in the forest without cutting any trees. I have had the pleasure of meeting and serving him many times in my life; often at my place in Lynbrook, Long Island.

Mr. Morgan, Sr., at the very time of the "Iron Chancellor's" departure, requested a carriage to take him to Monte Carlo. I went to the yard where they were assembled to pick one for him personally. He knew I wouldn't select just any carriage, coachman or horses, but would choose an outfit that befitted his dignity. For instance, I didn't want a carriage that lacked varnish on the wheels, that had a lantern missing, or wasn't clean. I wouldn't select a coachman who wasn't shaved, or who drove horses that didn't match in color. The coachman, carriage, horses, and harness must be clean and shining. After the inspection, and with the words *"C'est bien,"* I jumped onto the running board. The two brown, black, or white horses that I had chosen had lustrous hair and short ears, and a peppy coachman who was ready to fly with them. When we arrived at the front entrance even the horses co-operated, because they stopped with the same feet. I jumped down and announced, "Monsieur Morgan, your carriage awaits. Pierre, the coachman I have chosen, is yours to command." That made Mr. Morgan smile; he was always delighted with my choice.

Within the next few days many guests left; and the second, third, and fourth floors of the hotel were cleaned and closed for the season. The chambermaids and housemen covered the crystal chandeliers and furniture. Draperies were taken down, cleaned, and put away. Mattresses and rugs were renovated. Everything was made spic-and-span. Special coverings were placed on the waxed floors to protect them over the summer. Windows were washed, and the blinds closed and locked.

The only thing that remained was the memory of those lovely noble guests; it was a pleasure to think that next season they would be returning. I had a few dejected moments when I thought of each apartment and the guest or guests who had occupied it.

Empress Elizabeth of Austria, who had a suite of twenty rooms, was almost the last to leave, and when she did it really marked the end of the season. The only royal personage left in the vicinity of the hotel was Empress Eugénie, and she would soon leave Villa Cyrnos for Farnborough Hill.

I, too, was busy making preparations. I had had a tailor make a large special pocket which he stitched into my beautiful blue suit. That suit had been made to order by Monsieur Ulrick's tailor.

That inquisitive fellow asked, "Do you want to put a plate in it?"

"No, it's something to protect my heart."

"Oh, you have heart disease?"

"No," I replied, "but my heart is my sweetheart and I must take care of it." I became like Don Albini, who loved his mystery, and the tailor found out nothing. If he had known for what that pocket was to be used I might never have reached Contes. I didn't believe in telling anyone about a mission before it was accomplished; it could be told later but never before.

I opened the iron box in my trunk and took out the paper-wrapped coins. Altogether I had 7,000 francs, or $1,400. I put some of them aside for my own personal use. I put the rest into a large pouch and sewed each one down separately. Then I put the pouch into the large special pocket and pinned both securely together with four big safety pins. I locked my coat in the closet and began rearranging the things I had in my trunk. The one Jean Camous had given to me wasn't large enough, so I had to buy another. Michel accommodated me with one that had belonged to Mr. Marriott, the gentleman with the famous cane. The porter, who was going to remain in the hotel as a caretaker, had no need for it and sold it to me for ten francs. It was a wonderful bargain and was still good when the prohibition agents came to my place on Friday, June 6, 1930, and took it away. It was filled, then, with bottles of very old brandy that were worth $100 each; rarities that any cellar in the world would have been proud to possess. Before bottling, the brandy had remained in a wooden cask for 175 years. The spirit of Mr. Marriott must have had a final good laugh at my expense.

The trunk which had arrived at the hotel almost empty I filled to the top with suits, etc., which had been given to me to distribute around Contes. Some of the royal ladies had asked me whether my relatives could use certain garments. I always said, "Yes," and took everything I could get. Somebody in Contes might wear those clothes for his Sunday outfit. Most of the room in that big trunk was occupied with things from wardrobes other than my own. There were ties, gloves, shoes, dresses, suits, etc., including a silk sun umbrella. Maman Camous kept that umbrella all of her life, and now, 53 years later, it's in the possession of her daughter-in-law, Virginie.

I reserved part of the top section for my things. There were six suits of underwear, one dozen pairs of stockings, two dozen handkerchiefs, some of which were made of Lyon silk and some of Chinese, my old shoes, etc. A great many of those things were given to me as presents for services rendered to the noble guests.

On entering an apartment I would exclaim, "What beautiful linen you have, my prince!"

The prince would laugh and say, "I think you'd like to have a handkerchief."

"Not to use, my prince, but as a souvenir; like the flag of the regiment: to look at, but not to touch."

Because I had complimented him, he gave me a handkerchief worth $10.

My uniforms were to be left at the Cap Martin so that, after cleaning, they'd be ready for the next season.

The second trunk was filled with separately wrapped presents for everyone I could think of in Contes. I had several presents for Badou; these I wrapped into one package and held out. I was going to give it to him on our way home. I had purchased packages of smoking tobacco, snuff, chewing tobacco, candies, etc., including a fourteen pound box of candy for Madame Christini, the largest box that had ever been seen in Contes. When I showed it to the Duchess of Rutland, who was very interested in me, I said, "This one's for Madame Christini." Then I told her the story of the big piece of meat.

She kissed both my cheeks and said, "Don't ever change, Henri, my boy. I'll let you pay for this one yourself."

She put a beautiful silk, buff colored handkerchief into the breast pocket of my coat, and it wasn't until a few days later that I discovered she had folded a 100 franc note in it. I was lucky I didn't lose it, but then I never used the handkerchief; I kept it as a memento. The duchess, in the meantime, had left for England so I couldn't thank her until she returned the next season.

I marked "Handle with Care" on top of both my trunks. It was unnecessary because everything was tightly packed, contrary to the rattling trunk with which I had arrived.

Now it was my turn to leave. I was almost the last employee to go, and when my baggage was placed on the stagecoach I went to say goodbye to Madame and Monsieur Ulrick, who, with their French peasant maid, were to remain a few days longer. All three of them, then, would go to the Ulrick summer residence at Sospel, a little village at the top of the mountains.

Madame "Darling" said goodbye and kissed both my cheeks.

Monsieur Ulrick asked, "What about me?"

I jumped to his neck, happy to place my arms around him, and kissed him on both cheeks. There were a few tears.

He said, "Summer will soon be over, and you'll be back," and then he added, "by the way, here's a box of cigars that you must give to Papa Camous with the compliments of the Cap Martin."

There were fifty wonderful cigars in that box, of which Papa Camous said, "They're too beautiful to smoke."

But that was only until he smoked one; then he liked them so much he got up in the middle of the night to indulge in one, and that made Maman Camous say, "You smoke like a chimney."

He said, "I won't give any away, not even to Draghui or Don Albini. Henri said they were especially for me."

As I left the entrance of the Cap Martin I turned for a last look at the place that had been such a wonderland to me. I said, "Goodbye," but with my heart, so that the coachman wouldn't hear me. I stepped into the stagecoach, he cracked his whip, and we were on our way.

My Happy Return Home

THE COACHMAN CRACKED HIS WHIP several times during that one-and-a-half mile ride from the Cap Martin to Menton.

To each departing lady guest Monsieur Ulrick had presented a bouquet of flowers from the gardens of the hotel.

He had said, "*Madame la duchesse,* I hope these flowers will last until you reach home, and may the sight of them remind you that next season the plants will still be here to offer you more blossoms. The Cap Martin and its staff wish you and your family a bon voyage. I'm sure the aroma of these flowers will make you think of us and will convey the pleasure we have felt in having had the privilege of serving you."

As long as Monsieur Ulrick had not given me a bouquet, probably because I was a boy, I felt that every flower along the road to Menton belonged to me. They seemed to be saying, "Come back next year to see us; we'll still be here." I thought of the flowers of Contes that had spoken to and inspired me three years before to ask Don Albini about life.

I shook hands with the coachman when we reached the station and gave him a silver five franc piece, which made him remark, "Six months makes a lot of difference in a fellow who has brains." Well, I knew I was intelligent, and today I thank God that He has taken away only my money and has seen fit to leave my intelligence with me.

The French trains of 1890 were either too luxurious in their accommodations or they went to the other extreme and were too uncomfortable. Every one of the coaches for the third-class was divided into several compartments each having outside doors and a seating capacity of ten, five on each side. There were no washrooms and no aisles; so there was no room in which to move around. And there wasn't enough light inside to enable the reading of a newspaper. If the French Revolution lit the torch of liberty it certainly forgot to light up the coaches of the French railway system.

I bought a one-way ticket to Nice for which I paid twenty-two *sous*. I got into a third-class compartment that was reserved for women only, because I felt my money would be safer. I seated myself in a corner, and one of the ladies said, "This compartment is for ladies only."

I answered, "Madame, my mustache hasn't started to grow yet."

All of them laughed, and those few words served as an introduction. I looked at the nine ladies, who were packed in, and thought, "The French railway system thinks I'm a sardine." The women chattered among themselves, and I strained my eyes trying to read *Le Petit Niçois*. My mind, however, wasn't on the newspaper. I was anxious to arrive in Contes to present Maman Camous with the fortune I had pinned over my heart. The coins that I held out for personal use were in my back pocket inside a little bag that was also securely fastened with safety pins. I gave up reading the paper and looked out the window at the flowers along the tracks. I patted both of the pockets that held the bulk of my riches to be sure they were still bulging. I did that several times without paying any attention to the ladies, but nothing escaped them.

One said to another, "A nice looking boy; too bad he has St. Vitus' dance."

I didn't know what she meant. I knew I was as healthy as the first apple that had caused Eve to lose Paradise.

The lady on my left turned to me and asked, "What's the trouble? When did you first get sick?"

I replied, "Madame, I've never been sick in my life except for the measles."

They looked at each other in surprise, and I continued to make my incomprehensible movements. They never found out that I carried a fortune in those two pockets, the amount of which their husbands would probably never be able to accumulate in their lives. I was proud that I had made it in only six months.

Several of the women got off and others got on, which kept the compartment continually filled. We passed Roquebrune, Monte Carlo, Monaco, Turbie, Eze, Beaulieu, Villefranche, Riquiez, and finally we arrived at Nice. The ride had taken an hour and a half. I picked up Badou's present, bowed to the ladies, thanked them for accepting me into their compartment, wished them a bon voyage and said goodbye. I patted both of my pockets again, excused myself and went out. As I jumped off the train they all began talking at once, "Too bad he has St. Vitus' dance." When I found out what those words meant I felt sorry for those who really had it.

I watched as my trunks were taken from the train, and then found a porter who took my claim check. I gave him a tip so he'd give me better service and handle my baggage with care. At that age I had already discovered that a liberal tip, paid in advance, will always produce better results. It doesn't matter if the one who tips is a king or a peasant; the largest remuneration inspires the best service. It worked like a charm.

That porter said to another, "Be careful, don't throw the luggage down." Those two fellows handled my trunks as if they were filled with eggs. They carried them to a one-horse carriage, and I asked the coachman, in French, if he knew where the Place Garibaldi was. The language generally spoken in Nice is a patois, and when I asked him my question in French he answered in the same language.

"Yes, sir, step in."

He quickly started dusting the seats, and very politely helped me into his carriage. He spoke to his horse, and we were off. We turned down the wrong street, one that would take a roundabout way; but I had four hours to spare so I didn't care. Anyway, Badou wouldn't leave for Contes before the scheduled time. I was curious to know how people like the coachman, who never amounted to anything in life, got that way. His first idea, I decided, was to take the long route and make a man pay more money for the ride, whether he was in a hurry or not. The coachman when he saw anyone well dressed got the mistaken idea that that person had money, which very often was not so. His second idea was that anyone who rode in a carriage was more than the one who rode in a horse-car. He took me up and down a long road, and for an hour and a half I enjoyed a very beautiful panorama.

The horse sweated as we climbed a hill, and the coachman addressed him, saying in patois, *"Ti compri una capelina. Hie, Ronca! Ti compri una capelina,"* or, "Go on, Ronca! I'll buy you a hat."

I sat in back with my luggage, smoking a Turkish cigarette that I had helped myself to at the Cap Martin. As long as I'm on the subject of smoking I might add that the last cigar I ever smoked was on Sept. 2, 1910.

The horse and the coachman understood each other, and, because of the present he might get, the animal broke into a faster trot.

"The coachman is kind after all," I thought, "he considers his horse before himself."

We went up and down, up and down, until we finally approached Mont Boron.

When he yelled, *"Hie, Ronca! Mi compri e capuen,"* or, "Go on, Ronca! I'll buy myself a hat," I nearly swallowed my cigarette.

He didn't know that the fellow in his carriage understood and spoke patois, and that everything he had said had been understood. I was beginning to think that he expected to buy a house, too, with the money he made on that trip.

We arrived at the Place Garibaldi; the ten minutes it should have taken on the right route had extended to three hours. The horse was sweating, and the coachman was smiling as he stepped down from his seat and came back to me.

"Did you enjoy it, sir?"

At the same time he asked me for twenty-one francs and fifty *centimes,* in those days $4.30.

I lit another Turkish cigarette; its delightful aroma reached the coachman's nose. Even the horse turned his head; he wasn't accustomed to such good smoke. His boss smoked only cheap tobacco, which was enough to keep the flies away.

I handed him two francs and said in patois, "The trip is worth thirty *sous,* and ten *sous* for a tip makes it two francs."

His face turned red and then white and he perspired even though there was no sun. The horse began to whinny. The coachman could hardly believe his ears when he heard the patois, and he asked, "Are you from Nice?"

I said, "Oh, no! I'm from Contes."

When he heard that, he nearly had a fit. To think that a kid from a little village could make a city fellow from Nice think that he was a Russian prince or an English lord.

We both laughed until we were sick from it. The city fellow from Nice went up to his horse, patted its head, and said, "Ronca, you are a horse, but your coachman is a jackass. Goodbye to your hat and mine."

We laughed so much that people stopped and held up traffic. A policeman came over to find out what was going on. We told him, and the crowd joined him in laughing. Badou, who was waiting in his diligence until it was time to leave, saw the large gathering and, he too, had to come over. When he heard the story, he screamed.

He turned to the coachman whom he knew, introduced him as Titoun, and said, "You don't know the people of Contes, Titoun, but you're finding out about them."

I offered to buy Titoun a drink, but he said, "Oh, no, let me offer *you* a drink. As long as I took you for a prince let me act as your servant."

We went to an *auberge* and had some wine. Badou took care of my trunks, putting them on top of his diligence before joining us for a drink. In less than five minutes there were fifty people in the place listening to the story that the coachman seemed to think was funnier each time he told it. Everyone laughed. In those days a bottle of wine was worth five *sous,* or, five cents, and the one who bought it wouldn't ruin himself financially by drinking in an *auberge.* That same bottle would have cost five francs in the Cap Martin, and the duke, baron, or count who bought it would be entitled to his appellation because he paid for it.

It was almost time to leave so I said goodbye to Titoun, who had become flushed from too much wine. I slipped five francs to the proprietor of the *auberge* without anyone noticing, and said, "It'll help the coachman pay his bill."

Badou placed a feed bag of oats over the head of Titoun's horse because the coachman was too full of wine to remember the animal.

That story was told around until all the coachmen in Nice heard it. Years later they still joked, saying to one another, "Don't take a well dressed man for an English or Russian nobleman; he might fool you and prove to be somebody from Contes. Remember Titoun!"

I was sorry to learn in 1922, when I returned to Nice from America a very wealthy man, that Titoun had died a few years before. I had wanted, then, to buy him, not a horse's hat, but a horse with a hat. However, I looked up his wife, who was still alive and very, very old. I gave her an envelope that contained a thousand francs, and offered her my condolences on the death of her husband.

She started to cry and asked, "Why do you give this to me?"

I told her the story of thirty-two years before, and, like old Madame Gasiglia, she turned tears into laughter. She had heard that story from Titoun every time he had had a few drinks.

Badou and I started out for Contes. I rode on top with him and, after a few miles, handed him his present. I noticed, too, that the new whip I had ordered for him was in its place on the diligence, its red, white, and blue ribbons streaming with the wind. I had sent a letter to the man who supplied Badou with leather goods requesting a special one. He kept that whip for the rest of his life—replacing the ribbons as they wore out.

Badou, with tears in his eyes, opened his gift which contained a red foulard, two red handkerchiefs, and an English coachman's cap. Won-

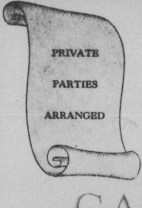

Café Henri Charpentier, Inc.
Rockefeller Center, New York City
1934
CARTE du JOUR

When You Come to Henri's You Not Only Dine But You Learn French

HORS D'OEUVRES

Caviar Frais 2.00 — Clovisse .45 Clams — Coupe de Fruits .50 Fruit Cocktail — Jambon de Virginie, Westphalie et d'York 1.00 Ham—Virginia, Westphalian and York — Jus de Tomates ou de Coquillages .40 Tomato Juice or Clam Juice

Canape Henri Charpentier .75 — Hors d'Oeuvres Varies 1.25 Assorted Hors d'Oeuvres — Melon en Saison .50 Melon in Season — Chair de Crabe Cocktail 1.00 Crab Meat Cocktail — Homard Cocktail 1.25 Lobster Cocktail

POTAGES—SOUPS

Petite Marmite Henri Charpentier .50

Creme a la Reine .50 Cream of Chicken — Soupe a l'Oignon .50 Onion Soup

Tortue Verte au Vieux Madere .80 Green Turtle with Old Madera

Puree de Petits Pois Frais .50 Puree of Fresh Peas — Gumbo Creole .40 Chicken Okra

Bouillon de Volaille .40 Chicken Broth — Bisque de Tomates .50 Bisque of Tomato

OEUFS—EGGS

Omelette .80

Brouille .80 Scrambled — Poche .50 Poached — Frit .50 Fried

Sur le Plat Farci .75 Shirred with Garniture — Cocotte .50 Boiled in Cocotte

POISSONS—FISH

Filet de Sole Anglaise Charpentier 1.75 Filet of English Sole Charpentier

Truite Meuniere 1.30 Trout Meuniere — Homard Henri Charpentier 2.50 Lobster Henri Charpentier

Sea Bass Nicoise 1.30

Darne de Saumon Pochee Sce. Mousseline 1.40 Salmon Steak Boiled Mousseline Sauce

Halibut, Bluefish, Kingfish, Scallops—Cuit au Gout 1.30 Halibut, Bluefish, Kingfish, Scallops—Cooked to Taste

Shade Roe 1.50

Grenouilles et Crabes Moux en Saison Frogs Legs and Soft Shell Crabs in Season

ENTREES

Poulet en Cocotte Beaulieu 4.00 Chicken in Cocotte Beaulieu — Noisette de Pre Sale Arlesienne 1.35 Noisette of Lamb Arlesienne

Cote de Veau en Casserole Maison 1.35 Veal Chop in Casserole Maison

Boeuf Braise a la Mode 1.35 Braised Beef a la Mode — Paupiette de Boeuf Provencale 1.35 Paupiette of Beef Provencale

Escargot a la Bourguignonne 1.35 Snails a la Bourguignonne — Viande Froides Cold Cuts

Entrecote Sautee Chez Soi 1.75 Minute Steak Chez Soi — Filet de Boeuf Maman Lecoq 1.90 Filet Mignon Maman Lecoq

Poitrine de Volaille Maison 1.75 Breast of Chicken Maison

Tripe Mantonnaise 1.35 Tripe Mentonnaise — Rognon de Veau Saute au Vin Blanc 1.35 Veal Kidneys Saute White Wine Sauce

Pates et Terrines de Foie Gras de Strassbourg 1.90 Pates and Terrines of Goose Liver of Strassburg

GRILLADES ET ROTIS
From the Grill and Roast

Grain Broiler — Pigeon 1.65 Squab — Pintade 3.50 Guinea Hen — Canard de Long Island (Henri Farm) 4.50 Long Island Duckling (Henri Farm)

Chapon Capon — Selle d'Agneau Saddle of Lamb — Agneau de Lait Milk Fed Lamb — Venaison et Gibier sur Commande Venison and Game (to order)

Sirloin 2.00 (2) 4.00 — Entrecote Minute 1.75 Minute Steak — Porter House

Chateaubriand (2) 4.50 — Filet Mignon 1.90 — Carre d'Agneau 3.25 Rack of Lamb

SALADES—SALADS

Laitue .50 Lettuce — Romaine .50 — Chiffonade .60 — Concombre .50 Cucumber — Poire d'Avocat .60 Alligator Pears

Salade de Legumes Frais .80 Fresh Vegetable Salad — Salade de Fruits .80 Fruit Salad

LEGUMES—VEGETABLES

Fresh Asparagus with Hollandaise Sauce .90

Haricots Verts .60 String Beans — Petits Pois .50 New Peas — Epinards .50 Spinach — Haricots de Lima .60 Lima Beans

Courgettes .50 Vegetable Marrow or Young Squash — Choux de Bruxelles .50 Brussell Sprouts — Tomates .50 Tomatoes — Artichauts .75 Artichokes

Choux Fleurs .75 Cauliflower — Nouilles .50 Noodles — Macaronis .50 Macaroni — Comme Garniture .40 As Garniture

POMMES: Frite .30 Potatoes: French Fried — Sautee .30 Saute — Lyonnaise .30 Lyonnaise — Souffles .30 Balloon — Douce .30 Sweet

Diner de Legumes Frais 1.25 Fresh Vegetable Dinner

ENTREMETS—DESSERT

Creme Caramel .50 Caramel Custard — Peche Cardinal .75 Peach Cardinal — Coupe Aux Marrons .75

Cerises Jubilees .90 Cherry Jubilee — Fraises Parisienne .75 Strawberries Parisienne — Friandises .30 Cookies — Glaces et Sorbets .40 Ice Cream & Water Ices

Patisserie .20 Pastries — Omelette Norvegienne 1.00 (2) 1.50 Baked Alaska — Souffles 1.00 (2) 1.50

Notre Crepe Original .75 Pancakes Suzette

FROMAGE IMPORTES DE FRANCE .45 Cheese Imported from France

Cafe Noir .20 Demi Tasse — Cafe Creme .30 Coffee & Cream — The .30 Tea

SI VOUS VENEZ CHEZ HENRI CHARPENTIER QUELLE QUE SOIT VOTRE ENVIE, POUR VOUS SATISFAIRE NOUS POUVONS TOUT FAIRE

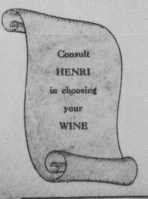

ORIGINAL
HENRI RESTAURANT
LYNBROOK, L. I. N. Y.   Lynbrook 759

derful fellow! He said he was sorry that he hadn't had more packages
for me to deliver before I left for the Cap Martin so that I could have
made more money. But he added, "No, maybe it's better because then
you might never have left to make your fortune."

People who passed us on the way noticed me sitting with Badou, so
when we arrived in Contes the whole village knew I was coming.
Maman Camous had already put two rabbits on to stew especially for
my arrival. She had noted, by my letters from the Cap Martin, that
there was always plenty of beef, veal, lamb, etc., but that I never mentioned rabbits. The family waited at home for me; even Madame Gasiglia was there representing Giroumetta. And all five were crying, which
made Papa Camous ask, "Why are we crying? We should be laughing."

Bacci and the rest of the animals were skeptical; I didn't look like
their Henri. My freckles had faded and my new blue suit gave me a
cosmopolitan air which they didn't like. Bacci looked at Blanchette as
if to say, "This fellow isn't our boss." Only when I talked did they
recognize me. They, too, found out what Titoun had learned, that
clothes were merely a masquerade and could not change a person. Bacci
jumped and ran around crazy with joy. His partner, Blanchette, was
tied and couldn't express her exhilaration. Bicou moved his ears and
said, "Hee haw!" The cow ruminated. There was another new Bismarck
in the pigpen. His predecessor had been butchered the week after
Christmas and here it was May and one of his cured hams still remained for me to taste. The new Bismarck grunted, "Who the devil is
this fellow that everybody should make such a fuss about him?" Fannie's
stall in the stable was still empty, but her old mule's hat still hung
on a nail.

Madame Gasiglia dined with us and we had a very intimate *soirée*.
Papa Camous went to the cellar and brought up a couple bottles of his
best wine. Slices of that cold cured ham were served with radishes and
black olives. We had bean soup *à la* Maman Camous. In all of my life
I have never tasted the equal of that superb dish of rabbit. For dessert
we had figs that had been dried the previous November. They filled a
soup plate which stood in the center of the table. I was impatient to

offer my fortune which was still imprisoned in the inside pocket of my coat, and I had no time for dessert. I emptied the soup plate of dried figs onto the tablecloth, and unfastened the safety pins that held the bag of gold pieces. All eyes were upon me as I cut the threads that held the coins in place. I emptied the bag into the plate with such a noise that Madame Gasiglia later said to her companion, "It's too bad you couldn't have seen it, Françoise; it rained gold over at the Camous home tonight. I wish Giroumetta could have seen it."

I presented the dishful of coins to Maman Camous, saying, "Maman, here is my first gift to you." Everyone was astonished. She stared in disbelief as she took the soup plate. Her hands shook and the coins gave a metallic tinkle, while Papa Camous, pale and with eyes that almost popped, looked out the window for fear the *gendarmes* were already at the door for me.

He asked incredulously, "You didn't steal it, did you, Henri?"

"No, I didn't Papa, each louis has been made honestly. But just a minute," I added.

I put my hand into my vest pocket and took out the twenty mark gold piece that the "Iron Chancellor" had given me as a tip.

I said, "Here, Papa, is a souvenir from the man you hate so much."

Instead of crying everybody laughed.

Papa Camous saw that it was the only foreign gold piece in the lot, and declared, "This twenty marks will just be enough to buy another pig, another namesake for the "Iron Chancellor."

By that remark I knew he was one of those old time unconquerable Frenchmen whom no German could buy.

RECIPES

✠

HORS-D'OEUVRE, GEORGE CLYMER

✠

SOUP, WILLIAM KELLY

✠

OMELET, EDWARD BELLAMY

✠

SCRAMBLED EGGS, W. O. ATWATER

✠

BAKED PIKE, SAMUEL CLEMENS

✠

PORK SAUTE, RUTHERFORD B. HAYES

✠

POTATOES, STEPHEN M. BABCOCK

✠

CELERY, EUGENE FIELD

✠

SALAD, GEORGE WASHINGTON CARVER

✠

APRICOTS, JEANNE EAGELS

✠

377

HORS-D'OEUVRE, GEORGE CLYMER

Boil 2 artichokes and remove the leaves. Only the hearts are used in this recipe. Let them become cold and then slice very thin.

Finely chop: ½ green pepper, 2 scallions, 1 peeled tomato, and 1 hard-boiled egg. Add 2 tablespoons of French Dressing, a pinch of red pepper, and the thinly sliced artichoke hearts. Mix thoroughly.

Finely cut ¼ head of lettuce and arrange it into nests on 2 serving plates. Place the above ingredients, green pepper, etc., in the center of the lettuce nests.

Finely chop 2 cold boiled beets. Place little piles around the outside of the lettuce nests and a little in the center. Sprinkle chopped parsley on each small pile of beets.

SOUP, WILLIAM KELLY

Wash and boil until tender: 2 chopped leeks, ½ chopped onion, and 2 peeled and quartered potatoes. Pass the vegetables through a sieve, separately retaining the water in which they have been cooked. Place the purée into a double boiler. Add 1 cup of the original water, 1 pint of milk, 1 cup of cream, and 1 tablespoon of butter. Season with salt and pepper. When it comes to a boil thicken it with the beaten yolks of 2 eggs. Before serving, sprinkle with very small croutons which have been fried in butter.

OMELET, EDWARD BELLAMY

Boil 2 potatoes with their skins. Peel and dice them.

Place 1 tablespoon of butter into a pan with 2 finely chopped shallots,

378

½ finely chopped green pepper, 2 thinly sliced mushrooms, and the potatoes. Stir, and when it becomes brown add 1 chopped peeled tomato and simmer for 10 minutes. Sprinkle with 1 pinch of salt and 1 pinch of pepper.

Prepare an omelet, using 6 eggs. Put the garniture in the center of the omelet before rolling it. Season.

SCRAMBLED EGGS, W. O. ATWATER

Place 2 pared, cored, and diced apples into a pan with 1 tablespoon of butter (or more if necessary). Let the apples become brown, but do not cook them until they become a purée. Sprinkle with 1 tablespoon of granulated sugar. Light 2 ponies of kirschwasser and stir into the apples.

Prepare 6 eggs for scrambling. When they are almost scrambled, add the apples, etc. Sprinkle a few small buttered croutons in at the same time. Mix and serve.

BAKED PIKE, SAMUEL CLEMENS

Take a 1 pound pike. Open and clean it. Remove head, tail, and, bones. Wash and dry thoroughly.

Place a generous piece of butter and 1 finely chopped shallot on a baking platter with the fish. Put into a preheated hot oven of 400° F. for 5 minutes. Baste it several times.

Cut ½ carrot and ½ leek julienne style and sprinkle it over the fish.

Mix 3 tablespoons of consommé with 2 tablespoons of dry white wine and 3 tablespoons of cream. Pour it over the fish, add another generous piece of butter, and put it back into the hot oven for 25 minutes. Season to taste.

PORK SAUTE, RUTHERFORD B. HAYES

Cut 1½ pounds of lean pork into small pieces. Place 1 finely chopped onion into a frying pan with 2 tablespoons of butter. Add the pork and sauté for 15 minutes until it becomes brown. Then put it into a casserole and add 2 sherry-glasses of white wine and ½ cup of cream. Place in a preheated hot oven of 400° F. for 10 minutes.

Cut 4 slices of bacon into pieces and put them into the frying pan in which the pork was cooked. Add 1 tablespoon of butter and 4 peeled and sliced cold boiled potatoes (that have been cooked with their skins). When the potatoes and bacon become hot, crush 1 clove of garlic into a little chopped parsley and sprinkle it over the top. Mix. Arrange the potatoes and bacon over the pork and leave in the hot oven 30 minutes longer. Ten minutes before removing from the oven sprinkle with a little grated cheese. Season to taste and serve with applesauce.

POTATOES, STEPHEN M. BABCOCK

Thinly slice 1 onion into a frying pan. Add 1 tablespoon of butter, 1 crushed clove of garlic, and 4 chopped slices of raw bacon. Cook for 10 minutes. Then add 4 peeled and sliced boiled potatoes (that have been cooked with their skins). Let it become hot, and then sprinkle with a little chopped parsley. Season to taste.

CELERY, EUGENE FIELD

Take 2 bunches of celery. Cut off the roots and leaves. Clean thoroughly. Leave whole. Boil until tender in plenty of water which has been salted.

Take them from the water and lay them on a clean cloth for a moment to remove all water. Place on a baking platter.

Mix 1 tablespoon of grated cheese, ½ clove of crushed garlic, and 1 tablespoon of bread crumbs. Sprinkle it over the celery.

Put 1 tablespoon of butter into a pan and add 2 finely chopped shallots, 2 finely chopped mushrooms, 1 clove of garlic which has been crushed into a little chopped parsley, 1 chopped peeled tomato, 1 sherryglassful of red wine, 1 tablespoon of grated cheese, and 1 teaspoon of Worcestershire sauce. Season with pepper and salt. Stir. Let it come to a boil, and then pour it over the celery. Place in a preheated hot oven of 400° F. for 10 minutes.

SALAD, GEORGE WASHINGTON CARVER

Shred the heart of 1 crisp Savoy cabbage lengthwise. Finely slice ½ onion and mix it with the cabbage. Sprinkle with a pinch each of salt, pepper, and paprika.

Separately mix: the juice of ½ lemon, 1 tablespoon of olive oil, 2 tablespoons of cream, 1 pinch of sugar, and 1 teaspoon of Worcestershire sauce. Pour it over the salad.

APRICOTS, JEANNE EAGELS

Cut 6 large ripe apricots in half, or you may use canned apricots if you wish.

Prepare 2 pieces of buttered toast and place them on a baking platter which contains 1 tablespoon of melted butter.

Put 1 cup of cooked rice into a mixing bowl and add 1 tablespoon of melted butter, 1 tablespoon of cream, 1 tablespoon of vanilla sugar, and 2 beaten egg yolks. Mix thoroughly.

Arrange the rice over the toast and place the apricots over the rice. Sprinkle with a little vanilla sugar, distribute 1 tablespoon of melted butter over the top, and bake in a preheated hot oven of 450° F. for 10 minutes.

Like great wine, Crêpes Suzette Sauce improves with age. Since it keeps for many months without spoiling, it can be prepared in advance. Above, Charpentier slices a lemon so thin that the pulp remains on the fruit, an important factor in preparing this delicate dish. Suzette Sauce can also be used on compotes, puddings, ice cream and sweet omelets.

HENRI SPECIALS

CAVIAR, ALEXANDRE PARIASDENSKY

No onion or chopped egg accompanies this caviar, which should be plentiful and of good quality—Beluga if you can afford it. Serve only a warm brioche, plenty of caviar and a few lemon tears. The caviar must, of course, be very cold. A glass of champagne served with it will make a very good beginning.

CAVIAR, ALEXIS RAGOVINE

Prepare 4 small thin pancakes from a batter of 1 egg, 1 tablespoon of milk, 1 tablespoon of flour and 1 pinch of salt. Keep the pancakes hot.

Whip ½ pint of heavy cream until it is stiff and stir in 1 tablespoon of melted butter (do not cook the butter). Take 4 large tablespoons of cold fresh caviar and mix them with the whipped cream very slowly so that the eggs are not destroyed.

Place a pancake on each serving plate and gently cover with 1 large tablespoon of the creamy caviar. Squeeze a few drops of lemon juice over it and cover with the 2 remaining pancakes. Serve with a small glass of vodka.

Never throw away the bones which remain from a veal or beef roast. A delicious soup or consommé can be made by slowly boiling them for a few hours with sufficient water to cover them, a few herbs and a pinch of salt and pepper. Left over vegetables, including potatoes, can be made into a purée of soup.

GREEN TURTLE SOUP, WILLIAM CASTLE

Take ¼ pound of canned green turtle meat. Put it into a casserole with 1 cup of beef consommé. Add 1 bay leaf and 1 pinch each of thyme, pepper and powdered cloves.

Separately boil 1 pint of clear, strong, beef consommé and pour it into a tureen. When the green turtle meat comes to a boil pour it, also, into the tureen.

Pour 2 ponies of brandy and 1 sherry-glass of Madeira wine into a dish, make it flame, and stir it into the tureen. Season to taste. A glass of delicious dry sherry should be served after the green turtle soup as an entr'act to the next course.

PETITE MARMITE, SARAH BERNHARDT

This rich consommé recipe will serve 6.

2 pounds of beef with marrow fat	2 celery stalk tops
	1 cabbage
4 pounds of beef and veal bones	Salt
1 chicken	Freshly ground black pepper
3 onions	¼ teaspoon of chervil
3 long turnips	¼ teaspoon of parsley
4 carrots	1 teaspoon of chives
1 leek	

Season the beef with a few pinches of salt and freshly ground black pepper. Place it into a casserole by itself and brown it over a hot fire for about 10 minutes. In another casserole similarly brown the chicken, moving it often so that it doesn't burn. Remove the marrow from one of the bones and put it aside. This is important. Then put all of the bones, the browned beef and the browned chicken into a large pot which contains 6 quarts of cold water. Roast the onions (unpeeled) over a hot fire until they become brown and fragrant. Add them to the pot. Peel and add the turnips and carrots. Then add the leek and the celery tops. Skim the broth whenever a froth forms during the first hour of boiling. The final broth must be clear and have a golden color. Place the cabbage in a separate pot, cover with cold salted water, and boil. When the cabbage is cooked, rinse it in cold water and continue boiling it in some broth taken from the soup pot. It must be cooked separately and eaten later with the other vegetables.

After the soup has boiled for 1 hour, remove the meat, chicken and vegetables (leave the bones) and continue to slowly boil the consommé for another 3 hours, skimming it when necessary. By that time it will contain enough nourishment to give a dwarf the strength of a giant. The beef, chicken and vegetables may serve as the other courses of your dinner. Steam them for 20 minutes in a covered pot containing just a little of the consommé. Slice the raw marrow as you would a banana and lay the slices in cold water. Toast croutons in the oven, covering them first with Parmesan cheese. Just before serving the consommé replace small pieces of chicken and carrot. When it is ready to be served, add 2 slices of marrow-fat to each portion. On each of these slices of marrow place minute quantities of chervil, chives, and parsley, which have been cut with a scissors and mixed. Add the croutons and serve. Season to taste.

ONION SOUP, THEODORE ROOSEVELT

Put 1 tablespoon of butter into a pan with 2 thinly sliced onions, a pinch of salt and a pinch of pepper. Cover and let them become very brown. They should be soft and not crisp. Add 1½ pints of hot consommé (chicken mixed with beef) and when it comes to a boil pour it into a casserole. Sprinkle large, thin, buttered Parmesan croutons over the top so that the soup is completely covered. Place in a hot oven of 400° F. for 15 minutes. Season to taste.

CREME DE FRANCE, WILLIAM K. VANDERBILT

Place 2 tablespoons of butter into a pan with 2 finely chopped shallots. Cook for 3 minutes. Then add 1 cup of milk, 3 cups of cooked fresh green peas, 1 pinch of salt and 1 pinch of pepper. Stir, and when it comes to a boil pass it through a sieve with the aid of a wooden spoon. Put the purée of peas into a double boiler with 1 cup of cream and 1 large tablespoon of butter. Let it come to a boil and thicken it with the beaten yolks of 2 eggs. Season to taste. The addition of 1 pony of brandy, if desired, is most satisfactory.

BORSCH, JULIUS BLOOMFIELD

Take 4 boiled beets. Peel and chop them fine. Put them into a pot with 1½ quarts of consommé. Add 1 finely chopped onion, 1 pinch of pepper, 1 pinch of salt and 1 finely chopped stalk of celery. Boil slowly for 30 minutes. Squeeze the juice of ½ lemon into 2 consommé cups (½ lemon for both). Add to each cup: 1 large tablespoon of sour cream and 1 pinch each of salt, pepper and sugar. Stir. Strain the consommé and pour it into the cups. It may be served either hot or cold. Season to taste.

SPAGHETTI, HUMBERT RICOLFI

Let 3 quarts of water come to a boil. Add 2 pinches of salt. When the water comes to a rolling boil, add ½ pound of spaghetti (unbroken). Boil for 16 minutes. It must not be cooked too much. While it is cooking, put 2 tablespoons of butter into a frying pan, add 4 finely chopped shallots and 3 thinly sliced mushrooms. Cook for 5 minutes. Then add 3 chopped, peeled, very ripe tomatoes.

Broil or fry 6 slices of bacon. Make them crisp and crumble them. Drain the spaghetti. Crush 1 clove of garlic, mix it with 1 tablespoon of melted butter and stir it into the spaghetti. Place it on a hot serving platter and sprinkle with the crushed bacon. Let the mushrooms, etc., come to a boil, season with a pinch of salt and pepper and pour over the spaghetti. Sprinkle 2 tablespoons of grated cheese over this. Season to taste. To appreciate the spaghetti, serve it with California claret.

RAVIOLI, CHARLES FAISSOLE

In this recipe prepare the sauce first. Put 2 tablespoons of butter into a frying pan, add 4 finely chopped shallots and 5 thinly sliced mushrooms. Cook for 10 minutes. Then add 3 chopped, peeled, very ripe tomatoes, 1 sherry-glass of claret, ½ cup of veal stock, 1 pinch of salt and pepper, 2 pinches of basil and 2 cloves of garlic which have been crushed into 1 tablespoon of chopped parsley. Let it boil slowly for ½ hour. Stand it aside. It is to be poured over the finished dish later.

Put 2 tablespoons of butter into a separate frying pan, add 4 finely chopped shallots and cook for 3 minutes. Then add 1 cup of chopped cooked spinach, 1 cup of finely chopped left-over roast chicken, roast veal or roast pork, and a few chopped chicken livers (cooked or uncooked). Crush 1 clove of garlic into a little chopped parsley and mix it with 2 tablespoons of bread crumbs. Add it to the frying pan. Stir and add 1 tablespoon of olive oil, 1 tablespoon of grated cheese, 2 raw eggs, 2 pinches of salt, 2 pinches of freshly ground black pepper and 1 pinch each of thyme, powdered cloves, and cinnamon. Mix it well.

387

Prepare a dough similar in stiffness to bread dough. Use 1 egg, 1 tablespoon of olive oil, 2 cups of sifted flour, 2 tablespoons of milk, 2 tablespoons of water and 1 pinch of salt. Place it in the refrigerator for an hour or two. Roll 2 sheets of dough as thin as possible with a rolling-pin. On one of the sheets of dough place 1 teaspoon of the stuffing in little heaps about 1 inch apart. Place the other sheet of dough over the top, dip your fingers into flour and pinch each one together, making each teaspoon of stuffing a prisoner. Then with a knife cut each one separate and sprinkle with flour.

Have 3 quarts of boiling consommé ready and place them carefully into it. Let them boil, not too rapidly, for 25 minutes. Strain and place on a serving platter. Let the prepared sauce come to a boil and pour it over the ravioli. Sprinkle with grated cheese. Season to taste. Accompany it with California claret.

LASAGNA, FRANCOIS DRAGHUI

Boil 1 cauliflower. Separately boil 6 potatoes with their skins. At the same time boil (separately) ½ pound of very broad noodles in salted water for 16 minutes. Start cooking the vegetables a little ahead of the noodles. When the vegetables are done, peel and slice the hot potatoes into a bowl. Break the hot cauliflower into pieces and mix with the potatoes. Add 2 tablespoons of melted butter and sprinkle with 2 tablespoons of grated cheese. Mix. Keep it hot.

Strain the boiled noodles and mix them with the potatoes and cauliflower. Crush 2 cloves of garlic into 2 tablespoons of chopped parsley, mix with 3 pinches of salt and 2 pinches of pepper, and sprinkle it over the top. Sprinkle with a little more grated cheese. Accompany with sliced raw tomatoes which have been sprinkled with finely chopped onions and celery, and a pinch of salt and pepper. Pour olive oil over the tomatoes, and be generous with it. Season to taste.

BOUILLABAISSE, AUGUSTE ESCOFFIER

This dish is seldom served to less than 4 people, since many kinds of fish are used. This recipe is sufficient for 6; it is served for lunch and constitutes the whole meal.

6 tablespoons of olive oil

3 finely chopped onions

3 finely chopped celery stalk tops

4 cloves of crushed garlic

2 bay leaves

2 pinches of thyme

1 whole parsley root

1 finely chopped leek

1½ pounds of lobster (chopped into pieces while still in the shells)

1 dozen mussels

6 chopped, peeled, very ripe tomatoes

2 quarts of beef or chicken consommé

3 tablespoons of butter

3 pinches of salt

2 pinches of pepper

1 teaspoon of saffron

1 pint of dry white wine

3½ pounds of mixed fish (equal quantities of halibut, catfish, sea bass, and pike which have been cut into large pieces)

Put the olive oil in a large pan and then add the onions, tomatoes, celery stalk tops, garlic, bay leaves, thyme, parsley root, leek, salt and pepper. Add the large pieces of pike, catfish, sea bass, halibut, lobster, mussels, white wine, butter, and saffron. Do not cover. Place in a pre-heated hot oven of 400° F. for 20 minutes. Pour 2 quarts of strong boiling beef or chicken consommé very gently over it. Cover tightly and place back in a very hot oven for 5 more minutes. Large slices of toasted French bread which have been rubbed with garlic and spread with olive oil should be served with the bouillabaisse. Or, the toasted French bread may be spread with olive oil which has been flavored with garlic. (To flavor, place garlic cloves in a cruet of olive oil.) Season to taste. An accompanying very cold bottle of dry white wine is imperative; if you have no wine don't make the bouillabaisse.

LOBSTER, PAPA JOFFRE

Place a live lobster weighing 1 pound into a pot with enough cold water to cover it. Cold and not boiling water must be used. Then the lobster, not knowing it is about to be cooked, will relax and go to sleep as the water gradually becomes warmer. To place it in boiling water will cause a tightening of the muscles, and the lobster will be tough.

To the pot add: 2 sliced carrots, ¼ onion (in one piece), 1 clove of unpeeled garlic, 1 stalk of celery (it isn't necessary to cut it), 1 bay leaf, 1 whole clove, 2 peppercorns, 2 pinches of salt and 1 slice of lemon. Cook the lobster 10 minutes, from the time it begins to boil. Then remove it from the water and twist off the claws. Turn the lobster on its back and cut it lengthwise from the head to the end of the tail. Use a stainless steel or silver knife; any other will discolor the meat. Crack open the claws. Remove the meat from the body, claws, and tail, and cut it into fair-sized pieces.

Put 1 tablespoon of butter into a casserole and add 2 finely chopped shallots, 3 thinly sliced mushrooms, 1 pinch each of salt, pepper and paprika, 1 pony of brandy and 1 sherry-glass of any good, dry sherry. Cook for 10 minutes and then add 1 cup of cream. Cover and let it come to a boil. Then add the cooked lobster. Let it remain on the fire for 3 minutes. To keep the lobster tender, it must not be kept boiling in the sauce. Separately serve with rice. Season to taste. It should be served accompanied by a glass of cold, sweet Sauterne.

LOBSTER, CHARLES DILLINGHAM

Take a 1½ pound live lobster. Remove and smash the claws. This is done in order to penetrate and cook the meat. Cut the tail into 4 pieces and split the body in half lengthwise. Sprinkle with a few pinches of salt and pepper. Place it into a frying pan and add 2 tablespoons of butter, 3 finely chopped shallots and 2 cloves of garlic which have been crushed into a little chopped parsley. Turn the fire high for 2 minutes. Then add 2 ponies of any good brandy, make it flame, and add 4 tablespoons of olive oil, 3 peeled and chopped ripe tomatoes, 2 tablespoons of meat stock and 1 pinch each of basil, thyme, tarragon, and red pepper. Let it come to a boil and then cover and place it in a preheated hot oven of 400° F. for 25 minutes. Season to taste. Serve with garlic croutons. Accompany it with a glass of Vouvray Rose (pink); it will please both you and the lobster.

FILLETS OF SOLE, JOSEPH MORAN

Take 1 pound of fillet of sole. Be sure that every particle of the black skin has been removed. Put 2 tablespoons of butter on a baking platter, melt it, and lay the fillets in the butter. Sprinkle with 2 finely chopped shallots and 3 sliced mushrooms. Add 1 sherry-glassful of white wine, 2 tablespoons of chicken consommé, 4 large whole oysters, 3 sliced shrimps and 1 cup of 40% cream. Sprinkle with 1 pinch each of salt, pepper and paprika. Place in a preheated oven of 400° F. for 30 minutes. Season to taste. Serve with buttered noodles. A glass of cold, dry white wine should accompany it.

HERRINGS, JULES WEBER

Place 2 marinated herrings into a serving dish.

Pare, core, and cut 1 apple julienne style. Mix it with a tablespoon of raisins which have been soaked to softness, 1 thinly sliced onion and 1 thinly sliced carrot. Cover the herrings with the mixed ingredients. Pour 2 tablespoons of vinegar over the top and sprinkle with 2 pinches of pepper.

Put 1 sherry-glassful of dry sherry into a pan. Add 1 tablespoon of Worcestershire sauce and 1 tablespoon of French mustard. When it comes to a boil remove it from the fire and stir in 1 cup of cream. Pour it over the herrings, etc. Season to taste.

SAUTEED CHICKEN LIVERS, J. P. MORGAN, SR.

Crush 1 clove of garlic into a little chopped parsley and mix it with 3 finely chopped shallots. Stand it aside.

Take 6 fresh chicken livers. Cut into halves.

Put 3 tablespoons of butter into a frying pan and when it begins to sizzle add the halved chicken livers. The hot butter often spatters when it comes in contact with the water inside the liver; so be careful and don't burn yourself. Turn the livers often and don't fry them longer than 8 minutes.

Make 2 slices of toast so that they will be ready the same time as the livers. Place the toast on a hot serving platter and arrange the sautéed livers over them. Sprinkle the prepared garlic parsley and shallots over the top. Then sprinkle with a pinch of salt and a pinch of freshly ground pepper. Put 1 tablespoon of butter into the frying pan in which the livers were sautéed and when it comes to a bubbling boil pour it over the finished dish. Season to taste. Serve with a glass of red port.

CHICKEN, "DIAMOND JIM" BRADY

Cut open and remove the entrails of 1 chicken. Wipe the inside with a clean cloth. Do not wash it. Chop the legs into 2 pieces each, the breast into 2 pieces and the remainder of the carcass into 4 pieces. Don't remove any of the bones. They will give the sauce of the finished dish more flavor.

Put 4 tablespoons of butter into a casserole with 5 finely chopped shallots and 3 thinly sliced mushrooms. Add the chicken and season with a pinch of salt and pepper. Cook for 5 minutes over a high fire, constantly turning the pieces. Pour 1 sherry-glass of brandy over it, make it flame, and stir. Place the casserole in a preheated hot oven of 400° F. for 40 minutes. Stir once in awhile. Dissolve 1 tablespoon of cornstarch in 3 sherry-glasses of dry sherry or white port. Mix with 1 pint of cream and stir it into the casserole, moving the whole thing back and forth over the fire until it boils. Before serving, add 2 tablespoons of meat stock. Serve with boiled rice. Season to taste. The addition of truffles will make this dish *non plus ultra*. An accompanying glass of cold, sweet white wine will make this an unforgettable dish. "Diamond Jim" Brady, however, drank only orange juice, which is not *à propos* at this time.

SQUAB CHICKEN, FRANK O. BURRIDGE

Take 2 squab chickens that weigh 1¼ pounds each. Prepare them for roasting. Clean and wipe the insides with a dry cloth. Do not wash them.

First make the stuffing. Put 2 tablespoons of butter into a casserole and add 2 finely chopped shallots, 4 finely chopped mushrooms and 2 tablespoons of diced bread. Cook for 2 minutes. Chop the livers taken from the squab chickens, as well as 2 additional chicken livers, into small pieces and sprinkle them into the casserole. Stir and cook for 2 more minutes. Add ½ clove of garlic which has been crushed into a little chopped parsley, 1 pinch each of salt, pepper and thyme, and 1 sherry-glassful of port wine. Stir it for a moment and then add ½ cup of cooked rice. Mix thoroughly, remove it from the fire, and stuff into the squab chickens. Place 2 strips of raw bacon over the breast of each and tie well. Put them into a roasting pan with 1 tablespoon of butter and place in a preheated hot oven of 400° F. Baste them often, adding more butter if necessary, and roast for 30 minutes, or until they are well browned, soft, but not dried.

Then remove the roasting pan from the oven and place it on top of the stove. Arrange the squab chickens on a hot serving platter and remove the strings. Add 1 tablespoon of butter to the roasting pan. Turn the fire up and add 1 teaspoon of meat stock, 1 sherry-glassful of dry sherry or port and a pinch of salt and pepper. Stir it with a wooden spoon until it comes to a sizzling boil and then pour it over the squab chickens. Serve immediately. Season to taste. A glass of cold, sparkling wine served with it will please both your heart and your palate.

CAFE DE PARIS CHICKEN

Roast 1 chicken. While it is roasting, boil the following vegetables so that they will be ready to use when the chicken is done: 2 tablespoons of diced carrots, 2 tablespoons of fresh green peas and 2 tablespoons of diced green beans. Cook until tender. Prepare 2 tablespoons of sautéed potatoes.

Place 2 tablespoons of butter into a separate pan and add 2 finely chopped shallots and 3 finely chopped mushrooms. Sauté for 5 minutes and then add 2 sherry-glasses of red wine and 1 cup of veal stock. Crush ½ clove of garlic into a little chopped parsley and sprinkle it into the pan. Let it come to a boil and add 1 more tablespoon of butter, 2 pinches of salt and 2 pinches of pepper.

Arrange the cooked carrots, peas, beans and potatoes in a casserole, making the shape of a nest. Lay the roasted chicken in the center, pour the sauce over it, cover and place in a preheated hot oven of 400° F. for 5 minutes. More vegetables may be used providing you make the sauce proportionately larger. Season to taste. This dish should be served with an accompanying glass of claret.

DUCKLING A LA BELASCO

The sauce recipe given here will suffice for several occasions; it will make about 2 quarts.

Put 4 tablespoons of butter into a casserole, add 4 finely chopped shallots and cook for 3 minutes. Then add 6 tablespoons of granulated sugar and stir until it becomes brown. Add the strained juice of 3 oranges and 1 lemon. Put the orange and lemon peels aside. Then add 2 sherry-glasses of sherry, 1 sherry-glass of white curaçao, 1 cup of currant jelly and 1 cup of Concord grape jelly. Stir well and when it comes to a boil add 1½ quarts of veal stock, 1 tablespoon of Worcestershire sauce and 1 tablespoon of beef stock. Let it boil slowly for 45 minutes. Keep removing the froth until it is clear.

While the sauce is cooking, take the orange and lemon peels which have been placed aside. With a paring knife, cut them julienne style and be sure they are free of all pulp. Mix the julienne orange and lemon peel with 1 pony of curaçao. Sprinkle with 1 tablespoon of granulated sugar, stir, and pour it all into the boiling sauce which has already cooked for 45 minutes. Stir thoroughly.

Take 1 duckling that weighs 5 or 6 pounds. Prepare it for roasting. Clean and wipe the inside with a dry cloth. Do not wash it. Put 1 pinch of salt and pepper inside the cavity as well as ½ raw onion (in one piece), and ½ stalk of celery which has been cut into pieces. Place the duckling into a roasting pan and pour 2 tablespoons of cold water over it to facilitate the rendering of the duck fat. Put it in a preheated hot oven of 400° F. Let it roast until the duckling is free of fat, about 45 minutes. Then remove all the fat and add 2 more tablespoons of consommé or water and 3 large tablespoons of butter. Roast for 30 minutes longer. Baste it often during that time. The duckling, when done, must be crisp and brown, with moist and tender meat. Season to taste. Serve the Belasco sauce separately. Place the sauce that is left over into the refrigerator for another time. It is excellent when served with roast pork, roast turkey, or any game, including venison. With the addition of gelatin this sauce, poured over slices of cold cooked ham, cold roast pork, roast turkey, squab, or guinea hen, etc., and placed in the refrigerator a few hours before serving, will make a delicious buffet. A glass of red Burgundy should be served with the Duckling *à la* Belasco.

ROUENNAIS DUCKLING, TOUR D'ARGENT PARIS

This is the famous duckling *à la presse au sang* as it is made in France. I wish, from the bottom of my heart, that some of America's farmers would raise this type of duck which, so far, is missing from the great American scene. The ones who do produce them will become the benefactors of our country's food industry. If those same farmers could produce the *poularde du Mans* and the *poularde de Bresse,* also, they would have birds superior in tenderness and taste to our own capon, which too often proves to be not a capon but just a large chicken. Then the restaurateur is fooled as well as the customer. The one who tries to fool another is a great fool himself.

Take 1 Rouennais duckling. Prepare it for roasting. Clean and wipe the inside with a dry cloth. Do not wash it. Put 1 stalk of celery, a piece of onion and a pinch of salt and pepper inside the carcass. This time place the duck on its back in a roasting pan. Pour 2 tablespoons of melted butter over the breast and put it in a preheated hot wen of 500° F. Baste it several times during the 12 minutes it takes to cook.

Have your duck press and casserole in the dining room ready to be used. Remove the duck from the oven, lay it on a hot serving platter, and take it to the dining room immediately. Remove the legs from the duck and send them back to the kitchen to be broiled. Cut the breast of the duck into long, thin fillets (about 14 to 16 fillets can be made from the breast). Arrange them on a platter and keep them warm, but not hot. Cut the carcass into pieces, put them into the duck press and remove all the juice (capture it in a receptacle of some kind).

Make the chafing dish very hot and put 1 large tablespoon of butter into it. Add 2 pinches of salt, 2 pinches of freshly ground black pepper, 1 pinch of red pepper, 2 ponies of brandy and 2 sherry-glasses of very old port. Make the brandy, etc., flame, add 1 more tablespoon of butter and then, with a fork, stir in the juice that was pressed from the duck.

The whole thing demands only 1 minute of cooking. Sprinkle the juice of ½ lemon over the duck fillets and then pour the boiling sauce over this. This is usually accompanied by boiled wild rice. Serve the broiled legs, which have been cut into pieces, but do not necessarily wait for them before eating the fillets. Season to taste. Serve with a very old red Burgundy.

TURKEY, FELOMENA CHARPENTIER

3 onions
4 apples
1 cup of seedless grapes
1 pound of roasted chestnuts
1 cup of hazelnuts
2 truffles
3 sherry-glasses of sherry
1 pinch of powdered cloves
2 pinches of thyme
2 tablespoons of Worcestershire sauce
2 tablespoons of meat stock
Consommé

1 carrot
7 shallots
2 pounds of roast pork (ground)
4 cloves of garlic
2 tablespoons of parsley
Salt
Freshly ground black pepper
2 cups of bread crumbs
2 tablespoons of grated cheese
Butter
2 ponies of brandy
1 sherry-glass of port
2 stalks of celery

Prepare a stuffing, using the above ingredients. Put 2 finely chopped onions and 4 tablespoons of butter into a casserole. Cook for 5 minutes and then add 4 pared, diced apples, 1 cup of seedless grapes, ½ pound of whole roasted chestnuts as well as ½ pound of chopped roasted chestnuts, 1 cup of chopped hazelnuts and 2 chopped truffles. Cook 5 more minutes. Remove it from the fire and add 2 sherry-glasses of sherry. Stir it well. Season with 4 pinches of salt, 3 pinches of freshly ground black pepper, 1 pinch of powdered cloves and 2 pinches of thyme. Add 1 tablespoon of Worcestershire sauce and 2 tablespoons of meat stock.

Put 3 tablespoons of butter and 5 finely chopped shallots into a separate casserole. Cook for 3 minutes and then add 2 pounds of ground roast pork (from a previous roast). Crush 4 cloves of garlic into 2 tablespoons of chopped parsley, mix with a pinch of salt and pepper and sprinkle it over the ground meat, etc. When it becomes hot remove it from the fire.

Grind the turkey liver and mix it with 2 ponies of brandy and 1 sherry-glass of port wine. Pour this over the diced apples, grapes, etc. Then add the ground roast pork, etc. Mix 2 tablespoons of grated cheese with 2 cups of bread crumbs and stir it into the stuffing. Stir the whole thing thoroughly.

Take a 14 to 16 pound turkey. Prepare it for roasting. Stuff it with the dressing and sew it well so it doesn't break open. Put ½ pound of butter into the roasting pan, melt it and add 2 cups of consommé. Cut 1 onion and 1 carrot into quarters. Add to the roasting pan. Add also 2 chopped stalks of celery. Place the turkey in the pan on its side. If you place it on its back the breast will become dry and lose its quality. Put it in a preheated hot oven of 500° F. After 5 minutes start to baste it and then keep on basting it every 5 minutes. Turn the turkey over every 20 minutes. Do this by taking hold of its legs with a cloth. Do not use a fork. It usually takes from 1 hour and 45 minutes to 2 hours to roast a turkey of this size. If you see that the butter and the consommé are getting low add a few more tablespoons of each. Turn the bird breast side up for the last 10 minutes of roasting. Then remove the turkey, the chopped celery and the quartered onion and carrot. Place the pan on top of the stove to prepare the gravy. There should be about 1 quart of gravy already in the pan. Add a generous piece of butter and 2 finely chopped shallots. Use a wooden spoon and stir in 1 sherry-glass of sherry, 1 pinch of pepper and 1 pinch of salt. Let it come to a bubbling boil and serve. Season to taste.

To perfect your cranberry sauce, mix ⅔ cranberry sauce with ⅓ apple sauce. Add the juice of 1 lemon, 2 tablespoons of granulated sugar and 1 pinch of cinnamon. Stir it well. The addition of 4 quarts of water to the carcass of the turkey, boiled slowly for 2 hours, will make an excellent consommé. Cold sparkling apple cider or cold punch should be served with the turkey. To make the punch, peel 2 lemons and 2 oranges. Mix the orange and lemon peel in a punch bowl with 6 tablespoons of granulated sugar. Let it stand 15 minutes. Then pour 1 sherry-glass of brandy or rum, and 1 sherry-glass of curaçao over it. Add 1 pint of hulled ripe strawberries. Stir thoroughly. Then add the juice of the 2 lemons and the 2 oranges, 1 quart of dry white wine and 1 pint or more of sparkling water. Place a large piece of ice in the punch bowl. Garnish with fresh green mint.

BEEF, MAMAN CAMOUS

Take 2 pounds of very lean beef from the buttock. Cut it into small pieces and place in a large casserole. Don't add butter or anything else. Let the pieces become brown by themselves. Then season with 1 pinch each of salt, pepper and powdered cloves. Add 2 bay leaves and 3 tablespoons of butter. Turn the meat in the butter and spices. Crush 2 cloves of garlic into a little chopped parsley, sprinkle it over the beef and mix well. Cover the casserole and let it cook over a moderate fire for 5 minutes. Then add 1 finely chopped onion and 6 quartered mushrooms. Again mix it well, cover and cook for another 5 minutes. After that pour 3 sherry-glasses of red wine over it, turn the fire up and stir it with a wooden spoon. Cook for 2 minutes. Then pour 3 cups of veal stock and 2 more sherry-glasses of red wine over the meat. Add 2 chopped, peeled, very ripe tomatoes, 1 more pinch of powdered cloves and 1 more bay leaf. Place the uncovered casserole in a preheated hot oven of 350° F. for 2 hours.

While it is in the oven, prepare your vegetables. Boil 1 cup of diced carrots and 1 cup of fresh green peas. Separately boil 1 cup of peeled small onions. Boil a few very small new potatoes with their skins. Then peel them (leave them whole). Place them into a separate casserole along with the drained carrots, peas and onions. Add 2 tablespoons of butter, a pinch of salt and pepper, 2 cups of veal stock and 3 sherry-glasses of claret. Crush 2 cloves of garlic into a little chopped parsley and sprinkle it over them. Let it all come to a boil and after the meat has been in the oven the required length of time add the vegetables. Stir and place it back in the oven for another 15 minutes. This dish may be served the way it is or with boiled noodles. Season to taste. Accompany it with California claret.

MINUTE STEAK, ROBERT HAGUE

This recipe calls for 1 pound of sirloin steak which has been cut no more than one-fifth of an inch thick. Cut the meat in two.

Have mixed and ready: 6 finely chopped shallots, 3 crushed peppercorns, 2 pinches of salt and a little chopped parsley.

Place 1 tablespoon of butter into a frying pan—just enough, when melted, to grease the pan. Turn the fire high and when it becomes very, very hot lay the steak into it. Fry it for 1½ minutes on each side. At the same time put 3 large tablespoons of butter into a separate pan and let it come to a bubbling boil. Place the steak on a hot serving platter and sprinkle with the chopped shallots, etc. Pour the boiling butter over the top. Season to taste. Serve with stewed tomatoes, and a glass of Musigny.

VENISON STEAK, GEORGE BUCKLEY

Take a 2 pound venison fillet which has properly ripened by hanging in a cool, dry place for a week or two, according to taste. Place it into a dish.

Crush 1 clove of garlic into a little chopped parsley and mix it with 2 finely chopped shallots and 2 pinches each of salt, thyme and freshly ground black pepper. Sprinkle it over the meat. Add 1 bay leaf and 4 sherry-glasses of very dry sherry. Cover the dish and keep it in a cool place for 2 days. Turn the meat twice a day.

Remove the marinated venison from the sherry. Retain the liquid.

Dry the fillet thoroughly by sponging both sides with a large bunch of parsley. Put it under a hot broiler for 20 minutes or until both sides acquire a crust and it is medium rare. Turn the meat often.

Just before taking the venison from the broiler put 2 tablespoons of butter into a frying pan and add 3 finely chopped shallots. Strain the sherry, etc., in which the venison was soaked and pour it into the pan when the butter comes to a bubbling boil. Then add 1 tablespoon of Worcestershire sauce, 1 tablespoon of meat stock and 1 teaspoon of French mustard. When this comes to a boil add 1 cup of 40% cream. Let it come to a boil again and remove it from the fire. Serve separately with the venison fillet. Venison is usually accompanied by a purée of boiled chestnuts. Season to taste. A Chambertin Burgundy is a polite requisite.

ROAST FILLET OF BEEF BELLEVUE, MAMAN LECOQ

This recipe must be made to serve at least 6 people because it necessitates the using of a whole beef fillet. It also calls for several vegetables which must be prepared ahead of time and kept hot.

Boil separately: 2 cups of diced green beans, 2 cups of fresh green peas, 2 cups of whole, small new carrots, 2 cups of fresh lima beans and 1 whole cauliflower. Drain, season and keep each vegetable separate. Boil and brown 2 cups of Brussels sprouts. Separately sauté 2 cups of diced potatoes. Keep them all hot.

Take 1 large, whole fillet of beef. Put 5 tablespoons of butter on a baking platter, melt it and lay the fillet in it. Roll the meat in the melted butter and season it with 2 pinches of salt and pepper. Place it in a preheated very hot oven of 500° F. for 5 minutes. Separately melt 5 more tablespoons of butter and stir 4 finely chopped shallots into it. Pour this over the fillet and reduce the heat to 400° F. Roast 30 minutes longer.

While the meat is roasting, make a separate sauce. Put 4 tablespoons of butter into a pan. Add 3 finely chopped shallots, 2 sherry-glasses of Madeira or port wine, 5 thinly sliced mushrooms, 3 chopped, peeled, very ripe tomatoes, 2 cups of veal stock, 1 tablespoon of French mustard and a few pinches of pepper and salt. Cook for 15 minutes.

Arrange the hot vegetables on a very large, hot serving platter, making a border of them. Put the whole cauliflower at one end and the lima beans at the other. Then put 1 cup of the diced green beans at each side of the platter next to the cauliflower so they are opposite each other. Next to each cup of green beans place 1 cup of the small carrots. Do the same with the peas, potatoes and Brussels sprouts until each side of the platter duplicates the other. Then place the filet in the center and arrange broiled halves of small tomatoes around it. Distribute 4 tablespoons of melted butter over the vegetables, with the exception of the cauliflower. Pour some Hollandaise sauce over the cauliflower (only the cauliflower). Serve the boiling sauce separately. Season to taste. A cold bottle of sparkling red Burgundy served with it will give it that magic touch.

VEAL CHOPS, ENRICO CARUSO

Put 2 tablespoons of butter into a frying pan and add 4 finely chopped shallots, 1 cup of button mushrooms, 5 whole cloves of unpeeled garlic, 1 finely chopped green pepper, 1 dozen ripe olives, 1 pinch of salt and 1 pinch of pepper. Cook for 10 minutes and then add 1 sherry-glass of Marsala wine. Cook for 5 more minutes.

While the garniture is cooking, sprinkle 2 thick veal chops with a pinch of salt, dip them into butter and broil them 4 minutes on each side. At the same time broil 2 tomatoes which have been cut into halves. Pour the mushrooms, etc., into a baking dish and place the broiled tomato halves on top. Arrange the chops next so that the end of each bone rests on the tomatoes. Add 1 tablespoon of butter and place it in a preheated hot oven of 400° F. for 20 minutes. Season to taste. Serve with a glass of cold Chablis.

HOT SALAD, DON ALBINI

This is a hot salad to be served on a Friday. I believe Don Albini enjoyed it on that day for over 85 years.

Clean and boil together 3 carrots, 3 potatoes, 3 turnips, 2 onions, 1 cup of green beans and ½ Savoy cabbage. While they are cooking, make a dressing which consists of: 1 crushed clove of garlic, 3 pinches of salt, 2 pinches of pepper, the juice of 1 lemon and 4 tablespoons of olive oil. Stand it aside for a moment.

When the vegetables are cooked, drain off the water and chop and mix them together while they are hot. Place them on a serving platter and keep them hot. Prepare 4 shirred eggs and arrange them over the vegetables. Stir the dressing (don't cook it) and pour it over the eggs. Sprinkle with chopped parsley. Season to taste.

PANCAKES, LILLIAN RUSSELL

Peel and core 1 ripe, juicy pear. Place it into a mixing bowl and crush it with a fork. Add 1 tablespoon of currant jelly, 1 tablespoon of melted butter, the juice of ½ lemon, 1 tablespoon of granulated vanilla sugar, 2 pinches each of grated lemon and orange peel, and 1 tablespoon of white curaçao. Mix it well.

Prepare a pancake batter, using 1 egg, 1 tablespoon of milk, 1 tablespoon of flour and 1 pinch of salt. Make 4 pancakes, spread them with the above ingredients and roll them. Place them on a hot serving platter and keep them hot. Sprinkle a little granulated sugar over the top.

Melt 1 tablespoon of butter in a small casserole and add 3 ponies of brandy. Make it flame and pour it over the hot pancakes.

DOUBLE DELIGHT FLAMBEE, MARY ANN GIESEL

Peel and slice 2 ripe peaches. Remove only the stems from 2 cups of black cherries. Add the juice of 2 strained lemons to the fruit, and mix it well. Sprinkle with 1½ cups of granulated sugar and then add 2 sherry-glasses of claret and 2 ponies of kirsch. Let it come to a boil and then pour 3 ponies of flaming rum over the top. Serve with vanilla ice cream.

FRUIT MACEDOINE, ETIENNE MARCEL

Prepare 1 cup each of diced apples, pears, oranges, peaches, pineapple and bananas. Add 2 cups of chopped English walnuts, 1 cup of granulated sugar, the strained juice of 3 lemons and 2 cups of maple syrup. Mix thoroughly. Place in the refrigerator for an hour to chill and then serve.

FRESH FIGS, ARTHUR FENTON

Peel 12 fresh figs and leave them whole. Moisten with white curaçao. Arrange them around a serving platter and place vanilla ice cream in the center. Sprinkle 1 cup of finely chopped hazelnuts over the top. Serve with thick raspberry syrup and *massepains*.

THE FIRST
CREPES SUZETTE

Edward, Prince of Wales, the son of Queen Victoria, came often to the Café de Paris in Monte Carlo where, at fifteen, I was striving to hold my position of *commis des rangs,* a kind of assistant waiter, against the growing hostility of the maître d'. Day after day the Prince came to the Café for his luncheon. I often helped serve him until one day, through a series of fortunate circumstances, it fell to my lot to wait upon him and his party.

"Good morning, your Highness," I said, and the maître d' scowled because he had forbidden me to speak first.

"*Bonjour,* Henri," the Prince said gaily. "What are we going to have for luncheon today?"

"Your Highness, today there will be a sweet never before served to anyone."

In the party that day were eight gentlemen and one little girl, the daughter of one of the gentlemen.

I had often experimented with what are called French pancakes, and I had watched Maman Camous make them with one egg and much flour. She prepared thin strips of lemon and orange peel with sugar syrup and then cooked the cake and syrup together. As a *commis des rangs,* who had his share of confidence, I believed I could improve on that. I was not hampered by the poverty of Contes and I had the advantage of my training under Jean Camous.

The pancakes had to be cooked twice, and since the first was a smoky operation it was performed in the kitchen. But the rest of the process occurred in the dining room right where a prince or a princess might watch how it was done. I stood in front of a chafing dish making the sauce. Everything was going along all right when suddenly the cordials caught fire! My heart leaped with the flames. "Now," I thought, "I'm ruined." The Prince and his friends were waiting. How could I begin all over?

I tasted it. I thought, "This is the most delicious melody of sweet flavors I've ever tasted." And I still think so. The accident which caused the cordials to flame was precisely what was needed to bring all those various instruments into one harmony of taste.

Graciously, in a manner to win approval even from Jean Camous, I plunged my supply of folded pancakes into the boiling sauce. I submerged them, I turned them deftly and, again inspired, I added two more ponies of a previously prepared blend of equal parts of maraschino, curaçao and kirschwasser. My wide pan was alive once more with blue and orange flame and as the colors died from the pan I looked up to see the Prince of Wales watching me.

That day he was dressed all in gray with a cravat in light blue. There was a carnation in his button hole. His gray beard was faultless. His chin went up and his nostrils inhaled. I thought then, and I think now, he was the world's most perfect gentleman. He ate the pancakes with a fork, but used a spoon to capture the remaining syrup. The Prince asked me the name of that which he had eaten with so much relish. I told him it was to be called Crêpes Princesse. He recognized it as a compliment, but protested with mock ferocity that there was a lady present. She was alert and rose to her feet and holding her little skirt wide with her hands she made him a curtsey.

"Will you," asked the Prince, "change the name from Crêpes Princesse to Crêpes Suzette?"

And so this confection was born and named, one taste of which, I really believe, would reform a cannibal into a civilized gentleman.

The next day I received a present from the Prince, a jeweled ring, a panama hat and a cane. After that how could the maître d' possibly dismiss the fifteen year old Henri?

CREPES SUZETTE

2 eggs

2 tablespoons flour

1 tablespoon cream

2 tablespoons milk

1 pinch of salt

Stir the ingredients smoothly to the consistency of olive oil, or until it will pour back silently and smoothly from a foot or more above the mixing bowl. Remember this is a French pancake and must be thin. Put 1 teaspoon of butter into a small round-bottomed frying pan (not aluminum) and when it bubbles pour in enough paste to cover the bottom of the pan. Be quick in moving the pan so as to spread the paste thinly. Keep the pan moving; that paste is a delicate substance. After 1 minute turn the pancake over, then turn it again and again until it is nicely browned. Fold the circle in half, and again to form a triangle. Make eight of these, which should serve four. This first step is a smoky one and should be done in the kitchen. The pancakes, however, are to be cooked a second time, a procedure which occurs in the dining room.

SUZETTE SAUCE

Vanilla sugar

Skin of 2 oranges

Skin of 1 lemon

Orange blossom water

Kirsch

White Curaçao

Juice of 2 oranges

Juice of 1 lemon

Butter

Rum

Maraschino

This sauce should be made in advance since it keeps for many months without spoiling. It can be made in great quantities; like good wine, it will improve with age. Vanilla sugar is one of the requisites for a fine cuisine. Put three or four vanilla beans into a quart jar of granulated sugar. After several days the sugar will be delicately flavored by the vanilla in the beans.

With a knife peel 2 oranges and 1 lemon so thin that the pulp remains on the fruit. Cut the peel julienne style and mix it with 4 tablespoons of vanilla sugar. Squeeze the strained juice of the 2 oranges and 1 lemon into a chafing dish. Add the vanilla sugar, etc., and ⅛ pound of butter. Let it come to a boil and then add 1 teaspoon of orange blossom water, 2 ponies of kirsch, 2 ponies of white curaçao, 2 ponies of rum and 1 pony of maraschino. When it comes to a boil remove it from the fire. This is the sauce which, if prepared in advance, will keep indefinitely.

After the Crêpes Suzette have been made and have been brought to the dining room, the final step is ready to be taken. Put some of the above prepared sauce into a large chafing dish (the quantity depends on your desire) and when it begins to bubble lay the pancakes in the sauce. Those who have no chafing dishes need not worry: it's not the chafing dish that makes the Crêpes Suzette, it's the sauce. If necessary, make it in the kitchen using a pan. Cut minute pieces of orange and lemon peel (no pulp), and put a little on top of each pancake. Blend 1 pony of each of the cordials used in the making of the sauce by placing them in a small preheated casserole. Make the cordials flame and pour it over the pancakes which are in the bubbling sauce. Serve immediately. The perfect Crêpes Suzette are not too liqueur-y. This is an equally delicious sauce for compotes, puddings, ice cream, or sweet omelets.

INDEX

INDEX

410

411

413

ITALIAN SPECIALTIES

VEGETABLES

414

CREPES SUZETTE

2 eggs
2 tablespoons flour
1 tablespoon cream
2 tablespoons milk
1 pinch of salt

Stir the ingredient
will pour back silentl
ing bowl. Remember
1 teaspoon of butter
aluminum) and wher